The

musicSocket

Music Industry Directory
2025

The

musicSocket

Music Industry Directory
2025

EDITOR
J. PAUL DYSON

JP&A
Dyson

Published in 2025 by JP&A Dyson
27 Old Gloucester Street, London WC1N 3AX, United Kingdom
Copyright JP&A Dyson

https://www.jpandadyson.com
https://www.musicsocket.com

ISBN 978-1-909935-54-9

**Registered with the IP Rights Office
Copyright Registration Service
Ref: 3504063018**

Foreword

This directory includes hundreds of listings of **record labels** and **managers**, updated in **MusicSocket**'s online databases between 2022 and 2025.

It also provides free access to the entire current databases, including over 1,200 record labels, and over 500 managers, with dozens of new and updated listings every month.

For details on how to claim your free access please see the back of this book.

Included in the subscription

A subscription to the full website is not only free with this book, but comes packed with all the following features:

Advanced search features

- Save searches and save time – set up to 15 search parameters specific to your work, save them, and then access the search results with a single click whenever you log in. You can even save multiple different searches if you have different types of work you are looking to place.
- Add personal notes to listings, visible only to you and fully searchable – helping you to organise your actions.
- Set reminders on listings to notify you when to submit your work, when to follow up, when to expect a reply, or any other custom action.
- Track which listings you've viewed and when, to help you organise your search – any listings which have changed since you last viewed them will be highlighted for your attention!

Daily email updates

As a subscriber you will be able to take advantage of our email alert service, meaning you can specify your particular interests and we'll send you automatic email updates when we change or add a listing that matches them. So if you're interested in labels dealing in hard rock in the United States you can have us send you emails with the latest updates about them – keeping you up to date without even having to log in.

User feedback

Our databases include a user feedback feature that allows our subscribers to leave feedback on each listing – giving you not only the chance to have your say about the markets you contact, but giving a unique artist's perspective on the listings.

Save on copyright protection fees

If you're sending your work away to record labels and managers you should first consider protecting your copyright. As a subscriber to **MusicSocket** you can do this through our site and save 10% on the copyright registration fees normally payable for protecting your work internationally through the Intellectual Property Rights Office (https://www.Copyright RegistrationService.com).

For details on how to claim your free access please see the back of this book.

Contents

Foreword..v

Contents...vii

Protecting Your Copyright 1

Record Labels
US Record Labels...3

UK Record Labels 33

Canadian Record Labels 67

Record Labels Index 69

Managers
US Managers 87

UK Managers..123

Canadian Managers 163

Australian Managers..165

Managers Index 167

Free Access
Get Free Access to the MusicSocket Website 185

Protecting Your Copyright

Protecting your copyright is by no means a requirement before submitting your work, but you may feel that it is a prudent step that you would like to take before allowing strangers to hear your material.

These days, you can register your work for copyright protection quickly and easily online. The Intellectual Property Rights Office operates a website called the "Copyright Registration Service" which allows you to do this:

- *https://www.CopyrightRegistrationService.com*

This website can be used for material created in any nation signed up to the Berne Convention. This includes the United States, United Kingdom, Canada, Australia, Ireland, New Zealand, and most other countries. There are around 180 countries in the world, and over 160 of them are part of the Berne Convention.

Provided you created your work in one of the Berne Convention nations, your work should be protected by copyright in all other Berne Convention nations. You can therefore protect your copyright around most of the world with a single registration, and because the process is entirely online you can have your work protected in a matter of minutes.

US Record Labels

For the most up-to-date listings of these and hundreds of other record labels, visit https://www.musicsocket.com/recordlabels

*To claim your **free** access to the site, please see the back of this book.*

4AD

Email: demos@4ad.com
Email: 4ad@4ad.com
Website: https://www.4ad.com
Website: https://www.facebook.com/fourad

Genres: Indie; Rock

Record label with offices in New York, Los Angeles, and London. Send demos by email.

825 Records

Website: https://www.825records.com
Website: http://youtube.com/825records

Genres: Pop; R&B; Rock; Singer-Songwriter

For the past decade, has served as a creative confidant from work-spanning independent recording artists to Fortune 500 companies. Owned by a Brooklyn-based record producer, this artist incubator turned multi-media company comprises a multi-disciplinary team of filmmakers, composers, editors, audio engineers, and musicians.

88 Rising

PO Box 45903
Los Angeles, CA 90045
Email: info@88rising.com
Website: https://88rising.com

Genres: All types of music

Record label based in Los Angeles, California.

A&M Records

2220 Colorado Avenue, 5th Floor
Santa Monica, CA 90404
Website: https://www.interscope.com
Website: https://www.facebook.com/interscope

Genres: Indie; Pop; Rock; Singer-Songwriter; Alternative; R&B

Part of a record label based in Santa Monica, California.

A389 Recordings

Website: http://www.a389records.com
Website: https://a389recordings.bandcamp.com

Genres: Hard Rock; Metal

DIY hard rock and metal label.

Accidental Entertainment

Email: hello@accidentalentertainment.com
Website: https://accidentalentertainment.com
Website: https://www.facebook.com/AccidentalEnt

Genres: Alternative; Indie; Rock; Acoustic; Latin; Electronic; Pop

We're a unique, independent boutique company, deeply rooted in Music Supervision and Production.

Acoustic Disc
PO Box 992
Port Townsend, WA 98368
Email: customerservice@acousticdisc.com
Email: business@acousticdisc.com
Website: https://acousticdisc.com

Genres: Acoustic Jazz; Acoustic Latin; Acoustic Folk; Classical; Acoustic Blues; Roots; World

Handles acoustic music only.

Affluent Records
New York, NY
Email: oscarsanchez@affluentrecords.com
Website: https://affluentrecords.com
Website: https://www.facebook.com/theaffluentrecords

Genres: Urban

Contact: Oscar Sanchez

A full service New York City entertainment company specializing in label and artist services consisting of artist development, music production, brand management, media, executive production, promotions and content creation.

Alias Records
838 EAST HIGH STREET # 290
Lexington, KY 40502
Email: accounts@aliasrecords.com
Website: http://www.aliasrecords.com
Website: https://www.facebook.com/Alias-Records-186847657059/

Genres: Indie Rock; Electronic; Singer-Songwriter

Record label based in Lexington, Kentucky.

Alive Naturalsound
Email: label@alive-records.com
Website: https://www.alive-records.com
Website: https://www.facebook.com/AliveNaturalsoundRecords

Genres: Rock; Soul

Rock and soul label established in 1993.

Alligator Records
P.O. Box 60234
Chicago, IL 60660
Email: info@allig.com
Website: https://www.alligator.com
Website: https://www.facebook.com/AlligatorRecords

Genres: Blues; Americana; Roots

Handles blues and blues-based music only. Send a maximum of four songs by post. Response by post only, so ensure legible postal address included. No email submissions or requests to visit artist's website. Response time of three months or more.

Alternative Tentacles Records
PO Box 419092
San Francisco, CA 94141
attn. Jello Biafra
Fax: +1 (510) 596-8982
Email: jb@alternativetentacles.com
Website: http://www.alternativetentacles.com

Genres: Country; Hardcore; Indie; Metal; Pop; Punk; R&B; Rock

Contact: Jello Biafra

Accepts demos on CD, tape, or vinyl. No MP3s. Will not listen to music online. Most demos get listened to, but response not guaranteed. No way to "check status" of your submission so don't ask for updates after you've submitted.

Amathus Music
Website: https://amathusmusic.com
Website: https://soundcloud.com/amathusmusic

Genres: Electronic Dance; Underground House; Trance; Commercial

Send query through demo submission form on website, with SoundCloud links. No MP3 attachments, or hard copy submissions. Response not guaranteed.

American Eagle Recordings
12 Lake Forest Court West
St. Charles, MO 63301-4540
Fax: +1 (636) 724-1325
Email: info@americaneaglerecordings.com
Email: americaneaglerecordings@earthlink.net
Website: http://www.americaneaglerecordings.com

Genres: All types of music

Contact: Dr. Charles Max E. Million

Record label based in St Charles, Missouri. Send demos by CD only, accompanied by completed Questionnaire (available for download from website). Extensive submission guidelines on website. Any submissions not adhering to the submission guidelines will be ignored. No MP3s or links by email.

American Laundromat Records
P.O. Box 85
Mystic, CT 06355-0085
Email: americanlaundromat@hotmail.com
Website: https://www.alr-music.com
Website: https://www.facebook.com/americanlaundromatrecords

Genres: Alternative; Folk; Indie; Pop; Rock; Singer-Songwriter

Record label based in Mystic, Connecticut. Not accepting new submissions as at January 2023.

American Recordings
Website: https://www.universalmusic.com/label/republic-records/#american-recordings

Genres: All types of music

An independent record label headed by the record producer and co-founder of Def Jam Recordings. The label was formed in 1988 and then changed its name in 1993.

Anti
Website: https://www.anti.com
Website: https://www.facebook.com/antirecords

Genres: Indie Rock

Record label based in Los Angeles, California.

Aphagia Recordings
San Francisco
Email: aphagia@outlook.com
Website: https://www.aphagiarecordings.com
Website: https://aphagiarecordings.bandcamp.com/

Genres: Experimental Electronic Industrial Progressive Glitch Instrumental Rock Soundtracks

A San Francisco based Independent Record Label focusing on odd forms of electronic and rock music.

API Records
PO Box 7041
Watchung, NJ 07069
Email: apirecords@verizon.net
Website: http://www.apirecords.com

Genres: Classical; Pop Rock

Record label based in Watchung, New Jersey. Accepts solicited demo submissions only. Unsolicited submissions will be discarded without being listened to.

Appleseed Recordings
1416 Larch Lane
West Chester, PA 19380
Website: https://appleseedmusic.com

Genres: Contemporary; Folk; Roots

An independent, idealistic and internationally distributed record label devoted to releasing socially conscious contemporary, folk and roots music by both established and lesser-known musicians. Send demo on CD or CD/R (no MP3s or cassettes) with bio and other relevant info. Listens to everything but response not guaranteed if not interested. See website for full guidelines.

Arabesque Recordings

1600 Harrison Avenue, Suite 307 A
Mamaroneck, NY 10543
Email: info@arabesquerecords.com
Website: https://www.arabesquerecords.com

Genres: Classical; Jazz

Record label based in Mamaroneck, New York, specialising in elegant classical and jazz music. Send query via form on website with info about you and your project and links to the music online.

Arctic Siren Records

4105 E Turnagain Blvd, Suite L
Anchorage, AK 99517
Email: artcsirn@acsalaska.net
Website: https://www.arcticsiren.com/arctic-siren-label.html
Website: https://www.facebook.com/arcticsiren

Genres: Acoustic

Dedicated to the production and distribution of quality recordings of independent artist and is committed to the financial independence of songwriters and performers.

Asthmatic Kitty Records

830 Glenwood Ave, Suite 510-414
Atlanta, GA 30316
Website: http://asthmatickitty.com
Website: https://www.facebook.com/asthmatickitty

Genres: Alternative Pop

Record label based in Atlanta. Not accepting submissions as at May 2023. Check website for current status.

Astralwerks Records

1750 Vine Street
Hollywood, CA
Email: astralwerks.astralwerks@gmail.com
Website: https://www.astralwerks.com
Website: https://www.facebook.com/astralwerks

Genres: Alternative; Electronic; Dance; Techno

Record label based in New York.

Atlantic Records

75 Rockefeller Plz Ste 3
New York, NY 10019
Website: https://www.atlanticrecords.com
Website: https://www.facebook.com/atlanticrecords

Genres: All types of music

Record label based in New York.

ATO Records

New York, NY 10016
Email: info@atorecords.com
Website: https://atorecords.com
Website: https://www.facebook.com/atorecords/

Genres: Alternative; Rock; Acoustic; Indie; Pop

Independent record label committed to artists and building their careers.

Average Joes Entertainment

3728 Keystone Avenue
Nashville, TN 37211
Email: info@averagejoesent.com
Website: https://averagejoesent.com

Genres: Country

Independent record label specialising in film, television, technology and country music.

Ba Da Bing Records & Management

181 Clermont Avenue, Suite 403
Brooklyn, NY 11205
Email: hello@badabingrecords.com
Website: http://www.badabingrecords.com
Website: http://soundcloud.com/badabingrecords

Genres: All types of music

Record label based in New York, operated by film and TV comedian.

Babygrande Records, Inc.

101 West 23rd Street Suite 296
New York, New York 10011
Email: inquiries@babygrande.com

Website: https://babygrande.com
Website: https://soundcloud.com/babygrande

Genres: Hip-Hop; Rock; Indie Rock; Electronic; Instrumental

Record label based in New York. Describes itself as "one of the premier independent record labels operating today". Send query by email with relevant info and streaming links only.

BackWords Recordings
334 Tonti St.
South Bend, IN 46617-1149
Email: tim@backwordsrecordings.com
Website: https://www.
backwordsrecordings.com

Genres: Avant-Garde; Alternative; Electronic; Melodic; Psychedelic; Traditional; Spoken Word; Singer-Songwriter; Rock; Mystical; Instrumental; Indie;; Guitar based; Classical

Contact: Tim Backer

An Independent Culture Production House.

Bar/None Records
PO Box 1704
Hoboken, NJ 07030
Email: glenn@bar-none.com
Website: http://www.bar-none.com
Website: https://soundcloud.com/barnonepop

Genres: Alternative; Indie; Rock

Record label based in Hoboken, New Jersey. Those looking to approach are asked to check out the website and artists currently worked with, then if you still think it's appropriate send a query by email with a link to music online. No large music file attachments by email.

Barbarian Productions
Email: talent@barbarianproductions.com
Website: http://www.
barbarianproductions.com

Genres: Pop; R&B; Hip-Hop; Singer-Songwriter; Soundtracks

Send submissions by email.

Barsuk Records
PO Box 22546
Seattle, WA 98122
Email: questions@barsuk.com
Website: https://www.barsuk.com
Website: https://www.facebook.com/barsukrecords

Genres: Indie; Rock

Record label based in Seattle. Send links to demos or electronic press kits online via form on website. Do not send audio files or physical CDs. Response not guaranteed.

BEC Recordings
Email: radio@becrecordings.com
Website: https://www.becrecordings.com
Website: https://www.facebook.com/becrecordingsmusic

Genres: Commercial Pop

Honored for more than 20 years to have worked with artists that have headlined sold-out festivals, secured #1 charting Billboard singles, and earned RIAA gold-certified albums. The label—best classified under the umbrella of commercial pop—has developed artists that have become staples across all CCM radio formats and digital marketing platforms.

Beggars Group (US)
Email: banquet@beggars.com
Website: https://beggars.com

Genres: Alternative; Dance; Electronic; Indie; Punk; Rock; Singer-Songwriter; World

International group with offices in the UK, US, and Canada. The group is not accepting demos itself, but individual labels are – see website for links.

Big Beat
Website: https://www.wearebigbeat.com
Website: https://www.facebook.com/wearebigbeat

Genres: House; Hip-Hop; Dance; Electronic

Originally a record label founder in 1987, imprint was re-launched in 2010.

Big Crown Records

PO Box 285
Centerport, NY 11721-1130
Email: demos@bigcrownrecords.com
Email: info@bigcrownrecords.com
Website: https://bigcrownrecords.com
Website: https://www.facebook.com/
bigcrownrecords/

Genres: Soul

Brooklyn based independent record label
started in 2016. Send soundcloud links only
by email.

Big Loud Records

Email: digital@bigloud.com
Website: https://bigloudrecords.com/
Website: https://www.facebook.com/
BigLoud/

Genres: Country

Record label dealing in country music.

The Birdman Recording Group, Inc.

Website: https://birdmanrecords.com

Genres: Underground Garage; Blues; Jazz;
Country; Modern Classical

Record label dedicated to quality music of all
genres, attempting to win over new fans by
"grassroots marketing and making the best
records around".

Black Dahlia Music

P.O. Box 631928
Highlands Ranch, CO 80163
Email: blackd@blackdahlia.com
Website: https://blackdahlia.com

Genres: All types of music

Record label based in Highlands Ranch,
Colorado.

Black River Entertainment

12 Music Circle South
Nashville, TN 37203
Email: info@blackrivernet.com
Website: https://www.blackriverent.com

Genres: Country; Christian

Entertainment company based in Nashville,
involved in music publishing and operating a
number of labels.

Blackheart Records Group

Fax: +1 (212) 353-8300
Email: blackheart@blackheart.com
Website: https://blackheart.com/
Website: https://www.facebook.com/
BlackheartRecordsGroup/

Genres: All types of music

Record label based in New York.

Blind Pig Records

Email: contact@blindpigrecords.com
Email: info@blindpigrecords.com
Website: https://www.blindpigrecords.com
Website: https://www.facebook.com/
Blindpigrecord/

Genres: Blues; Roots

Demo submissions are welcome as long as
they match the label's style. Do not attach
files to your email; provide link to YouTube,
Bandcamp, or other reputable location. Try
to listen to and consider every submission
but cannot answer each one. Response if
interested.

Blue Canoe Records

Email: contactbcr@bluecanoerecords.com
Website: https://www.bluecanoerecords.com
Website: https://www.facebook.com/
bluecanoerecords

Genres: All types of music

Only accepts recommendations from their
staff producers. Unsolicited material will not
be listened to.

Blue Elan Records

10880 Wilshire Boulevard, Suite 2000
Los Angeles, CA 90024
Email: info@blueelan.com
Website: https://blueelan.com
Website: https://www.facebook.com/
blueelan/

Genres: All types of music

A few years ago, we started out with a simple idea to become the most artist-friendly record label in the world. From the studio to release day and everything in between, we are passionate about our artists making the music they love, and support their growth at every step of the way.

Blue Note Label Group
Website: https://www.bluenote.com
Website: https://www.facebook.com/bluenote

Genres: Jazz; Pop; R&B

Record label founded in 1939, specialising in Jazz.

Bolero Records
18653 Ventura Boulevard, Suite 314
Tarzana, CA 91356
Email: info@bolero-records.com
Website: https://www.bolero-records.com

Genres: World; Jazz; Latin; New Age

Independent record label based in Tarzana, California, specialising in Nuevo Flamenco, Traditional Flamenco, World, Jazz, Latin and New Age.

Bomp Records
Email: MAILORDER@BOMPRECORDS.com
Website: https://www.bompstore.com
Website: https://www.facebook.com/bomprecords

Genres: Indie; Punk; Power Pop; Pop; Garage Rock; New Wave; Traditional Rock

An American indie label, featuring punk, pop, powerpop, garage, new wave, old school rock, and much more.

Brash Music
888 3rd Street NW, Suite A
Atlanta, GA 30318
Fax: +1 (678) 904-4790
Email: info@brashmusic.com
Website: http://www.brashmusic.com

Website: https://www.facebook.com/Brash-Music-168206919862613/

Genres: All types of music

Record label based in Atlanta, Georgia. Not accepting new music as at January 2018.

Bridge Nine Records
282 Rantoul Street
Beverly, MA 01915
Email: info@bridge9.com
Email: chris@bridge9.com
Website: http://www.bridge9.com
Website: https://www.facebook.com/bridge9

Genres: Hardcore

Contact: Chris Wrenn

Independent record label based in Beverly, Massachusetts.

Bright Antenna Records
10 E. Blithedale
Mill Valley, CA 94941
Email: info@brightantenna.com
Website: https://www.brightantenna.com
Website: https://www.facebook.com/BrightAntennaRecords/

Genres: Rock

Record label based in Mill Valley, California.

Brushfire Records
Website: http://brushfirerecords.com
Website: https://www.facebook.com/brushfirerecords

Genres: All types of music

Record label founded in Hawaii in 2002, and now based in Los Angeles. Strives to make music and films that are positive and works to connect like-minded musicians and artists in the surf community and beyond.

Bullet Tooth
Tinton Falls, NJ
Email: info@bullettooth.com
Website: https://www.bullettooth.com
Website: https://www.facebook.com/BulletToothHQ

Genres: Rock; Hardcore; Metal; Emo; Punk

Contact: Josh Grabelle

We are always on the lookout for music that is original, creative, and compelling. If you think you have it and you are HARD WORKING and will sacrifice your "9 to 5" for a life on the road, then we may be interested in your band!

Burnside Distribution
6635 N. Baltimore Ave. Suite 226
Portland, OR 97203
Email: skip@bdcdistribution.com
Email: info@bdcdistribution.com
Website: https://burnsidedistribution.com

Genres: All types of music

Contact: Skip Werner

Send the project you would like to release along with a marketing plan and outline of your need for national distribution. Please note our company does not offer physical distribution without your label/artist's digital distribution, although we will consider digital-only releases.

Burnt Toast Vinyl
PO Box 42188
Philadelphia, PA 19101
Email: btv@burnttoastvinyl.com
Website: https://www.burnttoastvinyl.com
Website: https://www.facebook.com/burnttoastvinyl

Genres: Alternative; Singer-Songwriter

Record label based in Philadelphia.

Cantaloupe Music
80 Hanson Place, Suite 301
Brooklyn, NY 11217
Fax: +1 (718) 852-7732
Email: info@cantaloupemusic.com
Website: https://cantaloupemusic.com

Genres: Classical; Electronic; Jazz; New Age; Punk; Rock; World

Contact: Cantaloupe A&R

Send demos on CD by post. All submissions listened to, but response not guaranteed.

Include details of past and upcoming performances.

Canyon
PO Box 61564
Phoenix, AZ 85082
Email: canyon@canyonrecords.com
Website: https://www.canyonrecords.com
Website: https://www.facebook.com/canyonrecords

Genres: Regional; World

Native American record label.

Capitol Christian Music Group
Website: https://www.capitolcmglabelgroup.com
Website: https://www.facebook.com/CapitolChristianMusicGroup

Genres: Christian; Gospel

Say of themselves that an unwavering vision combined with a commitment to excellence and an arsenal of exceptional talent continues to make them the leader in the faith-based entertainment industry.

Capitol Music Group
Website: https://www.capitolrecords.com
Website: https://www.facebook.com/capitolrecords

Genres: Dance; Indie; Pop; Rock; Urban

Accepts submissions through established sources (managers, etc.) only. All other material returned without being listened to.

Capitol Records Nashville
Website: https://www.umgnashville.com
Website: https://www.facebook.com/UMGNashville

Genres: Country

Country record label based in Nashville, Tennessee.

Carnival Music
Email: contact@carnivalmusic.net
Website: https://www.carnivalmusic.net
Website: https://twitter.com/CarnivalMusic

Genres: Americana; Country; Indie; Pop; Rock

Describes itself as neither a record label or publishing company, but doing the work of both.

Carpark Records
Email: info@carparkrecords.com
Website: https://www.carparkrecords.com
Website: https://soundcloud.com/carparkrecords

Genres: Alternative; Rock

An independent record label based in Washington, D.C and New York City. Established in 1999, the label began in New York City as an outlet for up-and-coming IDM, ambient, and experimental sounds. Moving to D.C. in 2005 led to releases from new Baltimore acts bringing new international attention to the roster.

Cascine
Los Angeles, CA
Email: demos@cascine.us
Email: info@cascine.us
Website: https://www.cascine.us
Website: https://soundcloud.com/cascine

Genres: Alternative Pop; Electronic

Independent record label based in Los Angeles. Known for its consistently stylish brand of alternative pop and electronic music. Send demos by email.

Cash Money Records
Website: https://www.cashmoney-records.com
Website: https://www.facebook.com/cashmoneyrecords

Genres: Hip-Hop; Urban; Pop

Hip-hop, urban, and pop record label.

Celestial Harmonies
PO Box 30122
Tucson, AZ 85751-0122
Email: celestial@harmonies.com
Website: https://harmonies.com

Genres: Ambient; Fusion; Modern Classical; Christian; World

Record label based in Tucson, Arizona, but active internationally. Covers lots of music from different religions, such as Christian, Jewish, and Hindu, among others.

Century Media Records (US)
Email: promotion@centurymedia.de
Website: https://www.centurymedia.com
Website: https://www.facebook.com/centurymedia

Genres: Metal; Rock; Traditional Metal; Gothic Metal; Black Metal; Hard Rock; Hardcore

Record label founded in 1988 and acquired by a large multinational in 2015. Main office in Berlin.

Cherrytree Records
2200 Colorado Ave
Santa Monica, CA 90250
Email: info@cherrytreemusiccompany.com
Website: https://cherrytreemusiccompany.com
Website: https://www.facebook.com/CherrytreeMusicCompany

Genres: All types of music

Pop Alternative Record label based in Santa Monica, California.

Chesky Records
1650 Broadway, Suite 900
New York, NY 10019
Email: info@chesky.com
Website: https://chesky.com

Genres: Classical; Jazz; World

Record label based in New York, specialising in classical, jazz, and world music.

Cleopatra Records
9417 Brodie Lane
Austin, TX 78748
Email: info@cleorecs.com
Website: https://cleorecs.com

Website: https://www.facebook.com/
CleopatraRecords
Website: https://myspace.com/cleorecs

Genres: Metal; Punk; Pop; Electronic; Rap;
Hip-Hop; Jazz; Gothic; Reggaeton;
Industrial

Record label based in Austin, Texas. Submit
music via form on website. Response only if
interested.

Closed Sessions
Email: alex@closedsessions.com
Website: https://www.closedsessions.com
Website: https://www.facebook.com/
ClosedSessionsChicago/

Genres: Hip-Hop

A record label with deep roots in Chicago's
Hip Hop scene, and the national Hip Hop
community. Started as a content partnership
during the wild west like environment of the
blog era. Beginning in late 2008, it hosted
first market plays from the era's most
innovative and emergent artists. In addition,
it took fans into the studio with these artists
to provide an examination of their art as well
as original recordings.

CMH Records
Website: https://www.cmhrecords.com
Website: https://www.cmhlabelgroup.com

Genres: Blues; Country; Gospel;
Instrumental; Rock; Pop

Dedicated to presenting the finest in
Bluegrass and roots music, through re-issues
of classic material by the greats and stellar
recordings from new voices.

Columbia Records
25 Madison Avenue
New York, NY 10010
Website: https://www.columbiarecords.com
Website: https://www.facebook.com/
columbiarecords

Genres: All types of music

Record label based in New York.

Communion Records US
Brooklyn, NY
Email: info@communionmusic.com
Website: https://www.facebook.com/
CommunionMusic

Genres: All types of music

Artist-led organisation combining elements
of live promotion, publishing and recording
to create a hub for artists to develop and
flourish. Founded in London in 2006.

Compass Records
916 19th Avenue South
Nashville, TN 37212
Fax: +1 (615) 320-7378
Email: submissions@compassrecords.com
Email: info@compassrecords.com
Website: https://compassrecords.com
Website: https://www.facebook.com/
CompassRecordsGroup

Genres: Blues; Folk; Americana; Jazz; Pop;
Alternative; Roots; World; Celtic

Record label based in Nashville, Tennessee.
No hip hop, rap, hard rock, or commercial
country. Send query by email with link to
music online. Explain why you think this
label is right for you and vice versa, and
provide details of last two years of touring
history.

Concord Music Group
5750 Wilshire Blvd, Suite 450
Los Angeles, CA 90036
Email: info@concord.com
Website: https://concord.com
Website: https://www.facebook.com/
concord/

Genres: Jazz; Pop; Rock; R&B; Blues; Soul;
Classical; World; Latin

Record label based in Los Angeles,
California. Describes itself as "one of the
largest independent record and music
publishing companies in the world".

Cowboy Rockstar Records
Email: william.mitchem@
cowboyrockstarrecords.com

Website:
https://www.cowboyrockstarrecords.com
Website: https://www.facebook.com/
cowboyrockstarrecords

Genres: Acoustic Alternative Christian
Extreme Funky Glam Hard Heavy Horror
Industrial Modern Non-Commercial Power
Progressive New Wave Thrash Americana
Black Metal Blues Country Folk Funk Deep
Funk Guitar based Hardcore Indie Metal
Nostalgia Psychebilly Punk Rock Rock and
Roll Rockabilly Singer-Songwriter
Soundtracks

Contact: William Mitchem

A dynamic new record label dedicated to
championing the voices of pioneering artists
and pushing the boundaries of sound. With a
fusion of a cowboy's spirit and rock 'n' roll
energy, this label is committed to celebrating
authenticity, creativity, and the relentless
pursuit of sonic excellence. Join us on the
journey where the spirit of the cowboy meets
the soul of rock 'n' roll.

Craniality Sounds
Email: cranialitysounds@gmail.com
Website: http://www.cranialitysounds.com
Website: https://www.facebook.com/
CranialitySounds/

Genres: Underground House; Underground
Dance; Funky House

An underground house music label dedicated
to bringing out the essence and eclectic of
underground dance music while having fun
at it. Focus is funky house music, but have
been known to drop other styles of house
music.

Curb Records
48 Music Square East
Nashville, TN 37203
Email: curb@curb.com
Website: https://www.curb.com
Website: https://www.facebook.com/
curbrecords

Genres: Christian; Country; Pop; Rock

A record label based in Nashville, Tennessee
which covers Christian, Country, Pop, and
Rock music.

Daemon Records
PO Box 1207
Decatur, GA 30031
Website: https://www.daemonrecords.com
Website: https://www.facebook.com/
DaemonRecords/

Genres: All types of music

An independent record label that was
founded in 1990 as a vehicle for recording
artists to express their artistic vision without
the confines and restrictions of a corporate
major record label. The label is operated
from the artist's perspective, with an
emphasis on community development on all
fronts including the arts, the environment,
and human rights. The label aims to help
break down barriers within the music
community, while providing an opportunity
for musicians to create and control their own
recordings within a free and nurturing
environment.

Dangerbird Records
3801 Sunset Boulevard
Los Angeles, CA 90026
Email: info@dangerbird.com
Website: http://www.dangerbirdrecords.com
Website: https://www.facebook.com/
dangerbirdrecords

Genres: Alternative; Indie; Rock

Record label based in Los Angeles,
California. Not accepting unsolicited demos
as at October 2024.

Daptone Records
115 Troutman
Brooklyn, NY 11206
Email: info@daptonerecords.com
Website: https://daptonerecords.com
Website: https://www.facebook.com/
daptonehouseofsoul

Genres: All types of music

Record label based in Brooklyn, New York.

Dauman Music
Email: jason@daumanmusic.com
Website: https://www.daumanmusic.com

Genres: Dance

Contact: Jason Dauman

Record label based in Los Angeles. Founder has procured songs for artists including U2, Bruce Springsteen, Garth Brooks, Billy Steinberg and Tom Kelly, Burt Bacharach and Carole Bayer Sager.

DCD2 Records
Website: http://dcd2records.com
Website: https://www.facebook.com/DCD2Records

Genres: All types of music

US record label.

Deep Elm Records
Maui, HI
Email: info@deepelm.com
Email: media@deepelm.com
Website: http://www.deepelm.com

Genres: Indie; Punk; Rock; Emo; Post Rock

Independent label based in Maui, Hawaii. Send submissions via online form on website, including links to music online. No submissions accepted by other means. No submissions by email.

Def Jam Recordings
Website: https://www.defjam.com
Website: https://www.facebook.com/DefJam/

Genres: Hip-Hop; R&B; Rap; Urban

Record label based in New York.

Delmark Records
4121 N. Rockwell
Chicago, IL 60618
Email: delmark@delmark.com
Website: https://delmark.com
Website: https://www.facebook.com/DelmarkRecords/

Genres: Blues; Jazz

Blues and jazz record label based in Chicago, Illinois.

Delos
Fax: +1 (415) 358-5959
Website: https://delosmusic.com
Website: https://www.facebook.com/DelosMusic

Genres: Classical

Classical music label.

Drag City
P.O. Box 476867
Chicago, IL 60647

UK OFFICE:
Drag City Inc.
Unit 409
Bon Marche Centre
241-251 Ferndale Rd
London, SW9 8BJ
Fax: +1 (312) 455-1057
Email: press@dragcity.com
Email: webmaster@dragcity.com
Website: https://www.dragcity.com

Genres: Pop; Rock; Alternative; Hard Rock; Experimental

Record label with offices in Chicago and London. No longer accepts demos "unless they're amazing".

Dualtone Records
Email: info@dualtone.com
Website: https://www.dualtone.com
Website: https://www.facebook.com/dualtonemusic

Genres: Americana; Folk; Indie Rock; Singer-Songwriter

American-based independent record label specializing in folk, singer/songwriter, Americana and indie rock.

Elton Audio Records
New Jersey
Website: https://www.eltonaudio.com

Genres: All types of music

An independent record label, online music news site, and management company based out of New Jersey.

Estrus Records

PO Box 2125
Bellingham, WA 98227
Email: website@estrus.com
Website: http://estrus.com

Genres: All types of music

Record label based in Bellingham,
Washington. No unsolicited demos.

Fair Trade

Website: https://fairtradeservices.com

Genres: Christian

Christian record label that aims to foster
relationships with artists in a spirit of
partnership and fairness.

Fantasy Records

Email: support@fantasyrecordings.com
Website: https://fantasyrecordings.com
Website: https://www.facebook.com/
FantasyRecords

Genres: All types of music

Established in San Francisco in 1949. A
home for innovative, authentic artists whose
music impacts the world.

Fever Records

PO Box 219
Yonkers, NY 10710
Email: fevermusic@aol.com
Website: https://feverrecords.com
Website: https://www.facebook.com/
FeverRecords

Genres: All types of music

Record label based in Yonkers, New York.

Fire Tower Entertainment

Los Angeles, CA
Email: artists@firetowerent.com
Website: https://firetowerent.com
Website: https://www.facebook.com/
firetowerent

Genres: Indie; Pop

Record label based in Los Angeles,
California. New artists can apply via system
on website.

First Access Entertainment (FAE)

Email: contact@faegrp.com
Website: https://www.faegrp.com
Website: https://www.facebook.com/faegrp

Genres: All types of music

Record label with offices in London, New
York, and Los Angeles.

Frontier Records

Sun Valley, CA
Email: info@frontierrecords.com
Website: https://www.frontierrecords.com
Website: https://www.facebook.com/
thefrontierrecords

Genres: Punk Rock; Classic Punk;
Alternative Rock

Punk label based in Sun Valley, California.

G² Records & Publishing

Website: https://www.
g2recordsandpublishing.com

Genres: Jazz; Guitar based Jazz

Record label founded in 2020 to offer jazz
musicians and solo guitarists with a jazz
focus a home in the digital world – always
with the aim of transforming their art
successfully from the traditional structures of
physical releases into the world of streaming
platforms.

Hacienda Records

Email: hacienda@haciendarecords.com
Website: https://www.facebook.com/
haciendarecords

Genres: Latin; Gospel

Record label based in Corpus Christi, Texas,
producing Latin, Tejano, Traditional Tex-
Mex, Conjunto and Norteño music, as well
as Banda, Merengue, Duranguense, Rock En
Español, Gospel and Christmas music.

Invisible Records

Chicago
Website: http://www.invisiblerecords.com
Website: https://www.facebook.com/
InvisibleRecords

Genres: Gothic; Metal; Rock

Contact: Katie/Jarin

Record label based in Chicago, specialising in goth, metal and rock.

Island Records (US)

1755 Broadway
New york, NY 10018
Website: http://www.islandrecords.com
Website: https://www.facebook.com/
IslandRecords

Genres: Contemporary; Indie; Metal; Pop; Punk; R&B; Rap; Hip-Hop; Rock; Urban

Record label based in New York.

Kemado Media Group

Brooklyn, NY 11222
Email: info@kemado.com
Website: https://kemado.com

Genres: All types of music

Record label, media rights acquisition, management, and distribution, based in Brooklyn, New York.

Kobalt Music

926 N Sycamore Ave
Suite 700
Los Angeles, CA 90038

2100 Ponce De Leon Blvd
Ste 1230
Coral Gables, FL 33134

907 Gleaves St
Suite 101
Nashville, TN 37203

2 Gansevoort St
6th Floor
New York, NY 10014
Website: https://www.kobaltmusic.com

Genres: All types of music

Founded in 2000 by a Swedish entrepreneur, the company represents some of the most iconic and exciting songwriters in the world. Today, the company, on average, represents over 40% of the top 100 songs and albums in the US and the UK.

Kranky

Email: krankyinfo@gmail.com
Website: https://kranky.net
Website: https://www.facebook.com/
krankyLTD

Genres: All types of music

Very specific aesthetic. Familiarize yourself with the label before contacting. Send links to two or three streaming MP3s hosted online (e.g. MySpace / bandcamp / Soundcloud etc. Do not send MP3 attachments or links to download MP3s.

Lazy Bones Recordings

10002 Aurora Ave. N
Suite 36 / PMB 317
Seattle, WA 98133
Email: scott@lazybones.com
Website: https://lazybones.com
Website: https://www.facebook.com/Lazy-Bones-Recordings-112143388514/

Genres: All types of music

Contact: Scott Schorr

An indie record label and music publishing company. The company started out in Seattle and has operated in the Big Island of Hawaii, Oahu, New Zealand and is currently headquartered in Melbourne, Australia, with a US office in Seattle.

Lazy S.O.B. Recordings

Website: https://lazysob.com

Genres: All types of music

Record label founded in 1995 by a six-time Grammy Award winning drummer, songwriter, engineer, producer and record mogul from Austin, Texas.

Leviathan Records
PO Box 745
Tyrone, GA 30290
Email: general@leviathanrecords.com
Website: http://www.leviathanrecords.com

Genres: Heavy Metal; Hard Rock; Rock

Record label based in Tyrone, Georgia.

Luaka Bop
New York
Email: iwasthinking@luakabop.com
Website: https://www.luakabop.com
Website: https://www.facebook.com/luakabop1989

Genres: World

Contact: David Byrne

Record label based in New York.

Mack Avenue
18530 Mack Avenue, #299
Grosse Pointe Farms, MI 48236
Email: info@mackavenue.com
Website: https://mackavenue.com
Website: https://www.facebook.com/mackavenue

Genres: Jazz

Jazz record label founded in Detroit in the nineties.

Malaco Music Group
PO Box 9287
Jackson, MS 39286-9287
Fax: +1 (601) 982-4528
Email: demo@malaco.com
Email: malaco@malaco.com
Website: https://www.malaco.com
Website: https://www.facebook.com/malacomusic

Genres: Blues; Gospel; R&B; Soul; Jazz

Record label based in Jackson, Mississippi. Send demos by email.

Manifesto Records, Inc.
1180 South Beverly Drive, Suite 510
Los Angeles, CA 90035-1157
Fax: +1 (310) 556-9801

Email: esc@manifesto.com
Website: https://manifesto.com

Genres: Alternative; Pop; Rock; Punk; Indie

Contact: Evan S. Cohen

Record label based in Los Angeles.

Mega Truth Records
Website: http://www.jonbare.net/jonbaremegatruth.htm

Genres: Blues; Rock

Contact: Jon Bare

Independent record label devoted to "capturing the world's best musicians playing music that makes you feel good".

Mello Music Group
Tucson, AZ
Email: info@mellomusicgroup.com
Website: https://www.mellomusicgroup.com
Website: https://www.facebook.com/MelloMusicGroup

Genres: Funk; Hip-Hop; Jazz; Soul

An internationally renowned record label based in the Sonoran Desert of Tucson, Arizona, that specializes in Hip-hop, Funk, Jazz, and Soul. Founded in 2007, they have released over 200 projects.

Mexican Summer
Brooklyn, NY
Email: demos@mexicansummer.com
Email: info@mexicansummer.com
Website: https://mexicansummer.com
Website: https://www.facebook.com/mexicansummer/

Genres: All types of music

An independent record label serving specialty formats from Brooklyn, New York since 2009. Our mission is to advocate the work of adventurous musicians without the limitations of genre or form.

Milan Records
Email: milanrecords@sonymusic.com
Website: https://www.milanrecords.com

Genres: Electronic; Soundtracks; World

Record label specialising in soundtracks for film, TV, and video games.

MNRK Music Group
New York, NY
Website: https://www.mnrk.com
Website: https://www.facebook.com/MNRKMusic

Genres: Americana; Alternative; Electronic; Hip-Hop; Heavy Metal; Rock

An independent music company based in New York, handling a diverse range of genres, including Americana, electronic, alternative, hip-hop, rock, and heavy metal.

Mountain Apple Company
P.O. Box 22569
Honolulu, HI 96823
Email: info@mountainapplecompany.com
Website: https://www.mountainapplecompany.com
Website: https://www.facebook.com/mountainapplecompany

Genres: Regional; Traditional; Contemporary

Record label releasing traditional and contemporary Hawaiian music.

Mountain Home Music Company
Email: info@mountainhomemusiccompany.com
Website: https://www.mountainhomemusiccompany.com

Genres: Roots

Record label specializing in bluegrass.

MRG Recordings
Email: submissions@mrgrecordings.com
Email: info@mrgrecordings.com
Website: https://mrgrecordings.com
Website: https://www.facebook.com/mrgrecordings

Genres: All types of music

Digital-focussed record label. Approach by email with links to music online. No audio file attachments (these will be deleted).

MTS Records
Email: michael@mtsmanagementgroup.com
Website: https://www.mtsmanagementgroup.com/mts-records/

Genres: All types of music

Send query by email or via contact form on website. Requires a promotions budget from artists.

My-Zeal Productions, Co.
Email: admin@myzealproductions.com
Email: Myzealproductions@gmail.com
Website: https://www.myzealproductions.com
Website: https://www.facebook.com/MyZealProductionsCo/

Genres: Gospel; Jazz; R&B; Pop; Country; Soul

A music production company founded in 2010 in Detroit, Michigan. Specialises in gospel music, but also produces music in other genres, such as R&B, jazz, pop, country, and soul.

New Pants Publishing
119 N. Wahsatch Ave
Colorado Springs, CO 80903
Fax: +1 (719) 634-2274
Email: rac@crlr.net
Website: http://www.newpants.com

Genres: Country; Folk; R&B; Rap; Pop; Rock

Contact: Robert A. Case

Company based in Colorado Springs, Colorado.

NoFace Records
Email: demos@nofacerecords.com
Website: https://www.nofacerecords.com
Website: https://soundcloud.com/nofacerecordsofficial

Genres: Electronic; Dubstep; House; Techno; Trance

Contact: Max Vangeli

Electronic music record label. Send demos by email. Promises to respond to every demo within two weeks.

Noisy Poet Records

276 5th Avenue, Suite 704
New York NY 10001
Email: admin@noisypoet.com
Email: booking@noisypoet.com
Website: https://www.noisypoet.com
Website: https://www.facebook.com/noisypoet/

Genres: All types of music, except: Doom Black Metal; Doom

Music arm of a multi-media company with worldwide music distribution. We deliver the sounds of tomorrow through ear-picked, unique, and authentic artists poised to breathe new life into the music industry. Doesn't aspire to reach the pinnacle of today's music landscape; we are driven to transform it.

Oh Boy Records

PO Box 150222
Nashville, TN 37215
Email: info@ohboy.com
Website: https://ohboy.com
Website: https://www.facebook.com/OhBoyRecords/

Genres: Folk; Roots

Folk / roots label based in Nashville, Tennessee.

1-2-3-4 Go! Records

420 40th Street #5
Oakland, CA 94609
Email: store@1234gorecords.com
Website: https://1234gorecords.com
Website: https://www.facebook.com/1234gorecords

Genres: Rock; Punk; Indie; Hardcore; Garage; Classic Rock; R&B; Soul; Jazz; Hip-Hop; Reggae; Ska; Funk; Country

An Independent record store and label based in Oakland, California.

The Orchard

Website: https://www.theorchard.com
Website: https://www.facebook.com/theorchard/

Genres: All types of music

Describes itself as the industry's leading distributor and artist and label services company.

Parma Recordings

44 Lafayette Rd
PO Box 1567
North Hampton NH 03862
Email: info@parmarecordings.com
Website: https://www.parmarecordings.com

Genres: Classical

Classical recording company based in North Hampton, New Hampshire.

Posi-Tone

PO Box 2848
Los Angeles, CA 90294
Email: info@posi-tone.com
Website: https://www.posi-tone.com
Website: https://soundcloud.com/posi-tone-records

Genres: Jazz

Jazz label based in Los Angeles, California, releasing both contemporary interpretations of classic material and fresh new ideas by innovative players.

Pravda Records

4245 N Knox, Suite 7
Chicago, IL 60641
Email: kenn@pravdamusic.com
Website: https://www.pravdamusic.com
Website: https://www.facebook.com/PravdaRecordsUSA/

Genres: Alternative Rock; Alternative Country; Rockabilly; Pop; R&B; Soul; Rock

Contact: Kenn Goodman

Independent record label based in Chicago. Full-service music licensing company with two in-house publishing companies.

Primarily A Cappella

Website: https://www.singers.com
Website: https://twitter.com/newsacappella

Genres: Contemporary; Jazz; Christian; World

Record label based in San Anselmo, California, specialising in a cappella. Releases include Christmas, Contemporary, Barbershop, Choral, Vocal Jazz, Christian, World, Vintage Harmony, Collegiate, Doo Wop, and Children's Choirs.

Quarto Valley Records

Email: info@quartovalleyrecords.com
Website: https://quartovalleyrecords.com
Website: https://www.facebook.com/quartovalleyrecords

Genres: Blues; Americana; Jazz; Rock

Independent label based in California.

R&S Records

Email: bandcamp@rsrecords.com
Email: merch@rsrecords.com
Website: https://www.rsrecords.com
Website: https://www.facebook.com/randsrecords

Genres: Dance; Electronic; Techno

Electronic label relaunched in 2008 with a number of remastered albums and remixes of classic tracks. Since the relaunch, the label has repositioned itself again as a forward-thinking electronic label releasing new, cutting-edge music.

Ramp Records

Email: info@ramprecords.com
Website: http://www.ramprecords.com

Genres: All types of music

Contact: Michael McDonald; Jeff Bridges; Chris Pelonis

Co-founded by a well-known Hollywood actor. Not accepting submissions as at February 2022.

Reach Out International Records (ROIR)

Website: https://roir-usa.com
Website: https://www.facebook.com/roirusa

Genres: Reggae; Rock; Punk; Indie

New York label begun in 1979 as a cassette-only label. Send demo via song and talent filtering service.

Relapse Records

Email: mailorder@relapse.com
Website: http://www.relapse.com
Website: https://www.facebook.com/RelapseRecords

Genres: Indie; Metal; Rock

Independent metal label.

Republic Records

Website: https://www.republicrecords.com
Website: https://www.facebook.com/RepublicRecordsOfficial

Genres: All types of music

Record label based in New York.

Revelation Records

PO Box 5232
Huntington Beach, CA 92615-5232
Email: webmaster@revhq.com
Website: http://www.revelationrecords.com
Website: https://www.facebook.com/revelationrecords/

Genres: Hardcore; Punk; Rock; Emo

Record label based in Huntington Beach, California.

Rhymesayers Entertainment

Minneapolis, MN
Website: https://rhymesayers.com
Website: https://www.facebook.com/Rhymesayers/

Genres: Hip-Hop

Independent hip hop record label based in Minneapolis, Minnesota, founded in 1995.

Rockzion Records
673 Valley Drive
Hermosa Beach, CA 90254
Fax: +1 (310) 379-6477
Email: rockzionrecords@rockzion.com
Website: https://rockzion.com

Genres: Christian; Rock

Record label based in Hermosa Beach, California, specialising in Christian and crossover rock.

Rotten Records
Website: https://www.rottenrecords.com
Website: https://soundcloud.com/rottenrecords

Genres: Extreme Metal; Hardcore; Punk

For the last 20 years, we have held an unyielding fist to the mainstream music industry. We've crushed all walls of conventional industry standards, carved our own niche and have always fought hard for our bands. With a staff of industry veterans and the power of major label distribution, we have always been on the cutting edge of extreme music, taking chances that other labels would never think about.

Round Hill Music
818 18th Ave. S, Suite 940
Nashville, TN 37203
Fax: +1 (615) 695-7706
Website: https://roundhillmusic.com

Genres: Roots

Record label with offices in New York, Los Angeles, Nashville, and London.

Rounder Records
Website: https://rounder.com
Website: https://www.facebook.com/RounderRecords/

Genres: Blues; Folk; Jazz; Rock; Roots; Americana

Describes itself as one of the world's most historic Americana and bluegrass record labels.

The Royalty Network, Inc.
Email: creative@roynet.com
Email: admin@roynet.com
Website: https://www.roynet.com
Website: https://www.facebook.com/RoyNetMusic

Genres: All types of music

Describes itself as one of the country's most esteemed independent music publishing companies, representing over 700,000 compositions. The company has been increasing its client roster dramatically from year to year, boasting a perpetually growing catalog of some of the most prolific songwriters, producers and artists across a multitude of genres.

Sacred Bones Records
Brooklyn, NY
Email: info@sacredbonesrecords.com
Website: https://www.sacredbonesrecords.com
Website: https://www.facebook.com/SacredBones

Genres: All types of music

Record label based in Brooklyn, New York.

Saddle Creek
Email: info@saddle-creek.com
Website: https://saddle-creek.com
Website: https://www.facebook.com/SaddleCreekRecords/

Genres: Indie Rock; Rock; Country Rock; Electronic

An independent record label founded in Omaha in 1993 with staff in Omaha, NE, Los Angeles, CA, New York, NY, Seattle, WA and Glasgow, Scotland (UK).

Schoolboy Records
Email: info@scooterbraun.com
Website: http://scooterbraun.com
Website: https://www.facebook.com/SBProjects

Genres: Pop

Part of a diversified entertainment and media company based in New York, with ventures integrating music, film, television, technology, and anthropology.

SCI Fidelity Records
Email: kevin@scifidelity.com
Email: allie@scifidelity.com
Website: https://scifidelity.com
Website: https://www.facebook.com/scifidelity

Genres: Blues; Electronic; Rock; Singer-Songwriter

Contact: Kevin Morris

Record label based in Boulder, Colorado.

Shady Records
Website: https://www.shadyrecords.com
Website: https://www.facebook.com/ShadyRecords

Genres: Hip-Hop; Rap; Urban

Record label specializing in hip hop music.

Shanachie Entertainment
37 East Clinton Street
Newton, NJ 07860
Email: facebook@shanachie.com
Website: http://www.shanachie.com
Website: https://www.facebook.com/shanachie.entertainment

Genres: Blues; Country; Electronic; Folk; Gospel; Jazz; R&B; Reggae; Singer-Songwriter; World

Record label based in New Jersey.

Shangri-La Projects, Inc.
PO Box 40106
Memphis, Tennessee 38174
Email: sherman@shangrilaprojects.com
Website: http://www.shangrilaprojects.com

Genres: Alternative Rock

Record label based in Memphis, Tennessee, with publishing and music tour arms to the business.

Shrapnel Records
Navato, CA
Email: shrapnel1@aol.com
Website: https://www.shrapnelrecords.com
Website: https://twitter.com/shrapnelrecords

Genres: Heavy Metal; Hard Rock; Blues; Progressive Metal; Blues Rock; Country; Guitar based; Jazz

Record label based in Navato, California.

Sick House Entertainment
Website: https://www.facebook.com/SickHouseEntertainment

Genres: All types of music

Contact: Nathan Sappington; Chandler Culler

Independent record label.

Side One Dummy Records
Email: info@sideonedummy.com
Website: https://sideonedummy.com
Website: https://www.facebook.com/SideOneDummy

Genres: Punk; Reggae; Hardcore; Ska; Alternative

Contact: Bill Armstrong; Joe Sib

Record label based in Los Angeles, California.

Signature Sound Recordings
32 Masonic Street
Northampton, MA 01060
Fax: +1 (509) 691-0457
Email: info@signaturesounds.com
Website: http://www.signaturesounds.com
Website: https://www.facebook.com/SignatureSoundsRecordings

Genres: Pop; Rock; Roots; Singer-Songwriter; Americana; Modern Folk; Indie

Record label based in Northampton, Massachusetts.

Silver Blue Productions / Joel Diamond Entertainment

3940 Laurel Canyon Boulevard, Suite 441
Studio City, CA 91604
Email: JDiamond20@aol.com
Website: https://www.joeldiamond.com

Genres: All types of music

Record label and publishing company based in Studio City, California. Handles a wide range of music, including classical.

Silver Wave Records

Boulder, CO
Email: jamesm@silverwave.com
Website: https://www.silverwave.com
Website: https://www.facebook.com/silverwaverecords/

Genres: Contemporary; World; Regional; New Age

Independent music label, specialising in World, New Age, and contemporary North American Indian music.

Six Degrees Records

PO Box 411347
San Francisco, CA 94141
Email: info@sixdegreesrecords.com
Website: http://sixdegreesrecords.com
Website: https://www.facebook.com/sixdegreesrecords

Genres: Electronic; Latin; Pop; Rock; World; Ambient; Folk; Contemporary; Classical; Dance

Record label based in San Francisco. Produces and markets accessible, genre-bending records that explore world music traditions, modern dance grooves, electronic music, and overlooked pop gems. Not generally accepting unsolicited demos, unless "you are determined", in which case send a private link to your music. No attachments.

Skaggs Family Records

PO Box 2478
Hendersonville, TN 37077
Fax: +1 (615) 264-8899
Email: info@skaggsfamilyrecords.com

Website: https://skaggsfamilyrecords.com
Website: https://www.facebook.com/rickyskaggsofficial

Genres: Blues; Country; Roots; Christian

Record label based in Hendersonville, Tennessee.

Skate Mountain Records

Email: info@skatemountain.com
Website: https://www.skatemountainrecords.com
Website: https://www.facebook.com/skatemountainrecords/

Genres: Alternative; Americana; Blues; Country; Hip-Hop; Pop; R&B; Rap; Rock; Rock and Roll; Roots Rock; Singer-Songwriter; Soul; Soundtracks; Classic; Commercial; Mainstream; Soulful Rock; Alternative Soul; Alternative Country; Garage; Punk

Bringing Alabama to the forefront of the music industry. With a history of success in film production, we are uniting Alabama's rich music scene with the global film business while concurrently developing and nurturing local and national talent.

This label is a family. With an ear to the street and an eye on quality, we are a close-knit group of artists, musicians, filmmakers and producers collaborating to create a truly unique one-stop shop for music and film production.

Currently creating a catalog of original music that's specifically for the filmmaker. Music from a variety of genres is available for licensing. With our vast resources in the entertainment industry from music and film experience, we uniquely provide the ability to connect artist with artist, filmmaker with musician. We produce custom music for film allowing the filmmaker to have a creative say as well as providing our traditional catalog of bad ass music.

Founded by music lovers with the artist in mind. The structure is not designed to just sell records; but to create damn good records. The rest will speak for itself.

Slip-N-Slide Records
Email: demos@slipnsliderecords.net
Email: ryan@slipnsliderecords.net
Website: https://www.slipnsliderecords.com
Website: https://soundcloud.com/
officialslipnsliderecords

Genres: Hip-Hop; Pop; Rap; Reggae; Urban; R&B

Record label hailing from South Florida. Responsible for selling over 30 million records. Send demos by email.

Slumberland Records
PO Box 19029
Oakland CA, 94619
Email: demos@slumberlandrecords.com
Email: slr@slumberlandrecords.com
Website: http://www.slumberlandrecords.com
Website: https://www.facebook.com/SlumberlandRecords

Genres: Post Punk; Indie; Pop; Punk; Lo-fi; Shoegaze

Record label based in Oakland, California. Send query by email with links to music online. No MP3 attachments.

Slush Fund Recordings
Email: david@slushfund.co
Website: https://www.slushfund.co

Genres: Rock

Rock record label established in 2007.

So Ridiculous Music Group
PO Box 18939
San Antonio, TX 78218
Email: info@srmgonline.com
Email: submit@srmgonline.com
Website: https://www.srmgonline.com/
Website: https://www.instagram.com/srmgonline

Genres: Electronic New Wave Melodic Mainstream Urban Soulful Psychedelic Progressive Acoustic Dubstep Drum and Bass Chill Country Hip-Hop Lo-fi Latin Metal Pop Punk R&B Ragga Rap Singer-Songwriter Rhythm and Blues Soul Soundtracks Spoken Word Techno Trance Trip Hop

An Independent label based out of San Antonio, Texas that tailors to the needs of creatives. We focus on a wide variety of services from Audio Production, Artist Development, Blog Placement, and Social Media Management. This is the core of where independent meets business.

Connect with us on our website to find out more!

Sonic Images Records
12400 Ventura Blvd #268
Studio City, CA 91604
Email: sonicimages@sonicimages.com
Email: AandR@sonicimages.com
Website: http://sonicimages.com

Genres: All types of music

Objective is to create an environment in which artistic expression is the norm rather than the exception. This is based on the belief that creative expression flourishes only when an artist is allowed to create free of restriction. Accordingly, the label is constantly seeking new and exciting projects that do not necessarily fit the conventional genres.

Sonic Safari Music
Jonkey Enterprises
663 West California Avenue
Glendale, CA 91203-1505
Email: chuck@sonicsafarimusic.com
Website: http://www.sonicsafarimusic.com
Website: https://www.facebook.com/SonicSafariMusic/

Genres: Ethnic; World; Traditional

Contact: Chuck Jonkey

Record label based in Glendale, California.

Sony Music Entertainment
25 Madison Avenue
New York, NY 10010
Website: https://www.sonymusic.com
Website: https://www.facebook.com/sonymusic/

Genres: All types of music

International music group with offices around the world. Only accepts demos submitted through an established music industry professional, such as a manager, lawyer, agent, producer, artist, programmer, or tastemaker.

Sony Music Nashville
Website: https://www.
sonymusicnashville.com
Website: https://www.facebook.com/
SonyMusicNashville/

Genres: Country

Country label based in Nashville, Tennessee.

Soulection
Website: https://soulection.com
Website: https://soundcloud.com/soulection

Genres: All types of music

Began as an independent radio show, now also an independent music label, festival, world-touring concert, and clothing line.

SoundScapes Media Group
1534 N. Moorpark Avenue #183
Los Angeles, CA 91360
Email: info@soundscapesmedia.com
Website: https://www.
soundscapesmedia.com
Website: https://www.facebook.com/
soundscapesmedia

Genres: Acoustic; Blues; Classic Rock; Classical; Jazz; Latin; Pop

Bringing high-definition boutique recordings of exotic music from around the world to the discerning ear.

Southern Lord Recordings
Email: info@southernlord.com
Website: https://southernlord.com
Website: https://www.facebook.com/
SLadmin

Genres: Metal; Hard Rock

Heavy metal label based in Los Angeles, California. Send demos as bandcamp stream

or similar. No zip files, MP3, or WAV. Do not submit via social media.

Spinefarm Records
1755 Broadway
New York, NY 10019

UK OFFICE
Beaumont House,
Kensington Village,
Avonmore Rd.,
London W14 8TS

FINLAND OFFICE
Merimiehenkatu 36 D
00150 Helsinki
Finland
Email: info@spinefarmrecords.com
Email: contact@spinefarm.fi
Website: https://www.spinefarmrecords.com
Website: https://www.facebook.com/
spinefarm

Genres: Hard Rock; Metal

Record label with offices in New York, London, and Helsinki.

Spiral Galaxy Entertainment
Los Angeles, CA 91343
Email: spiralgalaxyent@gmail.com
Website: https://spiralgalaxyent.com
Website: https://www.facebook.com/Spiral-
Galaxy-Entertainment-237987439580429/

Genres: Dance; Jazz; Hip-Hop; Gospel; Pop; R&B

Contact: Reggie Calloway

Record label based in Los Angeles, California.

Stackhouse & BluEsoterica
3516 Holmes Street
Kansas City, MO 64109
Email: jim@bluesoterica.com
Email: Stackhouse232@aol.com
Website: http://www.bluesoterica.com

Genres: Blues; World

Contact: Jim O'Neal

Record label based in Kansas City, Missouri.

Stef Angel Music

Email: musicsubmission@
stefangelmusic.com
Email: info@stefangelmusic.com
Website: https://stefangelmusic.com

Genres: All types of music

Send query by email with link to your music online, or for instructions on where to send physical submissions.

Stones Throw Records

2658 Griffith Park Boulevard #504
Los Angeles, CA 90039
Website: https://www.stonesthrow.com
Website: https://soundcloud.com/
stonesthrow

Genres: All types of music

Record label based in Los Angeles, California.

Strange Music Inc.

Peppergreen Media
2248 Broadway #1127
New York, NY 10024
Website: http://www.strangemusic.com

Genres: Alternative

Record label based in New York.

Strictly Rhythm

New York
Website: https://www.bmg.com/de/artist/
strictly-rhythm
Website: https://www.facebook.com/
strictlyrhythm/

Genres: House

House record label.

Stryker Records, Inc.

Greenwood, MS
Email: cdobry@strykerrecords.com
Website: http://www.strykerrecords.com
Website: https://www.facebook.com/
strykerrecords

Genres: Funky Hard Melodic Progressive; Blues Country Hip-Hop Indie Pop Rap Rock Rock and Roll

Contact: Chris Dobry

Record Label located in Greenwood Mississippi.

Sub Pop Records

2013 Fourth Avenue, Third Floor
Seattle, WA 98121
Fax: +1 (206) 441-8245
Email: info@subpop.com
Website: https://www.subpop.com
Website: https://soundcloud.com/subpop/

Genres: Americana; Electronic; Folk; Indie; Metal; Pop; Rock; Punk; Singer-Songwriter

Record label based in Seattle, the original home of Nirvana, Soundgarden and Mudhoney. Send demos via Soundcloud. See Facebook page for details.

Subliminal Records

Email: tracks@subliminalrecords.com
Website: http://www.subliminalrecords.com
Website: https://www.facebook.com/
subliminalrecords

Genres: Electronic; Dance; House; Techno

New York house and techno imprint. Send demos by email.

Suburban Noize Records

Burbank, CA
Website: https://suburbannoizerecords.com
Website: https://www.facebook.com/
suburbannoizerecords

Genres: Hard Rock; Hip-Hop; Punk; Underground

Record label based in Burbank, California.

Sugar Hill Records

Website: https://www.sugarhillrecords.com
Website: https://www.facebook.com/
sugarhillrecords

Genres: Blues; Roots; Americana

Label handling bluegrass, Americana and roots.

Sumerian Records

Email: info@sumerianrecords.com
Website: http://www.sumerianrecords.com
Website: https://www.facebook.com/
SumerianRecords

Genres: All types of music

Record label based in Los Angeles,
California.

Summit Records, Inc

PO Box 13692
Tempe, AZ 85284-3692
Email: sales@summitrecords.com
Website: https://www.summitrecords.com

Genres: Classical; Blues; Jazz

Record label founded in the late 1980s,
based in Tempe, Arizona.

Sunnyside Records

Email: francois@sunnysiderecords.com
Website: http://www.sunnysiderecords.com
Website: https://www.facebook.com/
SunnysideRecords

Genres: Jazz; Blues; World

Describes itself as a relaxed, independent
label, with an acceptance of any jazz style.

Surfdog Records

Attn: A&R
1126 South Coast Highway 101
Encinitas, CA 92024
Fax: +1 (760) 944-7808
Email: demo@surfdog.com
Website: https://surfdog.com

Genres: Contemporary; Folk; Indie; Pop;
Punk; R&B; Hip-Hop; Rap; Reggae; Rock;
Singer-Songwriter; Urban

Record label based in Encinitas, California.
Send demo by email as links to music online
(no MP3 attachments).

Symbiotic Records

Los Angeles, CA
Website: http://www.symbioticrecords.com
Website: https://www.facebook.com/
symbioticrecords

Genres: All types of music

Contact: Eric Knight; Jerjan Alim

Full service record label based in Los
Angeles, California. Send demo using form
on website.

T&R Recordings

7699 Brams Hill Drive
Dayton, Ohio 45459-4123
Fax: +1 (937) 360-3679
Email: info@tandr.us
Website: https://www.tandrrecordings.com/
Website: https://www.tandr.us/
Website: https://www.facebook.com/
tandrddp

Genres: Heavy Metal; Hard Rock; Noise
Core; Punk; Hardcore; Pop; Experimental

Contact: Justin Rissmiller

A small independent record label founded in
2015 and operated out of Dayton, Ohio. Send
links to music online via online contact form
on website.

Team Love Records

New Paltz, NY
Email: info@team-love.com
Website: https://test.team-love.com
Website: https://twitter.com/teamloverecords

Genres: All types of music

Record label based in New Paltz, New York.
Send submissions by email as Soundcloud or
Bandcamp track / playlist. No Microsoft
attachments or Google Drive links.

Tee Pee Records

Website: https://teepeerecords.com
Website: https://www.facebook.com/
teepeerecords

Genres: Indie; Metal; Punk; Rock

New York-based label dealing in indie,
metal, punk and rock.

Terminus Records

Atlanta, GA
Email: admin@terminusrecords.com
Website: https://terminusrecords.com

Website: https://www.facebook.com/
TerminusRecords/

Genres: Rock; Modern Rock; Blues

Record label based in Atlanta, Georgia.

Third Man Records
623 7th Avenue South
Nashville, TN 37203
Email: nashvillestore@thirdmanrecords.com
Website: https://thirdmanrecords.com
Website: https://www.facebook.com/
ThirdManRecords/

Genres: All types of music

Record label based in Nashville, Tennessee.
Considers itself "an innovator in the world of
vinyl records and a boundary pusher in the
world of recorded music".

37 Records & Management
3617 East Broadway Avenue #19PH
Long Beach, CA 90803
Email: Steven@37records.com
Email: Info37records@aol.com
Website: http://www.37records.com
Website: https://www.facebook.com/
37records/

Genres: All types of music

Contact: Steven McClintock

Record label and management company
based in Long Beach, California.

300 Entertainment
New York, NY
Email: info@threehundred.biz
Website: https://300ent.com

Genres: All types of music

Music company based in New York.

ThrillerTracks
Email: contact@thrillertracks.com
Website: https://www.thrillertracks.com

Genres: Electronic Ambient Instrumental
Soundtracks

Contact: Shane Cormier

An indie music label, specializing in
background production music for film and
video. Our music has been featured in BMW
and Lexus commercials in the Netherlands,
Germany and Italy.

Throne of Blood Records
New York, NY
Email: james@throneofbloodmusic.com
Website: http://www.
throneofbloodmusic.com
Website: https://www.facebook.com/
tobrecnyc/

Genres: Electronic; Club; Disco; House

Record label based in New York,
specialising in House, Electro, Disco, and
Club music.

Thump Records
Email: customersupport@thumprecords.com
Website: https://thumprecords.com
Website: https://www.facebook.com/
thumprecords

Genres: Dance; Electronic; Latin; Pop;
R&B; Rap; Hip-Hop; Urban

Home of the World's Favorite Party Music!
We specialize in music from the streets
representing decades of great sounds.

Tommy Boy
Website: https://www.tommyboy.com
Website: https://twitter.com/
TommyBoyRecords

Genres: Electronic; Hip-Hop; Latin Hip-
Hop; Dance; Alternative; Pop

Hip Hop and Electronic label founded in
New York City in 1981.

TommyBoy Entertainment LLC
New York, NY
Website: https://www.tommyboy.com
Website: https://twitter.com/
TommyBoyRecords

Genres: Hip-Hop; Dance; Electronic;
Alternative; Pop

Legendary Hip Hop and Electronic label founded in NYC in 1981.

Tooth & Nail Records
P.O. Box 12698
Seattle, WA 98111
Email: resume@toothandnail.com
Website: https://www.toothandnail.com
Website: https://www.facebook.com/toothandnail

Genres: Alternative; Rock

Record label based in Seattle, tracing its origins back to the early '90s punk and hardcore music scene. Send your best three tracks on CD by post.

Topshelf Records
540 NE Tillamook Street
Portland, OR 97212
Email: info@topshelfrecords.com
Website: https://www.topshelfrecords.com
Website: https://soundcloud.com/topshelfrecords

Genres: All types of music

Record label based in Portland, Oregon. Not accepting demos as at August 2022.

Toucan Cove Entertainment
800 Fifth Avenue #101-292
Seattle, WA 98104-3191
Email: info@toucancove.com
Website: https://toucancove.com
Website: https://twitter.com/toucancove

Genres: All types of music

Full service entertainment company.

Triple Crown Records
PO Box 222132
Great Neck, NY 11022
Email: info@triplecrownrecords.com
Website: http://www.triplecrownrecords.com
Website: https://www.facebook.com/triplecrownrecords

Genres: Alternative; Rock

Record label based in Great Neck, New York.

True Panther Sounds
New York
Email: sounds@truepanther.com
Website: https://truepanther.com
Website: https://www.facebook.com/truepanthersounds

Genres: All types of music

New York-based independent record label.

Ultra Music
Email: info@ultrarecords.com
Website: https://www.ultrarecords.com
Website: https://www.facebook.com/UltraRecordsOfficial/

Genres: Electronic; Pop; Rap; Hip-Hop; Reggae; World; Dance

Describes itself as "one step ahead in the world of dance music" and "the leading independent electronic label".

Unfun Records
PO Box 40307
Berkeley, CA 94704
Email: johnny@unfunrecords.com
Email: unfunrecords@hotmail.com
Website: http://unfunrecords.com

Genres: All types of music

Record label based in California. Send demo on CD by post.

Union Entertainment Group (UEG), Inc.
Email: info@ueginc.com
Website: http://www.ueginc.com

Genres: All types of music

Record label based in the Los Angeles area since 1987, with offices in California, Texas, Florida, Washington, Canada, and Amsterdam.

UniversalCMG World Entertainment 1954
Wells Fargo Center
Straiter Enterprise Inc. BAO
355 South Grand Avenue
Los Angeles, CA 90071

Email: universalrecord@yahoo.com
Website: https://www.unicmg.com

Genres: All types of music

Record label based in Los Angeles, California.

Urband & Lazar
Los Angeles, CA
Email: help@urbandlazar.com
Website: https://www.urbandlazar.com

Genres: Indie Rock; Alternative; Singer-Songwriter

A premier, Grammy-Award winning music publishing company.

Vagrant Records
Website: https://vagrant.com
Website: https://www.facebook.com/vagrantrecords

Genres: All types of music

Record label based in California. Focuses on rock, but features artists in a variety of other genres including folk, soul, electronic, and pop.

Valley Entertainment
Email: jon@valley-entertainment.com
Email: erika@valley-entertainment.com
Website: https://www.valley-entertainment.com
Website: https://www.facebook.com/valleyent

Genres: Jazz; New Age; Rock; World; Blues; Country; Celtic; Instrumental

A privately owned record label that was founded in the mid-nineties. The label includes an eclectic repertoire from pop to alternative, with focus on singer-songwriters, modern Irish musicians and World music.

Van Richter
Email: manager@vanrichter.net
Email: vanrichterrec@gmail.com
Website: https://www.vanrichter.net
Website: https://www.facebook.com/vanrichter.net/

Genres: Industrial; Gothic; Ambient; Synthpop

Our Artists cover the entire spectrum of the Industrial sub genres including Aggro, Electro, Darkwave, Noise, and Ambient.

Verve Label Group
Universal Music Group
2220 Colorado Ave
Santa Monica, CA 90404
Website: https://www.vervelabelgroup.com
Website: https://www.facebook.com/ververecords/

Genres: Jazz; Contemporary; Pop; R&B

Record label based in Santa Monica, California.

Victory Records
Fax: +1 (312) 666-8665
Email: info@victoryrecords.com
Website: https://victoryrecords.com
Website: https://www.facebook.com/VictoryRecords

Genres: Metal; Rock; Indie; Hardcore; Punk

Formed in 1989, it separated itself from the pack as the definitive independent label for punk, hardcore, emo, metal and alternative. Supplying 30 years of formative music to diehard audiences everywhere, the Chicago-bred and -based label cranked up the voices of three generations of iconoclasts and built a culture without compromise.

Vineyard Worship
Email: info@vineyardworship.com
Website: https://www.vineyardworship.com
Website: https://www.facebook.com/VineyardWorship

Genres: Christian

Record label releasing Christian music.

Viper Records
Website: https://www.viperrecords.com
Website: https://www.facebook.com/viperrecords/

Genres: Hip-Hop; Rap

A boutique indie label created to level an uneven playing field between artists and labels. Approach via online contact form. Tries to respond, but not always possible due to volume of submissions.

Visionary Music Group

Website: http://www.teamvisionary.com
Website: https://www.facebook.com/VisionaryMusicGroup

Genres: Urban

Not accepting enquiries as at October 2022.

VP Records

89-05 138th Street,
Jamaica, NY 11435

FLORIDA:
6022 S.W. 21st Street
Miramar, FL 33023

LONDON:
Room 302, Edinburgh House
170 Kennington Lane
London
SE11 5DP
UK

JAMAICA, WI:
1 Upper Sandringham Ave,
Kingston 10, Jamaica
Fax: +1 (718) 658-3573
Email: information@vprecords.com
Website: https://www.vprecords.com
Website: https://soundcloud.com/vp_records

Genres: Reggae

Record label based in Jamaica, New York, with offices in Florida, London, and Jamaica.

Warner Music Group (WMG)

1633 Broadway
New York, NY 10019
Website: https://www.wmg.com
Website: https://www.facebook.com/warnermusicgroup

Genres: All types of music

No direct submissions. Demos should be submitted to specific label via an established

industry professional, such as a manager, agent, lawyer, journalist, or existing artist, etc.

Warner Music Nashville

Website: https://www.warnermusicnashville.com
Website: https://www.facebook.com/WarnerMusicNashville

Genres: Country

Country label based in Nashville Tennessee.

Warner Records

1633 Broadway
New York, NY 10019
Website: https://www.warnerrecords.com

Genres: All types of music

Record label based in New York.

Watertower Music

Email: wtmsupport@Warnerbros.com
Website: http://www.watertower-music.com
Website: https://soundcloud.com/watertowermusic

Genres: Soundtracks

Record label based in Los Angeles, California, specialising in movie soundtracks.

Waveform Records

Email: webguest@waveformhq.com
Website: https://www.waveformrecords.com
Website: https://www.facebook.com/waveformrecords

Genres: Downtempo Electronic; Chill; Ambient

Handles mid to downtempo chill and ambient music they call "exotic electronica". Send query by email with links to music online.

Wax Records Inc.

Email: info@waxrecords.com
Website: https://www.waxrecords.com

Genres: Pop; Rock

Always looking to expand their roster with new and exciting talent. Send query by email with links to music online. No large file attachments.

Waxploitation Records
Los Angeles
Email: artists@waxploitation.com
Website: https://waxploitation.com
Website: https://soundcloud.com/waxploitation

Genres: Hip-Hop

Record label based in Los Angeles, California.

Wicked Cool Records
New York
Website: http://wickedcoolrecords.com
Website: https://www.facebook.com/WickedCoolRecords/

Genres: Garage Rock; Rock and Roll

Label based in New York, created in 2005 to support new Rock and Roll.

Wild Records
Los Angeles, CA
Website: https://wildrecordsusa.com
Website: https://twitter.com/wildrecords

Genres: Blues; Garage; Rockabilly; Soul; Surf

Contact: Reb Kennedy

Record label based in Los Angeles, California.

Word Records
Website: https://www.curb.com/WordRecords/
Website: https://www.facebook.com/curbrecords

Genres: Contemporary; Christian; Country; Hip-Hop; Rap; Rock

Faith-based record label.

Yep Roc Records
Email: info@yeproc.com
Website: https://www.yeproc.com
Website: https://www.facebook.com/yeproc

Genres: Blues; Country; Folk; Pop; Rock; Roots

We believe in the vision of each of our Artists. We strive to serve each project based on its unique characteristics. Through strong promotional and marketing efforts, our goal is to reach as large an audience as possible with each new release.

UK Record Labels

For the most up-to-date listings of these and hundreds of other record labels, visit https://www.musicsocket.com/recordlabels

*To claim your **free** access to the site, please see the back of this book.*

0207 Def Jam Recordings

London
Website: https://www.0207defjam.com
Website: https://www.facebook.com/
0207defjam

Genres: Urban; Hip-Hop; R&B; Soul

A dynamic London-born label which endeavours to deliver high quality music alongside groundbreaking artist campaigns. Founded in 2020, it provides a space where impactful and unfiltered music can find its way to the world. It is also the UK home of the iconic American label which has shaped and propelled cutting-edge hip hop culture around the world for over 35 years.

1043 Recordings

Riverside
New Bailey Street
Salford
M3 5FS
Email: label@futureworksmusic.co.uk
Website: https://1043recordings.com
Website: https://www.youtube.com/user/
futureworksmusic/videos

Genres: All types of music

We pride ourselves on our high-quality production values and eclectic mix of genres. Our release roster is full of singer-songwriters, DJs, bands, and multimedia

artists, and we would be excited to add your music to this list, whether you're making beats, tracks, scores, sound design, or game audio. Please connect with us on our socials, use the contact form or drop us a mail.

Acorn Records

Website: https://twitter.com/acornrecordsuk

Genres: All types of music

Global label involved worldwide with all different types of music.

The Adult Teeth Recording Company

Website: https://www.adultteeth.co.uk
Website: https://www.facebook.com/
adultteeth/

Genres: Alternative Rock; Experimental Pop; Indie; Electronic; Ambient

Record label founded in 2012, dealing in alternate rock, experimental pop, indie, electronic, ambient and spoken word. Formats: vinyl, CD, cassette and digital.

Akira

London
Email: info@akirarecords.com
Website: https://www.akirarecords.com

Website: https://www.facebook.com/ AkiraRecords/

Genres: Folk; Rock; Indie; Electronic

Label and Production House intent on exposing the best new talents and the most exciting music.

Alya Records
Room 16
The John Banner Centre
620 Attercliffe Road
Sheffield
S9 3QS
Email: hello@alyarecords.com
Website: https://alyarecords.co.uk
Website: https://www.facebook.com/ AlyaRecords/

Genres: All types of music

Exists to help develop artists of all genres, backgrounds and levels. If you want to know more then get in touch by email.

AnalogueTrash Ltd
2 Unity Street
Todmorden
West Yorkshire
OL14 7SR
Email: hello@analoguetrash.com
Email: label@analoguetrash.com
Website: https://www.analoguetrash.com
Website: https://soundcloud.com/ analoguetrash

Genres: Alternative

Small independent record label run from a spare bedroom in Todmorden, West Yorkshire. Send demos by email.

Axtone
Website: https://www.axtone.com
Website: https://www.labelradar.com/labels/ axtone/profile

Genres: Dance; House; Disco; Dubstep; Electronic; Techno; Trance

Send demos via online submission system. See website for details.

Bad Bat Records
Chester
Email: badbatrecords@gmail.com
Website: https://badbatrecords. bandcamp.com
Website: https://soundcloud.com/ badbatrecords

Genres: Alternative; Electronic; Ambient; Experimental; Dance

An eclectic label supporting independent artists. Dabbling in electronic and ambient music.

Birdland Records
Email: hq@birdlandrecords.com
Email: nick@birdlandrecords.com
Website: https://birdlandrecords.com
Website: https://soundcloud.com/ birdlandrecords

Genres: Singer-Songwriter

Independent record label.

Black Butter Records
London
Email: info@black-butter.co.uk
Email: demos@black-butter.co.uk
Website: https://www.black-butter.com
Website: https://soundcloud.com/black-butter-records

Genres: Dance; Hip-Hop; Urban

Record label based in London. Send query by email with "Demo" in the subject line, including Soundcloud links.

Blindsight Records
Email: info@blindsightrecords.co.uk
Website: http://www.blindsightrecords.co.uk
Website: https://soundcloud.com/blindsight-records

Genres: Rock; Electronic; Ambient; Post Rock; Hardcore; Metal

Record label based in the United Kingdom. For demo submissions make contact by email, or use Soundcloud.

Bloo Coo Records

Email: contact@bloocoorecords.com
Website: https://www.bloocoorecords.com
Website: https://www.facebook.com/
BlooCooRecords/

Genres: All types of music

Independent record label.

Bluesky Pie Records

Folkestone
Kent
Email: Blueskypielive@gmail.com
Website: https://www.facebook.com/
blueskypierecords/

Genres: All types of music

Not-for-profit, ethical record label. Send query by email with MP3s or links to music online.

Bohemian Jukebox

Email: recordings@bohemianjukebox.com
Website: https://www.bohemianjukebox.com
Website: https://soundcloud.com/bencalvert

Genres: Post Folk; Singer-Songwriter; Psychedelic; Alternative Acoustic; Leftfield Acoustic; Experimental

Contact: Ben Calvert

Record label with offices in Birmingham. Works with Post-Folk, Alternative and Psychedelic lyric-centric songwriters who have a way with poetics.

Bomber Music Ltd

125-135 Preston Road
London
BN1 6AF
Email: postbox@bombermusic.com
Website: https://www.bombermusic.com
Website: https://www.facebook.com/
bombermusic

Genres: Punk; Rock and Roll; Rockabilly; Reggae; Ska; Underground;

Label set up in 2010 by an independent music company, describing itself as the UK's leading alternative music publisher.

Border Community

Website: http://www.bordercommunity.com
Website: https://soundcloud.com/border-community

Genres: Electronic

Record label based in London. Send streaming links via online contact form.

Boslevan Records

Email: boslevanrecords@gmail.com
Email: vinosangre@gmail.com
Website: https://boslevanrecords.co.uk
Website: https://www.facebook.com/
BoslevanRecords

Genres: Hardcore; Indie; Punk; Punk Rock

DIY record label based in Cornwall.

Botchit & Scarper Records

Website: https://www.botchitandscarper.com
Website: https://www.facebook.com/botchit

Genres: Break Beat

Record label founded in 1995. Describes itself as unique in present times, in that it concentrates on artist development; and "has reinvented the way breakbeats impact the dance world".

Brain Bomb Productions (BBP)

Website: https://www.brainbomb.com/
Website: https://soundcloud.com/brainbomb

Genres: Ambient; Chill; Downtempo; Break Beat; House; Techno; Tribal; Trance; Drum and Bass

Contact: Luke Harrison

Small indie label that has grown organically over many years into a high impact producer of music audio and video productions.

Bread Records

Manchester
Email: michael@breadrecords.co.uk
Website: https://breadrecords.co.uk
Website: https://www.facebook.com/
breadrecords

Genres: Alternative Rock; Folk; Indie; Rock

A Manchester-based record label and promotions team specialising in live music, events and releases. We put on a range of events across Manchester and aim to promote local and unsigned bands, artists and songwriters.

Breakfast Records LLP

Bristol
Email: submissions@breakfastrecords.co.uk
Email: josh@breakfastrecords.co.uk
Website: https://breakfastrecords.co.uk
Website: https://www.facebook.com/breakfastlabel

Genres: Folk; Garage; Guitar based; Indie; Punk; Punk Rock

Contact: Dan Anthony; Josh Jarman

An independent record label based in Bristol that specialises in releasing punk, indie and folk records. Send demos by email.

Burning Shed Limited

Unit B, Yarefield Park
Old Hall Road
Norwich
NR4 6FF
Email: support@burningshed.com
Website: https://burningshed.com

Genres: Ambient; Electronic; Singer-Songwriter; Progressive; Rock

Contact: Tim Bowness; Peter Chilvers; Pete Morgan

Online label and record store. Send demos by post or as emails with download links. No attachments. Response not guaranteed unless interested.

Buzz Records

Email: studio@thebuzzgroup.co.uk
Website: https://thebuzzgroup.co.uk
Website: https://www.facebook.com/buzzpublicity

Genres: Alternative Roots; Blues; Country; Folk; Alternative Blues

A small independent alternative bluses label focusing on "music that has an insurgent twist and an original angle, dragging old-time sounds kicking and screaming into the 21st century." Focussing now on a single artist, so not taking on any new acts.

Candlelight Records

Beaumont House
Kensington Village
Avonmore Rd
London
W14 8TS
Email: info@spinefarmrecords.com
Website: https://www.candlelightrecords.co.uk
Website: https://www.facebook.com/candlelightrecords/

Genres: Metal

Metal record label based in London, with offices in New York and Helsinki.

Caritas Records

Achmore
Moss Road
Ullapool
Ross-shire
IV26 2TF
Email: caritas-records@caritas-music.co.uk
Email: info@caritas-music.co.uk
Website: https://www.caritas-music.co.uk

Genres: Classical

Contact: Katharine Douglas

Record label handling Classical and Choral music.

CCT Records

45 Staple Lodge Road
Northfield
Birmingham
B31 3BZ
Website: https://milwaukie2003.wixsite.com/cctrecords

Genres: Alternative; Electronic; Ambient; Dubstep; Hip-Hop; Techno

Always interested in new amazing artists, so if you feel you're making cutting edge sounds (especially futuristic tech-house vibes) email a link or use the dropbox. You can also send a CD by post.

Chalkpit Records Ltd
Isle of Wight
Email: chalkpitrecords@gmail.com
Website: https://www.chalkpitrecords.com
Website: https://www.facebook.com/
chalkpitrecords/

Genres: Alternative; Funk; Indie; Pop; Soul

Contact: Silas Gregory

Record label based on the Isle of Wight.
Send query by email with links to music
online. No MP3 attachments.

Champion Records
181 High Street
Harlesden
London
NW10 4TE
Email: rob@championrecords.co.uk
Email: raj@championrecords.co.uk
Website: https://www.
championrecords.co.uk
Website: https://www.facebook.com/
championrecords/

Genres: Garage; House; Singer-Songwriter

Record label based in Harlesden, London.

Chandos Records Ltd
Chandos House
1 Commerce Park
Commerce Way
Colchester
Essex
CO2 8HX
Fax: +44 (0) 1206 225201
Website: https://www.chandos.net

Genres: Classical

Classical record label, based in Colchester,
Essex.

Chemikal Underground Records
Glasgow
Email: info@chemikal.co.uk
Website: https://chemikal.co.uk
Website: https://soundcloud.com/chemikal-
underground

Genres: Alternative

Record label based in Glasgow, Scotland.

Cherry Red Records
Power Road Studios
114 Power Road
London
W4 5PY
Fax: +44 (0) 20 8747 4030
Email: infonet@cherryred.co.uk
Email: ideas@cherryred.co.uk
Website: https://www.cherryred.co.uk
Website: https://www.facebook.com/
CherryRedRecords

Genres: All types of music

A proudly independent record label making
noise in West London for more than 40
years.

Chocolate Fireguard Music Ltd
PO Box 461
Huddersfield
West Yorkshire
HD5 8WL
Email: info@chocolatefireguard.co.uk
Website: http://www.
chocolatefireguard.co.uk
Website: https://www.facebook.com/
ChocolateFireguardMusic
Website: http://www.myspace.com/
chocolatefireguardmusic

Genres: Dance; Electronic; Hip-Hop; Rock

Record label based in Huddersfield, West
Yorkshire. Always looking for new music,
so submit your tracks if you think they are
right for this label after consulting the
website.

Circuit Records
c/o Higher Rhythm Ltd
53-57 Nether Hall Road
Doncaster
South Yorkshire
DN1 2PG
Email: mail@circuitrecords.co.uk
Website: https://www.circuitrecords.co.uk

Website: https://www.facebook.com/
circuitrecordsuk

Genres: All types of music

Record label from a Yorkshire based music
and media company, also running a radio
station, a recording studio, artist
development programmes, live events, and
lots of other things. Accepts approaches from
artists from Yorkshire.

Circus Recordings
Website: https://www.circusrecordings.com
Website: https://www.facebook.com/
CircusRecordings

Genres: House; Techno

Record label than runs parallel to the events
side of the business, which has been
releasing music since 2009. Describes itself
as a serious go to label for house and techno
and serious electronic music.

Circus Records
17 Chocolate Studios
7 Shepherdess Place
Shoreditch
London
N1 7LJ
Email: info@circus-records.co.uk
Website: https://circus-records.co.uk
Website: https://soundcloud.com/
circusrecords

Genres: Electronic

Electronic record label based in Shoreditch,
London. Send query by email with
soundcloud links for up to two tracks.

Clue Records
Leeds
Email: info@cluerecords.com
Website: https://cluerecords.bandcamp.com
Website: https://www.facebook.com/
ClueRecords

Genres: Alternative; Indie; Rock

An independent record label based in Leeds,
UK. "We work with artists we adore and
release music we love."

Cold Spring
Unit 4B, Canal Foundry
Albion Road
New Mills
Derbyshire
SK22 3EZ
Email: demos@coldspring.co.uk
Email: info@coldspring.co.uk
Website: https://coldspring.co.uk

Genres: Ambient; Industrial; Noise Core;
Power Electronic; Doom; Experimental;
Soundtracks

Record label / mailorder store / distributor
based in Derbyshire. Send demos by post or
send links to music online by email, but do
not send attachments by email. Replies to all
demos, but do not expect an immediate
reply.

Coloursounds
Leeds
Website: https://soundcloud.com/
coloursoundsuk
Website: https://www.facebook.com/
coloursoundsuk

Genres: Electronic; House; Disco; Indie; Pop

Represents an eclectic range of
contemporary electronic music.

Columbia Records
9 Derry Street
London
W8 5HY
Website: https://www.columbia.co.uk
Website: https://www.facebook.com/
ColumbiaRecordsUK/

Genres: All types of music

UK office of the oldest surviving brand name
in pre-recorded sound.

Come Play With Me
Yorkshire Dance
3 St Peter's Square
Leeds
LS9 8AH
Email: label@cpwm.co
Website: https://cpwmrecords.com

Website: https://www.facebook.com/
cpwmrecords

Genres: All types of music

Our aim is to support and develop diverse
artists and demographics, showcasing the
best in new Northern talent.

Cooking Vinyl
12 & 13 Swainson Road
London
W3 7XB
Email: info@cookingvinyl.com
Website: https://www.cookingvinyl.com
Website: https://www.facebook.com/
cookingvinylrecords/

Genres: All types of music

Record label based in London. Home to an
eclectic mix of acclaimed artists.

Cr2 Records
Email: demos@cr2records.com
Email: info@cr2records.co.uk
Website: http://www.cr2records.co.uk
Website: https://soundcloud.com/cr2records

Genres: Dance; House; Techno; Electronic

Contact: Mark Brown

Send demos by email as private Soundcloud
links, or via online submission system. No
MP3 email attachments.

CRD Records Limited
TRURO
TR2 5YJ
Email: info@crdrecords.com
Website: https://www.crdrecords.com
Website: https://www.facebook.com/
CRDrecords

Genres: Classical

Classical record label based in Truro,
Cornwall.

Critical Music
Email: badger@criticalmusic.com
Website: https://criticalmusic.com
Website: https://www.facebook.com/
criticalmusicdnb

Genres: Drum and Bass; Electronic; Dance

Electronic dance music label committed to
shining a light on the new generation of
Drum & Bass artists. Submit demos via
online form on website.

Cruise International Records
Alerton Grange Vale
Leeds
LS17 6LS
Email: info@cruisedigital.co.uk
Website: https://www.cruisedigital.co.uk
Website: https://www.facebook.com/
cruisedigitalmusic/

Genres: All types of music

Record label based in Leeds, West
Yorkshire. Send query through form on
website.

Dance To The Radio
Email: demos@futuresoundgroup.com
Website: https://www.dancetotheradio.com
Website: https://www.facebook.com/
dancetotheradio

Genres: Experimental; Indie

Music group including label, publishing, and
artist management. Send demos as streaming
links by email. No attachments.

Dead by Mono Records
Email: info@deadbymono.com
Website: https://www.deadbymono.com
Website: https://www.facebook.com/
DeadbyMonoRecords

Genres: Garage Rock Rhythm and Blues
Rock and Roll Surf Rockabilly Psychebilly
Punk Instrumental Blues Horror Alternative
New Wave Psychedelic

Independent record label and mail order
based in the UK. Dedicated to garage rock,
surf music and rock'n' roll since 2005.

Decca Records
Universal Music
4 Pancras Square
London
N1C 4AG

Email: info@decca.com
Website: http://decca.com
Website: https://www.facebook.com/
deccarecords

Genres: All types of music

Describes itself as a legendary British record label, which has been home to "some of the greatest recording artists ever".

Deek Recordings
Email: deekrecordings@gmail.com
Website: http://www.deekrecordings.co.uk
Website: https://www.facebook.com/
deekrecordings

Genres: All types of music

Contact: Nathan Jenkins

Record label established in 2012.

Defected
Email: demos@defected.com
Website: https://defected.com
Website: https://www.facebook.com/
DefectedRecords

Genres: Dance; House

Record label based in London. Dedicated to the finest in house, from its label and numerous associated imprints, to its events and festivals.

Demon Music Group
BBC Worldwide Ltd
Television Centre
101 Wood Lane
London
W12 7FA
Email: info@demonmusicgroup.co.uk
Website: https://www.
demonmusicgroup.co.uk
Website: https://www.facebook.com/
DemonMusicGroup

Genres: Alternative; Indie

Describes itself as the UK's largest independent record company. Specialises in the reissues of catalogue titles so does not sign new acts.

Dirty Bingo Records
Email: sacha@dirtybingorecords.com
Website: http://www.dirtybingo.co.uk
Website: https://www.facebook.com/
DirtyBingoRecs/

Genres: Alternative; Electronic; Indie; Indie Pop

First a club now an independent record label. We capture what is vital in music today with limited runs of vinyl pressings, digital downloads and live shows. Every release is tailored, every release is personal, and our bands' sound and vision are paramount. Approach via contact form on website.

Dirty Hit
Email: info@dirtyhit.co.uk
Website: https://dirtyhit.co.uk
Website: https://www.facebook.com/
DirtyHit/

Genres: Alternative

Independent record label formed in 2009, with a desire to develop and nurture homegrown artists. Frustration with outdated record company models means a commitment to long-term career building principals. Send query by email with links to music online.

Disconnect Disconnect Records
Website: https://
disconnectdisconnectrecords.bigcartel.com
Website: https://www.facebook.com/
disconnectdisconnectrecords

Genres: Emo; Pop Punk; Post Punk; Punk; Punk Rock; Hardcore

UK punk rock label focusing on independent punk rock bands from the UK and further afield.

Dissention Records
Website: https://www.dissentionrecords.com
Website: https://twitter.com/dissentionmgmt

Genres: Punk; Alternative

Independent record label started in Boston but now based in the UK. Heavily influenced by punk rock music, specifically the DC hardcore scene.

Divine Art Record Company
176-178 Pontefract Road
Cudworth
Barnsley
S72 8BE
Email: info@divineartrecords.com
Website: https://divineartrecords.com

Genres: Classical

Classical music label with offices in the UK and US. See website for brochure on recording with the label, and the new project proposal form. No forms of current popular music. Offers both recording service arrangement and traditional royalty arrangement, covering up-front costs. See website for full details.

Do As You Please
Email: niall@doasyouplease.uk
Website: https://www.doasyouplease.uk
Website: https://www.facebook.com/doasyoupleaseuk

Genres: Break Beat; Acid House; Garage; House; Techno

Record label specialising in Acid House, Breakbeat, Techno, Garage, and House.

Dog Knights Productions
Email: info@dogknightsproductions.com
Email: dogknightsproductions@hotmail.co.uk
Website: https://dogknightsproductions.com/
Website: https://www.facebook.com/dogknights

Genres: Hardcore; Punk

UK-based independent record label.

Doing Life Records
Liverpool
Email: info@doinglifiterecords.com
Website: https://doinglifiterecords.bandcamp.com
Website: https://www.facebook.com/doinglifiterecords/

Genres: Alternative; Emo; Indie; Rock; Singer-Songwriter

Not-for-profit label focused on community and developing the next generation of alternative Liverpool musicians.

Domino Recording Company
Website: https://www.dominomusic.com
Website: https://soundcloud.com/dominorecordco

Genres: Alternative

Founded in Putney, South West London, in 1993. Send demos via Soundcloud.

Donut Records
Bristol
Email: donutrecords@hotmail.com
Website: https://donutrecords.bandcamp.com
Website: https://soundcloud.com/donut-records

Genres: Indie; Psychedelic Rock; Rock and Roll

Independent record label based in Bristol.

Dorado Music
19A Douglas Street, Unit B
London
SW1P 4PA

US OFFICE:
4770 Biscayne Blvd. Suite 900
Miami, FL 33137
United States
Email: contact@dorado.net
Email: ollie@dorado.net
Website: https://dorado.net
Website: https://www.facebook.com/doradorecords/

Genres: Acid Jazz; Drum and Bass; Jazz; Electronic; Hip-Hop; Soul

Record label with offices in London and Florida.

Double Denim Records
Email: jack@doubledenimrecords.com
Website: https://www.doubledenimrecords.com

Website: https://www.facebook.com/
doubledenimrecords

Genres: Electronic; Pop

Record label founded in 2010. Send query by email.

Droma Records
Website: https://dromarecords.
bandcamp.com
Website: https://www.facebook.com/
dromarecords/

Genres: All types of music

Describes itself as a West Midlands based musical projects machine. Releases music by Midlands based bands.

Drongo Records
Norwich
Website: https://drongorecords.
bandcamp.com
Website: https://facebook.com/
DrongoRecords

Genres: Alternative; Rock

Record label based in Norwich.

Drum With Our Hands
Email: info@drumwithourhands.com
Email: steve@drumwithourhands.com
Website: http://www.drumwithourhands.com
Website: https://www.facebook.com/
DWOHrecords

Genres: Electronic; Alternative Folk; Classic Pop; Ambient

Contact: Andy; Steve

Indie/DIY record label from North Wales.

Earache London
Email: tim@earache.com
Email: dan.hardingham@earache.com
Website: https://www.earache.com

Genres: Metal

Send submissions via Artist Submission Form on website.

Easy Life Records
Email: info@easyliferecords.com
Website: https://easyliferecords.com
Website: https://www.facebook.com/
easyliferecords/

Genres: Alternative

Independent label formed in 2014.

Electric Honey Music
Email: electrichoney1992@gmail.com
Website: https://www.facebook.com/
electrichoneymusic
Website: https://linktr.ee/
electrichoneyrecords

Genres: All types of music

Independent student-run record label.

Elevate Records
Email: hello@elevaterecords.co.uk
Website: https://www.elevaterecords.co.uk
Website: https://soundcloud.com/
elevaterecordsuk

Genres: Drum and Bass

Submit demos via online submission system. See website for details.

EMI Records
Website: https://emirecords.com
Website: https://www.facebook.com/
EMIRecordsUK

Genres: All types of music

Describes itself as "one of the most defining labels in popular music. With an illustrious history and a diverse and ground-breaking roster of acts, the label has been at the forefront of every seminal musical movement."

Engineer Records
Email: label@engineerrecords.com
Email: info@engineerrecords.com
Website: https://www.engineerrecords.com
Website: https://www.facebook.com/
engineerrecords

Genres: Hardcore Punk; Emo; Alternative; Indie

Independent, alternative record label from England since 1999 sending over 300 releases out to the world. Send query by email with bio, band pic, and any record artwork, with mp3s or links to music online. No large files.

Enhanced Music
20-24 Old Street
London
EC1V 9AB
Email: info@enhancedmusic.com
Email: shop@enhancedmusic.com
Website: https://www.enhancedmusic.com
Website: https://www.labelradar.com/labels/enhancedmusic/portal

Genres: Ambient; Chill; Electronic; Trance

Record label based in London. Send demos via online upload system. See website for link.

Erased Tapes Records
London
Website: https://www.erasedtapes.com

Genres: All types of music

A truly independent record label that has disrupted the industry and rejuvenated the musical landscape. The London-based label has consistently nurtured genre-defying artists from all around the world without losing its avant-garde ethos.

Esoteric Recordings
Email: esotericrecordings@aol.com
Website: http://www.esotericrecordings.com
Website: https://www.facebook.com/EsotericRecordings/

Genres: Progressive Rock; Psychedelic Rock; Classic Rock; Electronic; Alternative Pop

Contact: Vicky Powell

The home of quality reissues in the Progressive, Classic Rock and Psychedelic genres.

Fantastic Plastic
Unit 6 Trident House
London
SE1 8QW
Email: info@fpmusic.org
Website: https://www.fpmusic.org
Website: https://www.facebook.com/fpmusicco

Genres: Alternative Guitar based

Independent record label also offering artist management and music publishing.

Far Out Recordings
Email: info@faroutrecordings.com
Website: https://www.faroutrecordings.com
Website: https://soundcloud.com/faroutrecs

Genres: Regional; Electronic

London-based record label dealing in Brazilian and electronic music.

Fast Static
Website: https://faststatic.co.uk
Website: https://www.facebook.com/FastStatic

Genres: Alternative

Independent record label and events collective.

Fat Hippy Records
c/o Captain Tom Music
11 – 15 Ann Street
Aberdeen
AB25 3LH
Email: info@fathippyrecords.co.uk
Website: http://www.fathippyrecords.co.uk
Website: https://www.facebook.com/fathippyrecords

Genres: All types of music

Independent record label based in Aberdeen, Scotland. Founded in 2002 to help raise the profile of the burgeoning North East Scotland music scene, and with the hope of overthrowing the "evil tyranny of the $ driven corporate music industry" and replacing it with their own "slightly nicer one".

FatCat Records UK
PO Box 3400
Brighton
BN1 4WG
Email: info@fat-cat.co.uk
Website: http://www.fat-cat.co.uk
Website: https://soundcloud.com/
fatcatrecords

Genres: All types of music

Record label with offices in the US and UK.
Send email with links to music online. Also
accepts physical demos by post.

Fellside Recordings
Website: https://www.fellside.com
Website: https://www.facebook.com/
fellsiderecordings

Genres: Folk; Traditional; Roots

Record label specialising in Folk, Traditional
and Roots music. A wide range of styles and
presentation and an equally wide range of
artists, from those well-established to those
making their debut albums.

Fiction Records
Website: https://fictionrecords.co.uk
Website: https://soundcloud.com/
fictionrecords

Genres: All types of music

London-based record label originally
founded in 1978 and then, after a period of
inactivity, re-started in 2004.

Fierce Panda Records
Email: simon@fiercepanda.co.uk
Email: chris@fiercepanda.co.uk
Website: http://www.fiercepanda.co.uk
Website: https://www.facebook.com/
fiercepanda

Genres: Indie; Rock

Indie rock label based in London. Approach
by email with links to music on Soundcloud
or Bandcamp or Facebook.

Fika Recordings
Email: demos@fikarecordings.com
Email: info@fikarecordings.com
Website: http://fikarecordings.com
Website: https://www.facebook.com/
fikarecordings

Genres: Folk; Guitar based; Indie

Send query by email with bio, details of
artists you like, bands you've played shows
with, links to press or radio coverage, and
links to streaming music online (e.g.
Soundcloud or Bandcamp). Discriminates
against artists based on their political beliefs.

Finger Lickin' Records
6 Windmill Street
London
W1T 2JB
Email: info@fingerlickin.co.uk
Website: http://www.fingerlickin.co.uk
Website: https://soundcloud.com/
fingerlickinmanagement

Genres: Break Beat; Dance; Hip-Hop;
Electronic

Record label based in London.

Fire Records
4 Tyssen Street
Dalston
London
E8 2FJ
Email: james@firerecords.com
Website: https://www.firerecords.com
Website: https://www.facebook.com/
Firerecords

Genres: Experimental; New Wave; Post
Punk; Psychedelic Rock

Contact: James Nicholls

Record label with offices in London, New
York, and Bologna.

Fired Up Records
Lincoln
Email: sarahc@fireduprecords.com

Website: https://fireduprecords.com
Website: https://soundcloud.com/
fireduprecords

Genres: Hard Dance

Contact: Sarah Curtis

Record label based in Lincoln, UK.
Specialises in hard dance. Submit demo via
online submission form.

First Night Records
Website: http://first-night-records.co.uk

Genres: Soundtracks

Contact: John Craig OBE

Mainly deals in theatre, film and TV
soundtracks.

First Run Records
Glasgow
Email: billy@23rdprecinctmusic.com
Email: susan@23rdprecinctmusic.com
Website: https://www.
23rdprecinctmusic.com/collections/first-run
Website: https://www.
23rdprecinctmusic.com/

Genres: Commercial; Indie; Pop

Record label based in Glasgow, Scotland.

Flair Records
1st Floor
25 Commercial Street
Brighouse
HD6 1AF
Email: info@now-music.com
Website: https://www.now-music.com
Website: https://www.facebook.com/Now-
Music-388961064509727/

Genres: Pop

Record label based in West Yorkshire,
dealing with pop artists.

Flat50 Records
Stratford
London
Email: info@flat50.co.uk
Email: paul@flat50.co.uk
Website: http://www.flat50.co.uk
Website: https://www.facebook.com/
Flat50Arts

Genres: Alternative; Blues; Country; Folk;
Indie; Punk; Rock

Arts collective providing arts events,
management, and promotional organisation,
as well as running an independent record
label working with bands and singer-
songwriters. Always looking for exciting
new artists and acts.

Flowers in the Dustbin
Glasgow
Email: info@flowersinthedustbin.org
Website: http://flowersinthedustbin.org
Website: https://www.facebook.com/
flowersinthedustbin

Genres: All types of music

Contact: Stephen McKee

Record label based in Glasgow.

Folkroom Records
Email: stephen@folkroom.co.uk
Email: ben@folkroom.co.uk
Website: http://folkroom.co.uk
Website: https://www.facebook.com/
Folkroom

Genres: Folk

Folk label based in London. Acts are
generally discovered by playing at the
fortnightly live gigs. Best method of
approach is therefore to apply to play at one
of the gigs.

Fox Records
Email: jd@foxrecords.net
Website: http://www.foxrecords.
limitedrun.com
Website: https://www.facebook.com/
foxrecordings/

Genres: Alternative

Alternative label.

Freaks R Us
Email: freaks@freaksrus.net
Website: https://www.freaksrus.net
Website: https://www.facebook.com/
freakartists

Genres: Alternative; Electronic;
Experimental; Post Punk

Record label and artist management.

Fury Records
PO Box 7187
Ringstead
Kettering
NN16 6DJ
Email: furyrecords@btconnect.com
Website: http://www.fury-records.com

Genres: Rockabilly; Rock and Roll

Record label based in Kettering,
Northamptonshire. Specialises in all styles
related to Rockabilly and Rock'n'Roll
music.

Futurist Recordings
45 Staple Lodge Rd
Birmingham
Email: shawndavis22@hotmail.com
Website: https://milwaukie2003.wixsite.com/
futuristrecordings
Website: https://www.facebook.com/
Futuristrecordings/

Genres: Experimental; Acid House; Techno;
Underground

Deep cutting-edge experimental techno and
acid house label.

Fuzzkill Records
Email: fuzzkillrecords@gmail.com
Website: https://www.facebook.com/
FUZZKILLrecords
Website: https://twitter.com/
FUZZKILLRECORDS

Genres: Garage; Lo-fi; Psychedelic Rock;
Rock and Roll

Scottish record label and party planner.

Gerry Loves Records
Website: http://gerrylovesrecords.com
Website: https://twitter.com/gerryloves

Genres: All types of music

Describes itself as a "tiny DIY label
producing quality musical artifacts". Send
query using form on website, including links
to streaming tracks. Listens to all demos, but
cannot guarantee a response.

Glasstone Records
Bath
Email: submit@glasstonerecords.com
Email: info@glasstonerecords.com
Website: https://glasstonerecords.com

Genres: Indie; Rock; Metal; Electronic;
Punk; Electronic Punk; Alternative

Contact: Greg Brooker

Independent label based in Bath. Send
music, plus EPK if you have one, in an email
via dropbox (preferred), soundcloud, or
youtube. Listens to everything but cannot
guarantee response.

Graphite Records
c/o Northern Music Co.
Piazza Offices, Salts Mill
Saltaire
Shipley
West Yorkshire
BD18 3LA
Fax: +44 (0) 1274 730097
Email: andy@northernmusic.co.uk
Email: george@northernmusic.co.uk
Website: http://www.graphiterecords.net
Website: https://www.facebook.com/
GraphiteRecords

Genres: Alternative; Rock; Metal

Independent record label based in Shipley.

Green Pepper Junction
Website: https://greenpepperjunction.com

Genres: All types of music

Contact: Asher Halle

Originally founded in the early seventies as a production company, now a record label based in Glasgow.

Greentrax Recordings
Cockenzie Business Hub
Edinburgh Road
Cockenzie
East Lothian
EH32 0XL
Email: info@greentrax.com
Website: https://www.greentrax.com
Website: https://www.facebook.com/greentrax/

Genres: Regional; Traditional; Celtic

Contact: Ian Green

Record label dealing in traditional Scottish, Celtic, and Gaelic music.

Gruuv
Email: demos@gruuv.net
Email: label@gruuv.net
Website: https://soundcloud.com/gruuv
Website: https://www.facebook.com/gruuv

Genres: House; Techno

Send query by email with links to streaming or download links online.

Hand in Hive
Email: contact@handinhive.com
Website: http://www.handinhive.com
Website: https://www.facebook.com/handinhive

Genres: Indie; Pop

An independent music company, formed in 2014 by two friends with a shared love of music, specialising in records, management, publishing and sync.

Handsome Dad Records
Email: handsomedadrecords@gmail.com
Website: http://www.handsomedadrecords.com
Website: https://www.facebook.com/handsomedadrecords

Genres: All types of music

Record label releasing CDs and vinyl.

Hassle Records
Email: mease@fulltimehobby.co.uk
Email: tom@fulltimehobby.co.uk
Website: http://www.hasslerecords.com
Website: https://www.facebook.com/HassleRecords/

Genres: Alternative; Emo; Hardcore; Indie Rock; Punk; Metal; Pop Punk

A fully independent record label based in London, UK. Releases heavy guitar music.

Heavenly Recordings
Email: daisy@heavenlyrecordings.com
Website: https://heavenlyrecordings.com
Website: https://www.facebook.com/HeavenlyRecordings

Genres: Indie; Alternative; Rhythm and Blues; Underground; Country Pop

Send submissions by email.

Hit And Run Records
Email: Joe@hitandrunrecords.com
Website: https://www.facebook.com/hitandrunrecords

Genres: Pop Punk; Rock; Alternative

Independent record label from Birmingham, UK, specialising in Pop Punk, Rock and alternative music.

Hope Recordings
Unit 4.16 The Paintworks
Bath Road
Bristol
BS4 3EH
Email: la@hoperecordings.com
Website: https://www.hoperecordings.com
Website: https://www.facebook.com/HopeRecordings/

Genres: Dance

Record label based in Bristol. Send demos as WeTransfer or Soundcloud links through online submission form.

Hospital Records
Unit 4 Bessemer Park
250 Milkwood Road
London
SE24 0HG
Fax: +44 (0) 20 8613 0401
Email: Chris@HospitalRecords.com
Email: Dan@HospitalRecords.com
Website: https://www.hospitalrecords.com
Website: https://www.facebook.com/
hospitalrecords

Genres: Drum and Bass

Contact: Chris Goss

Record label based in London. Send demos
via demo submission page on website. No
demos by email.

Houndstooth
Email: houndstooth@fabriclondon.com
Website: https://www.houndstoothlabel.com
Website: https://soundcloud.com/
HoundstoothLBL

Genres: Electronic

Artist-led electronic label based at a London
nightclub.

I'm Not From London
The Old Bus Depot
Upstairs 1st Floor
1 Fisher Gate Point
Lower Parliament Street
Nottingham
NG1 1GD
Email: info@imnotfromlondon.com
Website: https://www.imnotfromlondon.com
Website: https://soundcloud.com/
imnotfromlondonrecords

Genres: Guitar based

A group of Nottingham based DIY
promoters, regularly putting on gigs in
Nottingham and sometimes in Leeds,
Sheffield and Blackpool. Launched label in
2010 and released first record in 2011.

Ignition Records
London
Fax: +44 (0) 20 7258 0962
Website: https://ignitionrecords.co.uk

Website: https://twitter.com/
IgnitionMusicUK

Genres: Alternative; Rock

Independent record label with offices in
London and LA. Send query via online
contact form, including links to as many of
your social media accounts as possible.

Infidelity Records
Email: demos@infidelityrecords.co.uk
Website: http://infidelityrecords.co.uk
Website: https://www.facebook.com/
Infidelityrecords

Genres: Drum and Bass

Record label specialising in D&B. Vocalists
and producers can approach through through
email.

Infinite Hive
Website: https://infinitehive.com
Website: https://www.facebook.com/
infinitehive

Genres: Indie; Metal; Punk; Rock

Contact: Mr John

Edinburgh-based Independent Record Label.

Innerground Records
Website: https://www.innergroundmusic.com
Website: https://soundcloud.com/
innergroundmusic

Genres: Dance; Drum and Bass

Record label based in London. Send demo
via submission system on website.

InTime Records
Nairn
Scotland
Email: admin@intimerecords.co.uk
Website: https://intimerecords.co.uk/
Website: https://www.facebook.com/
Intimerecordslabel

Genres: Electronic; Indie; Pop; Rock

An independent record label based in Nairn,
Scotland combining a love of music with a

passion for quality, covering rock, pop and electronica. Send electronic press kit via online form. Do not send raw MP3s or .wav files.

Iron Man Records
Website: https://ironmanrecords.net
Website: https://twitter.com/IronManRecords

Genres: Alternative; Metal; Rock; Punk

Independent record label working out of Birmingham, Cardiff and London. The label also provides Tour Management Services to Musicians, Theatre groups and Film production companies.

Island Records
4 Pancras Square
Kings Cross
London
N1C 4AG
Website: https://www.islandrecords.co.uk

Genres: All types of music

Record label based in London.

Jeepster Recordings Ltd
Email: info@jeepster.co.uk
Website: https://jeepster.co.uk
Website: https://www.facebook.com/jeepsterrecordings

Genres: All types of music

Send demo by email with info and links to your music online.

JohnJohn Records
61b Stepney Green
London
E1 3LE
Email: theboss@johnjohnrecords.com
Website: http://www.johnjohnrecords.com

Genres: Folk; Jazz; World

Contact: Benoit Viellefon

Record label based in London.

Jungle Records
Suite B2 Livingstone Court
55 Peel Road
Wealdstone
Harrow
HA3 7QT
Email: enquiries@jungle-records.com
Website: https://www.jungle-records.net
Website: https://www.facebook.com/JungleRecords

Genres: All types of music

Record label based in London. Rarely signs new acts, and the only usually ones with an established sales base. Send query by email with links to music online, or submit CD by post. No MP3s by email.

Just Music
Just House
9 Gladwyn Road
London
SW15 1JY
Email: justmusic@justmusic.co.uk
Website: https://www.justmusic.co.uk
Website: https://soundcloud.com/justmusiclabel

Genres: Electronic; Acoustic; Ambient; Downtempo; Chill

Contact: John Benedict; Serena

Record label founded out of a belief that all music of artistic merit should have the opportunity to "enrich our lives". Accepts demos by post or email, but cannot return material or reply to unsuccessful submissions.

JW Music Limited
Website: https://jwmusic.uk
Website: https://facebook.com/jwmusichq

Genres: Electronic; House; Pop; R&B; Urban

Record label based in Carlisle. Also offers artist management, hosts branded events, and operates YouTube channel and radio show / podcast. Send demo through demo submission form on website.

Killing Moon Records
Email: info@killing-moon.com
Website: https://killing-moon.com
Website: https://www.facebook.com/
killingmoonrecords

Genres: Indie; Pop; Rock; Hardcore; Post
Hardcore

Record label based in London. Accepts
demos electronically.

Kscope
Snapper Music plc
1st Floor
52 Lisson Street
London
NW1 5DF
Website: https://kscopemusic.com
Website: https://soundcloud.com/
kscopemusic

Genres: Rock; Post Progressive

Record label based in London. Due to the
high level of submissions, cannot answer all
demo enquiries.

Kudos Records Limited
77 Fortress Road
Kentish Town
London
NW5 1AG
Email: info@kudosrecords.co.uk
Website: https://kudosrecords.co.uk
Website: https://www.facebook.com/
kudosrecords

Genres: House; Leftfield; Hip-Hop; Jazz;
Techno

London distributor that will work with artists
willing to act as their own label.

Kufe Records Ltd
Fax: +44 (0) 20 8898 8649
Email: info@kuferecords.com
Website: https://www.kuferecords.com

Genres: Reggae; Classic R&B; Country

Specialised in Sixties & Modern R & B,
Reggae, Soca and Country Music.

Lab Records
Email: info@labrecs.com
Website: https://labrecs.com
Website: https://www.facebook.com/
labrecords/

Genres: Pop Rock; Acoustic; Alternative;
Folk; Hip-Hop; Reggae; World

Pop-rock label based in Manchester. Send
demo by post.

The Leaf Label Ltd
PO Box 272
Leeds
LS19 9BP
Email: contact@theleaflabel.com
Website: http://www.theleaflabel.com
Website: https://www.facebook.com/
theleaflabel

Genres: Alternative; Experimental

Record label based in Leeds. Send demo on
CD, vinyl, or cassette. No emails with
attachments. See website for full details.

Learn Fear
Bradford
Website: https://www.learnfear.com
Website: https://www.facebook.com/
learnfear/

Genres: All types of music

Record label based in Bradford.

Lewis Recordings
95A Hackney Road
London
E2 8ET
Email: info@LewisRecordings.com
Website: http://www.lewisrecordings.com
Website: https://www.facebook.com/
LewisRecordingsLDN

Genres: Alternative Hip-Hop; Rap;
Electronic; Dubstep

Record label founded in 2001.

Lex Records Ltd
Email: word@lexrecords.com
Website: https://lexrecords.com

Website: https://www.facebook.com/
Lexprojects/

Genres: Alternative

A record label, music publisher, and film production company based in London.

Limbo Records
Glasgow
Website: https://www.
23rdprecinctmusic.com/collections/limbo

Genres: All types of music

Record label based in Glasgow, Scotland.

Linn Records
Email: info@linnrecords.co.uk
Website: https://www.linnrecords.com
Website: https://www.facebook.com/
linnrecordsmusic

Genres: Celtic; Classical; Jazz; Traditional

Describes itself as "one of the world's leading audiophile labels specialising in Classical, Jazz and Scottish music."

Lismor Recordings
46 Elliot Street
Glasgow
G3 8DZ
Website: http://www.lismor.com

Genres: Traditional; Regional; Celtic

Record label based in Glasgow. Describes itself as one of the premier Scottish music labels of all time.

Loose Music
14 Shaftesbury Centre
85 Barlby Road
London
W10 6BN
Email: info@loosemusic.com
Website: https://www.loosemusic.com
Website: https://soundcloud.com/loose-music

Genres: Americana; Alternative Country

Describes itself as Europe's premier Americana and alt Country record label.

Send query by email with links to streams. No attachments.

MadTech Records
181 High Street
Harlesden
London
NW10 4TE
Email: demos@madtechrecords.com
Email: tom@championrecords.co.uk
Website: https://www.madtechrecords.com
Website: https://www.facebook.com/
madtechrecords

Genres: Contemporary Electronic

London label releasing contemporary electronic music. Send query by email.

Marshall Records
Website: https://www.marshall.com/gb/en/
artist-services/record-label
Website: https://www.facebook.com/
marshallrecords

Genres: Alternative; Guitar based; Indie; Metal; Punk; Rock

Submit EPK via online submission system.

Measured Records
5 Eagle Street
Glasgow
G4 9XA
Email: info@nohalfmeasures.com
Website: https://nohalfmeasures.com
Website: https://www.facebook.com/
nohalfmeasures

Genres: All types of music

Record label based in Glasgow, Scotland. Part of a group including artist management and publishing divisions.

Memphis Industries
Email: info@memphis-industries.com
Website: https://www.memphis-industries.com
Website: https://twitter.com/memphisind

Genres: Alternative; Indie

Record label based in London.

Moksha Recordings Ltd
PO Box 102
London
E15 2HH
Email: recordings@moksha.co.uk
Website: https://www.moksha.co.uk

Genres: Alternative Electronic Fusion

Record label based in London. Send query by email with links to music online.

Mook Records
Authorpe Road
Leeds
LS6 4JB
Email: mail@mookhouse.ndo.co.uk
Website: http://www.mookhouse.ndo.co.uk

Genres: Alternative; Indie; Punk

Label based in Leeds, founded in 1995 out of a desire to "make records with a live vibe and a minimum of overdubs". Has own recording studios and rehearsal rooms. Send query by email.

Mute Records
Email: demos@mute.com
Email: mute@mute.com
Website: https://mute.com
Website: https://www.instagram.com/muterecords/

Genres: Alternative; Electronic

Send query by email with three or four streaming links. No attachments.

National Anthem
Email: hello@national-anthem.co.uk
Website: http://www.national-anthem.co.uk
Website: https://www.facebook.com/nationalanthemmusic

Genres: All types of music

Independent record label specialising in limited edition vinyl releases pressed on high quality 7″, 10″ or 12″ vinyl, also released digitally.

Needwant
Email: demos@needwantmusic.com
Email: info@needwantmusic.com
Website: https://needwantmusic.com
Website: https://soundcloud.com/seanneedwant

Genres: Chill; Electronic; House; Techno; Dance

Send query by email with links to music online.

Neighbourhood
London
Email: l@iliantapebooking.de
Website: https://neighbourhood-ldn.bandcamp.com
Website: https://www.facebook.com/Neighbourhood.LDN

Genres: Techno

Techno label based in London.

Nervous Records
5 Sussex Crescent
Northolt
Middx.
UB5 4DL
Email: info@nervous.co.uk
Website: https://www.nervous.co.uk
Website: https://www.facebook.com/Nervous-Records-90855264733/

Genres: Psychebilly; Rockabilly; Rock and Roll

Record label based in Northolt, Middlesex. Aims to to bring rock and roll into the present day – NOT a nostalgia label.

Nettwerk Records
15 Adeline Place, 3rd Floor
London
WC1B 3AJ
Fax: +44 (0) 20 7456 9501
Website: https://nettwerk.com
Website: https://www.facebook.com/nettwerkmusicgroup

Genres: Acoustic; Folk; Singer-Songwriter

Record label with head office in Canada and other offices in Los Angeles, New York City, London, and Hamburg.

New State Music
58 Rochester Place
Camden Town
London
NW1 9JX
Email: info@newstatemusic.com
Website: https://www.newstatemusic.com
Website: https://soundcloud.com/newstatemusic

Genres: Trance; Dance

Record label based in London. Send demos as soundcloud links through online contact form.

Ninja Tune
PO Box 4296
London
SE11 4WW
Email: demos@ninjatune.net
Website: https://www.ninjatune.net

Genres: Hip-Hop; Electronic; Break Beat; Downtempo; Leftfield; Jazz

Record label with offices in London, UK, and Los Angeles, California. Send demo by email only, with links to MP3 files, soundcloud pages, or websites, but No MP3 attachments. Keep demos short and sweet with your best track first. Do not chase for response.

No Dancing Records
Email: info@nodancing.co.uk
Website: https://www.nodancing.co.uk
Website: https://soundcloud.com/nodancing

Genres: Indie; Rock; Leftfield; Alternative

Record label based in Belfast. Loves to hear new music, but not currently that active.

No Front Teeth
PO Box 27070
London
N2 9ZP
Email: NFTpunx@nofrontteeth.co.uk
Website: https://www.nofrontteeth.co.uk

Genres: Punk Rock

Record label based in London.

Nutopia Music
London
Email: hello@nutopiamusic.com
Website: https://nutopiamusic.com
Website: https://www.instagram.com/nutopiamusic/

Genres: All types of music

Record label based in London. Works with artists of all genres.

One Inch Badge (OIB) Records
Second Floor Central Block
St Augustine's Church
Stanford Avenue
Brighton
BN1 6EA
Email: submissions@oneinchbadge.com
Email: office@oneinchbadge.com
Website: https://www.oneinchbadge.com
Website: https://www.facebook.com/oneinchbadge

Genres: Rock; Pop; Electronic; Folk

Concert promotions, record label and venue management company based in Brighton. Send demos by email.

One Little Independent Records
34 Trinity Crescent
London
SW17 7AE
Email: demos@olirecords.com
Email: contact@olirecords.com
Website: https://www.olirecords.com
Website: https://www.facebook.com/olirecords

Genres: All types of music

Send email with links to MP3 files, SoundCloud pages or websites. Include contact details in the body of the email.

101BPM
20-22 Wenlock Road
London
N1 7GU
Email: demos@101bpm.com
Email: team@101bpm.com
Website: https://www.101bpm.com
Website: https://www.facebook.com/
101BPM

Genres: Electronic; Urban

Music agency and record label based in
London. Send music submissions by email.

Ostereo
International House
61 Mosley Street
Manchester
M2 3HZ

LONDON
23 Tileyard Studios
Tileyard Road
London
N7 9AH
Email: info@ostereo.com
Website: https://ostereo.com

Genres: All types of music

Record label with offices in Manchester and
London.

PAPERecordings
Email: hello@paperecordings.com
Website: https://paperecordings.com
Website: https://soundcloud.com/
paperecordings

Genres: House; Disco; Leftfield

Style ranges from deep house and disco to
Balearic and leftfield.

Paradise Palms Records
41 Lothian Street
Edinburgh
EH1 1HB
Email: booking@theparadisepalms.com
Website: https://www.theparadisepalms.com

Genres: Dance; Electronic; Indie

Devoted to emerging indie/electronica, loose
dance music and cosmic bangers. The label
has been part of the music scene in
Edinburgh for around 8 years, championing
both emerging and established acts from the
local area as well as around the world.

Park Records
PO Box 651
Oxford
OX2 9RB
Email: parkoffice@parkrecords.com
Website: https://parkrecords.com
Website: https://www.facebook.com/profile.
php?id=100063531371464

Genres: Folk

Folk record label based in Oxford.

Parlophone Records
Website: https://www.parlophone.co.uk
Website: https://www.facebook.com/
parlophone

Genres: All types of music

Long-standing label that has boasted such
acts as the Beatles, Blur, Radiohead, and
Kylie.

Perry Road Records Ltd
75 Perry Road
Buckden
Cambridgeshire
PE19 5XG
Email: enquiries@perryroadrecords.co.uk
Website: https://www.
perryroadrecords.co.uk

Genres: Blues; Country; Indie; Rock

Record label based in Cambridgeshire. Send
demo by post, or by email with the name of
your music page online. No attachments or
links.

Phantasy Sound Ltd
5a Bear Lane
Southwark
London
SE1 0UH
Email: demos@phantasysound.co.uk
Email: phantasyhq@gmail.com

Website: https://shop.phantasysound.co.uk
Website: https://www.facebook.com/
phantasy.sound

Genres: Alternative; Dance; Electronic

Record label based in London. Send demo
by email.

Philophobia Music
Email: philophobiamusic@gmail.com
Website: https://www.facebook.com/
philophobiamusic
Website: https://linktr.ee/PhilophobiaMusic?
fbclid=
IwAR1YJvdfuf9jdiqXeLRhagetk2WtM5mh
hOwxkBnLX79RPqmgR2taGFv9WNo

Genres: Indie; Pop

Independent record label based in Wakefield,
West Yorkshire.

Pinball Records
Email: frank@pinballrecords.co.uk
Website: http://www.pinballrecords.co.uk
Website: https://soundcloud.com/
pinballrecords/

Genres: Electronic; House

Record label focussed on electro and house.

Pinky Swear Records
Website: http://pinkyswearrecords.
limitedrun.com
Website: https://www.facebook.com/
pinkyswearrecords

Genres: Emo; Hardcore; Pop; Punk

Independant Record Label focussing on
vinyl and tape releases.

Play It Again Sam
1 Bevington Path
London
SE1 3PW
Website: http://www.playitagainsam.net
Website: https://www.instagram.com/
playitagainsamrecs/

Genres: All types of music

Record company based in London. Part of
one of the biggest independent record
distributors in Europe.

Polydor Records
4 Pancras Square
London
N1C 4AG
Website: https://www.polydor.co.uk
Website: https://www.facebook.com/
polydorrecords

Genres: All types of music

Record label based in London.

Positiva Records
London
Website: https://positivarecords.com
Website: https://soundcloud.com/
positivarecords

Genres: Dance

Send submissions as Soundcloud link via
online submission system. Response not
guaranteed unless interested.

Public Pressure
London
Website: https://we.publicpressure.io
Website: https://soundcloud.com/
jointhepressure

Genres: Alternative; Heavy Blues;
Psychedelic Hip-Hop; Progressive Metal;
Electronic

We empower artists and labels connecting
them directly to their audience and allowing
them to retain control over their work and
revenue.

Pumpkin Records
Website: https://pumpkinrecords.co.uk
Website: https://www.facebook.com/
pumpkinrecordsuk

Genres: Dub; Garage; Psychebilly; Punk;
Rockabilly; Ska; Ska Punk

Describes itself as more of a collective than a
record label.

Purple Worm Records
Hull
Website: https://www.facebook.com/
purplewormrecords/
Website: https://twitter.com/purplewormrec

Genres: All types of music

Independent record label based in Hull.

Quatre Femmes Records
London
Email: quatrefemmesrecords@gmail.com
Website: https://quatrefemmesrecords.
bandcamp.com
Website: https://www.facebook.com/
QuatreFemmesRecords

Genres: Folk; Indie; Pop; Psychedelic; Rock

Record label based in London.

Ram Records
5 Merchant Square
8th Floor
London
W2 1AS
Email: info@ramrecords.com
Website: https://www.ramrecords.com
Website: http://soundcloud.com/ramrecords/

Genres: Drum and Bass

Drum & bass label based in London. Send demos via Soundcloud or Wavo submission on Facebook.

Ramber Records
7 Winfell Drive
Manchester
M40 7BX
Email: rob@ramberrecords.com
Website: https://ramberrecords.com
Website: https://www.facebook.com/
Ramberrecords

Genres: Electronic Pop; Garage; Psychedelic
Rock

Home-dubbed cassette enthusiasts based in Manchester, specialising in dark-edged electro-pop. Send demos by post or by email.

Rare Vitamin Records
Email: RareVitaminRecords@gmail.com
Website: https://rarevitaminrecords.
bandcamp.com
Website: https://www.facebook.com/
rarevitaminrecords

Genres: Garage; Post Punk; Punk;
Psychedelic Rock

If music be the food of love, are you the indigestion?

RareNoiseRecords
Suite 509
Britannia House
1-11 Glenthorne Road
London
W6 0LH
Email: info@rarenoiserecords.com
Website: https://www.rarenoiserecords.com
Website: https://www.facebook.com/
rarenoise

Genres: Ambient; Dub; Jazz; Progressive

Record label based in London, with a mission to detect and amplify contemporary trends in progressive music, by highlighting their relation to the history of the art-form, while choosing not to be bound by pre-conceptions of genre. Send query by email with Soundcloud links or equivalent, with bio and background information.

Raven Black Music
Email: info@ravenblackmusic.com
Website: https://www.facebook.com/
ravenblackmusic

Genres: All types of music

UK-based record label. Promotes new melodic intelligent music which is both passionate and positively life affirming.

RCA Label Group UK
2 Canal Reach
London
N1C 4DB
Email: reception.enquiries@sonymusic.com
Website: https://www.rca-records.co.uk

Genres: All types of music

UK record label. Accepts demos via post only in USB or CD format. Mark submissions for the attention of a specific label, followed by "demos".

Real World Ltd
Box Mill
Mill Lane
Box
Wiltshire
SN13 8PL
Website: https://realworld.co.uk
Website: https://www.facebook.com/ realworldrecords

Genres: All types of music

Home to a group of music-loving companies in Box, Wiltshire.

Release / Sustain
East London
Email: info@releasesustain.com
Email: gabbi@releasesustain.com
Website: http://www.releasesustain.com
Website: https://www.facebook.com/release. sustain

Genres: Chill; House; Techno; Underground

Contact: Gabriel Arierep; Eduardo Tavares

Record label based in East London.

Relentless Records
Email: demos@relentlessrecs.com
Email: emily@relentlessrecs.com
Website: https://www.relentlessrecs.com
Website: https://www.facebook.com/ relentlessrecs/

Genres: Alternative

Record label based in London. Contact A&R team by email.

Revolver Records
152 Goldthorn Hill
Wolverhampton
WV2 3JA

Email: submissions@revolverrecords.com
Email: music@revolverrecords.com
Website: https://revolverrecords.com
Website: http://soundcloud.com/ revolverrecords

Genres: Rock; Metal; Jazz

Record label based in London. Prefers to receive demos via email, but also accepts via post. When submitting by email, send no more than MP3 or WAV files as attachments. If sending more, use streaming platforms (e.g. Spotify; Soundcloud) or digital storage platform (e.g. Dropbox; Google Drive). Physical discs submitted by post cannot be returned.

Roadrunner Records
Website: https://www. roadrunnerrecords.co.uk
Website: https://www.facebook.com/ roadrunnerrecordsuk

Genres: Metal; Rock

Hard rock and metal record label.

Rock Action Records
Glasgow
Email: info@rockactionrecords.co.uk
Website: https://rockaction.scot
Website: https://www.facebook.com/ rockactionrecords

Genres: Alternative; Electronic; Indie; Rock

Independent record label based in Glasgow. Happy to receive demos, but cannot guarantee individual response or feedback.

Rose Coloured Records
Email: records@rosecoloured.com
Website: https://www.rosecoloured.com
Website: https://www.facebook.com/ RoseColouredRecords/

Genres: All types of music

Small independent label. Tries to listen and respond to all submissions. Send links to videos or tracks by email or through form on website.

Rough Trade Records
66 Golborne Road
London
W10 5PS
Email: demos@roughtraderecords.com
Website: https://roughtraderecords.com
Website: https://www.facebook.com/
roughtraderecords

Genres: Indie; Rock

Record label based in London with offices in New York. Send demos by email as links only. No attachments.

Saint Productions
Sheffield
Email: mark@saintproductions.co.uk
Website: http://saintproductions.co.uk

Genres: Dance; Pop

Record label based in Sheffield, Yorkshire.

Sapien Records Limited
Clarendon House
Clayton Street
Newcastle
NE1 5EE
Email: info@sapienrecords.com
Email: david@sapienrecords.com
Website: http://www.sapienrecords.com
Website: https://www.facebook.com/
sapienrecords

Genres: Hip-Hop; Metal; Pop; Punk; Rock; R&B

Contact: David Smith; Ollie Rillands

Independent record label based in Newcastle.

Saved Records
Maidstone, Kent
Email: info@savedrecords.com
Website: http://www.savedrecords.com
Website: https://soundcloud.com/
savedrecords

Genres: House; Techno; Electronic

Record label based in Maidstone. Send demos by email.

Saving Grace Music
Email: info@saving-grace.co.uk
Website: https://www.saving-grace.co.uk
Website: https://www.facebook.com/
housesginc/

Genres: Grime; Hip-Hop; House; Garage; Indie; Folk; Rock; Soul; Pop; Drum and Bass; Dubstep

A creative imprint and talent development hub working with aspiring, developing and established artists alike, releasing, marketing, promoting and distributing creative works in the fields of music, video, art and fashion.

Schnitzel Records Ltd
Leigh On Sea
Email: talent@schnitzel.co.uk
Email: info@schnitzel.co.uk
Website: https://schnitzel.co.uk
Website: https://www.facebook.com/
schnitzelrecords

Genres: Alternative; Rock

Record label based in Leigh On Sea. Send submissions by email.

Scotdisc
62 Telford Road
Cumbernauld
B67 2AX
Email: info@scotdisc.co.uk
Website: https://scotdisc.co.uk

Genres: Regional

Record label based in Cumbernauld, specialising in Scottish music.

Scruff of the Neck (SOTN)
36-40 Edge Street
Manchester
M4 1HN
Email: info@scruffoftheneck.com
Website: https://scruffoftheneck.com
Website: https://www.facebook.com/
scruffoftheneck

Genres: All types of music

Independent record label and music collective promoting concerts and tours, releasing records and developing artists.

Approach via Artist Contact Form on website.

Shabby Doll Records
Email: hello@shabbydoll.co.uk
Website: http://www.shabbydoll.co.uk
Website: https://www.facebook.com/ShabbyDollRecords

Genres: Underground House

Record label specialising in bespoke underground house music.

Signum Records
Unit 14
21 Wadsworth Road
Perivale
Middlesex
UB6 7LQ
Email: info@signumrecords.com
Website: https://signumrecords.com
Website: https://www.facebook.com/signumrecords

Genres: Classical

Independent classical record label based in Perivale, Middlesex.

SLAM Productions
c/o 3 Thesiger Road
Abingdon
OX14 2DX
Email: slamprods@aol.com
Email: ZirconRover@aol.com
Website: http://www.slamproductions.net

Genres: Contemporary Jazz; Experimental

Independent CD label based in Abingdon, and founded in 1989. Not releasing CDs by any more new artists as at May 2023.

Slapped Up Soul Records
Bristol
Website: https://www.facebook.com/slappedupsoul/
Website: https://twitter.com/slappedupsouluk

Genres: Soul

Independent record label specialising in music with soul.

Small Pond Record Label
27 Castle Street
Brighton
BN1 2HD
Email: info@smallpondrec.co.uk
Website: https://smallpondrec.com
Website: https://soundcloud.com/small-pond

Genres: All types of music

Unlike many indie labels, we do not work in one particular genre. We love everything from ambient techno to progressive metal. We do, however, like music that is left-field, alternative, and different. We are always looking for that little je ne sais quoi, no matter the genre.

Snapper Music
52 Lisson Street
London
NW1 5DF
Website: https://snappermusic.com

Genres: Alternative; Rock; Metal; Post Progressive

Record label based in London.

So Recordings
Email: info@sorecordings.com
Website: http://sorecordings.com
Website: https://www.facebook.com/SoRecordings

Genres: Alternative; Indie; Rock

Record label founded in 2009. In 2023, celebrated its first number one album in the UK.

SOMM Recordings
13 Riversdale Road
Thames Ditton
Surrey
KT7 0QL
Email: sales@somm-recordings.com
Website: https://somm-recordings.com
Website: https://soundcloud.com/siva-oke

Genres: Classical

Classical label based in Thames Ditton, Surrey.

Sonic Cathedral
Office 44
78 Golders Green Road
London
NW11 8LN
Website: https://soniccathedral.co.uk
Website: https://www.facebook.com/
soniccathedral.uk

Genres: Electronic; Psychedelic Rock;
Shoegaze

Record label based in London.

Sony Music Entertainment UK Ltd
2 Canal Reach
London
N1C 4DB
Email: reception.enquiries@sonymusic.com
Website: https://www.sonymusic.co.uk

Genres: All types of music

London office of large international record
label. Accepts demos via post only, in USB
or CD format.

Sotones Music Co-Operative
13 Mansion Road
Southampton
SO15 3BQ
Email: demos@sotones.co.uk
Email: andy@sotones.co.uk
Website: http://sotones.co.uk
Website: https://www.facebook.com/sotones

Genres: All types of music

Contact: Andy Harris (Managing Director)

Music collective based in Southampton,
generally only working with local acts. Will
accept demos, however. See website for
more details.

Soul II Soul
Email: info@soul2soul.co.uk
Website: https://soul2soul.co.uk
Website: https://soundcloud.com/
soul2souluk

Genres: R&B; Rap; Urban

Record label based in London.

Soundplate
London
Website: https://soundplate.com
Website: https://www.facebook.com/
Soundplate/

Genres: Electronic; House

A London based independent record label
and music technology company.

Southern Fried Records
Email: andy@anglomanagement.co.uk
Website: https://www.
southernfriedrecords.com
Website: https://soundcloud.com/
southernfriedrecords

Genres: Electronic; Dance

A London-based independent electronic
dance music record label. Send demos by
email.

Southpoint
Email: info@southpointmusic.co.uk
Website: https://www.southpointmusic.co.uk
Website: https://soundcloud.com/
southpointmusic

Genres: Dubstep; Garage; Grime

Record label based in Hove, dedicated to
promoting local and lesser known talent and
reviving Brighton's fading bass and grime
scene.

Speedowax
Birmingham
Email: speedowax@gmail.com
Website: https://www.facebook.com/
speedowax
Website: https://twitter.com/Speedowax

Genres: Hardcore; Indie; Rock; Post Rock;
Thrash; Punk

Non-profit record label based in
Birmingham, established in 1997. Has
released over 125 records. One-man
operation run for fun from the back room of
a record shop.

Spiritual Records
4 Ferdinand Street
Camden
NW1 8ER
Fax: +44 (0) 7748 593758
Email: rafael@spiritualrecords.co.uk
Email: elliot@spiritualrecords.co.uk
Website: https://www.spiritualrecords.co.uk
Website: https://www.facebook.com/
spiritualrecordslabel

Genres: Alternative Blues; Acoustic; Folk;
Rock; Singer-Songwriter

Born in September 2015, in Camden.

We started to record some of our best
featured artists in our own studio upstairs at
the Bar.

Our hope is that we can bring out the best of
our artists musically and support them long
and short term. We encourage all our artists
to help each other and help us build the label
and to make it stand out in an industry that
continues to be plagued by false hope and
promises.

Staylittle Music
Email: press@staylittlemusic.com
Email: shows@staylittlemusic.com
Website: https://www.staylittlemusic.com
Website: https://soundcloud.com/
staylittlemusic

Genres: Acoustic; Folk; Indie

Record label with strong DIY ethos.

Stolen Recordings
Email: stolenrecordings@googlemail.com
Email: stolen@stolenrecordings.co.uk
Website: https://stolenrecordings.co.uk
Website: https://www.facebook.com/Stolen.
Recordings.Ltd

Genres: Alternative; Indie

Record label, management, and publishing
company. Closed to demos as at July 2023.

Sunbird Records
4 The Circus
Darwen

BB3 1BS
Website: https://www.sunbirdrecords.com
Website: https://www.facebook.com/
SunbirdRecords

Genres: All types of music

Independent record label and live music
venue, based in Darwen.

Sunday Best Recordings
Unit 1
50-52 Hanbury Street
London
E1 5JL
Email: info@sundaybest.net
Website: http://www.sundaybest.net
Website: https://www.facebook.com/
sundaybestrecordings

Genres: Indie; Electronic; Alternative;
Leftfield

Originally founded as a leftfield club night in
1995, the label emerged in 1997. Renowned
for its expansive and eclectic roster, as well
as an unswerving dedication to the leftfield.

Supersonic Media
London
Email: demos@supersonic-media.co.uk
Email: heidi@supersonic-media.co.uk
Website: https://www.supersonic-
media.co.uk
Website: https://soundcloud.com/
supersonicmedia

Genres: Alternative; Dance; Drum and Bass;
House; Post Hardcore

Independent record label and publisher,
based in London. Send query by email with
streaming links and artist bio.

Superstar Destroyer Records
Manchester
Website: https://superstardestroyer.co.uk
Website: https://www.facebook.com/
ssdrecords

Genres: Alternative; Progressive; Post Rock;
Shoegaze

Record label based in Manchester.

Talking Elephant
37 Eastgate Street
North Elmham
NR20 5HE
Email: info@talkingelephant.co.uk
Website: http://www.talkingelephant.co.uk
Website: https://www.facebook.com/talkingelephant

Genres: Blues; Folk; Classic Rock

Record label based in North Elmham.

Teide Records
Website: https://www.teiderecords.com
Website: https://www.facebook.com/TeideRecordsofficial/

Genres: All types of music

A vibrant and versatile record label committed to transforming artist compensation within the industry. From the outset, our label has remained steadfast in its mission to champion emerging talent, offering comprehensive support across numerous fronts. Send demos as private SoundCloud links via online contact form on website.

37 Adventures
London
Email: hello@37adventures.co.uk
Website: http://37adventures.co.uk
Website: https://www.facebook.com/37Adventures/

Genres: Electronic; Dance; Indie; Pop

Contact: Alex Bean; Nick Worthington

Record label based in London. Always looking for exciting new music projects. Contact by email.

Three Galleys Records
Farrar Road
Sheffield
South Yorkshire
Email: threegalleys@gmail.com
Website: https://www.threegalleys.com
Website: https://www.facebook.com/ThreeGalleys/

Genres: Alternative; Folk

A micro label specialising in folk, alternative, and art house releases.

Tonotopic Records
4 Capricorn Centre
Cranes Farm Road
Basildon
Essex
SS14 3JJ
Email: laura@tonotopicrecords.com
Website: https://www.tonotopicrecords.com

Genres: Avant-Garde Alternative Acoustic Electronic Experimental Melodic

Contact: Laura Evans

An independent UK record label founded in 2015. We work closely with artists of all genres to record, publish and promote their music internationally.

Run by musicians and music lovers, we sign every artist with long term development in mind. We don't drop an act once their music stops selling, we support and grow their creative output so they can continue to write amazing music. We look for raw talent we can work with, not hits handed to us on a silver platter. If you are interested in becoming an artist, send us a demo and we'll get back to you as soon as possible.

Tontena Music
Email: info@tontenamusic.com
Website: http://www.tontenamusic.com
Website: https://soundcloud.com/tontena

Genres: All types of music

Record label and studio (also production and music publishing). Send queries by email with links to music online. No attachments.

Toolroom Records
Email: info@toolroomacademy.com
Website: https://toolroomrecords.com
Website: https://soundcloud.com/toolroomrecords

Genres: House

House record label based in Maidstone, Kent. Send demos via online submission system. Endeavours to listen to all of them, but cannot guarantee a response.

Tough Love Records
Email: info@toughloverecords.com
Website: http://toughloverecords.com
Website: https://www.facebook.com/ToughLoveRecordings/

Genres: All types of music

Record label based in London.

Traffic Cone Records
Glasgow
Email: traffic.cone.records@gmail.com
Website: https://www.facebook.com/Traffic.Cone.Records
Website: https://www.youtube.com/user/TrafficConeLive

Genres: All types of music

Music news, Gig nights, Club nights, Podcasts, Radio, Festivals, etc.

Trestle Records
Email: info@trestlerec.com
Website: http://www.trestlerec.com
Website: https://twitter.com/trestlerecords

Genres: Electronic; Classical; Pop; Contemporary; Instrumental

Record label dedicated to putting out new instrumental music.

Tumi Music Ltd
Mill Cottage
St Catherine
Bath
BA1 8EU
Fax: +44 (0) 1225 858545
Email: info@tumimusic.com
Website: http://www.tumimusic.com

Genres: Latin; World

Record label based in Bath, specialising in Latin American and Caribbean music.

Universal Music UK
4 Pancras Square
London

N1C 4AG
Email: contact@umusic.com
Website: https://www.umusic.co.uk

Genres: All types of music

Always looking for the hottest new emerging talent.

Upbeat Recordings
Waverley House
6 The Bramblings
Rustington
West Sussex
BN16 2DA
Email: info@upbeat.co.uk
Website: https://upbeatrecordings.co.uk
Website: https://upbeatmailorder.co.uk

Genres: Jazz

Jazz record label based in Rustington, West Sussex.

Vallance Records
East London
Website: https://www.vallancerecords.com
Website: https://www.facebook.com/VALLANCERECORDS/

Genres: Garage; Indie; Psychedelic Rock; Punk

Record label based in East London, founded in 2016.

Venn Records
Email: shop@vennrecords.com
Website: https://vennrecords.com
Website: https://www.facebook.com/vennrecords

Genres: Metal; Punk; Rock

Genre fluid UK record label.

Vertical Records
16 Woodlands Terrace
Glasgow
G3 6DF
Email: info@verticalrecords.co.uk
Website: https://verticalrecords.co.uk
Website: https://twitter.com/verticalrecords

Genres: Celtic; Roots

Celtic and roots label based in Glasgow, Scotland.

Voltage Records
Units 7,8,10,11
St. Stephen's Mill
Newton Place
Ripley Street
Bradford
West Yorkshire
BD5 7JW
Email: enquiries@voltagerecords.com
Email: info@voltagerecords.com
Website: http://www.voltagerecords.com
Website: https://www.facebook.com/voltagerecords1

Genres: Guitar based; Electronic

Send demos on audio CDs only – no MP3s. Include brief bio, one or two photos, and contact details on the CD itself.

Wagg Records
25 Commercial Street
Brighouse
HD6 1AF
Email: info@now-music.com
Website: https://www.now-music.com
Website: https://www.facebook.com/profile.php?id=100057275875429

Genres: All types of music

A small independent label used mainly for nurturing new artists. Parent company also offers music management and music publishing services, as well as operating another record label.

Wah Wah 45s
London
Email: dom@wahwah45s.com
Website: https://www.wahwah45s.com
Website: https://www.facebook.com/WahWah45s

Genres: Soul; Funk; Acoustic; Jazz; Electronic; Dub; Reggae

Contact: Dom Servini

Genre defying, vinyl cutting, gig loving independent UK label. Releasing beautiful music since 1999.

Warp Records
PO Box 25378
London
NW5 1GL
Website: http://warp.net
Website: https://www.facebook.com/warprecords

Genres: Alternative; Ambient; Electronic; Experimental; Guitar based; Dance; Shoegaze

Record label based in London.

Wichita Recordings
Email: info@wichita-recordings.com
Website: https://www.wichita-recordings.com
Website: https://www.facebook.com/wichitarecordings

Genres: All types of music

Send query by email with links to music online. No MP3 attachments. Response not guaranteed.

WW Records
London
Email: info@wwrecords.co.uk
Website: http://www.wwrecords.co.uk
Website: https://www.facebook.com/WEAREWWRECORDS

Genres: Alternative Dance; Electronic

A cutting-edge record label that cultivates electronic music and artists that are influenced by its culture.

XL Recordings
Website: https://xlrecordings.com
Website: https://www.facebook.com/xlrecordings

Genres: Alternative; Electronic

Independent UK record label.

Xploded
Blackburn
Website: https://www.xploded.co.uk
Website: https://www.facebook.com/XplodedMusic/

Genres: Dance; Pop

A UK-based record label distributed by Universal Music Group – set up in late 2018 by former founders of one of the UK's most successful independent labels over the past 30 years.

Young Poet Records

Email: info@young-poet.com
Website: https://young-poet.com
Website: https://facebook.com/youngpoetrecords

Genres: All types of music

A place where music and business work in harmony, and where artists are given the space to build careers on sustainable terms.

Above all, we're focused on releasing music we love, that reflects and transcends the everyday. We support our artists in becoming the very best versions of themselves, via a label operation that draws upon hard-earned know-how and uses data to inform but never lead.

ZTT Records

Website: http://www.ztt.com
Website: https://www.facebook.com/zttrecords

Genres: Alternative; Acoustic; Indie; Electronic

British record label founded in 1983 which has produced 45 UK top 40 hits.

Canadian Record Labels

For the most up-to-date listings of these and hundreds of other record labels, visit https://www.musicsocket.com/recordlabels

*To claim your **free** access to the site, please see the back of this book.*

Beggars Group Canada

333 King Street East
Toronto, Ontario
M5A 0E1
Email: canada@beggars.com
Website: https://www.beggarsgroup.ca
Website: https://twitter.com/BeggarsCanada

Genres: Alternative; Pop; Rock

Record label based in Toronto, Ontario.

Biscornus Records

Montreal, QC
Email: biscornusrecords@gmail.com
Email: biscornus@gmail.com
Website: https://bscrecords.bandcamp.com
Website: https://www.facebook.com/
bscrecords

Genres: Experimental; Post; Instrumental;
Soundtracks; Trip Hop

A Montreal-based independent digital micro-label for improvised, experimental, drone, post-rock, neo-classical, soundtrack.

Dine Alone Records

864 Eastern Avenue
Toronto, ON M4L 1A3
Email: info@dinealonerecords.com
Website: https://dinealonerecords.com
Website: https://www.facebook.com/
dinealonerecords

Genres: Emo; Indie; Hip-Hop; Post
Hardcore; Punk; Rock

Record label with offices in Toronto,
Nashville, Los Angeles, and Sydney.

NorthernBlues Music Inc.

39 Birch Ave.
Ottawa ON
K1K 3G5
Email: info@northernblues.com
Website: http://www.northernblues.com
Website: https://www.facebook.com/
NorthernBlues-Music-209455625926/

Genres: Blues; World; Roots; Gospel

Record label based in Ottowa, Ontario. Aims
to be a friendly home to Canadian blues
artists.

Sound of Pop Inc.

Wolfville, Nova Scotia
Email: glenn@soundofpop.com
Website: http://soundofpop.com
Website: https://www.facebook.com/
soundofpop

Genres: Alternative; Pop

Record label based in Wolfville, Nova
Scotia.

Sparks Music
219 Dufferin Street
Unit 12A (Liberty Street Entrance)
Toronto
Ontario
M6K 3J1
Fax: +1 (416) 862-8364
Email: andy@sparksmusic.com
Website: https://sparksmusic.com
Website: https://www.facebook.com/
SparksMusicLabel

Genres: Alternative Pop; Rock

Contact: Andy Crosbie

Record label based in Toronto, Ontario,
handling "rock, pop, and everything
between".

Sphere Music
Website: http://www.spheremusique.com
Website: https://www.facebook.com/
spheremusique

Genres: All types of music

Record label based in Quebec.

Stony Plain Records
PO Box 170
Waterdown, Ontario
L0R 2H0
Email: info@stonyplainrecords.com
Website: https://stonyplainrecords.com

Genres: Blues; Folk; Classic R&B; Country;
Rock and Roll; Roots

Contact: Holger Petersen

A record company based in Waterdown,
Ontario, a small town right outside of
Toronto. The label specializes in what its
founder calls roots music: Contemporary
music with roots in the past that stands on its
own, but which influences almost all the pop
music you hear around you.

Record Labels Index

This section lists record labels by their genres, with directions to the section of the book where the full listing can be found.

You can create your own customised lists of record labels using different combinations of these subject areas, plus over a dozen other criteria, instantly online at https://www.musicsocket.com.

*To claim your **free** access to the site, please see the back of this book.*

All types of music
1043 Recordings (*UK*)
88 Rising (*US*)
Acorn Records (*UK*)
Alya Records (*UK*)
American Eagle Recordings (*US*)
American Recordings (*US*)
Atlantic Records (*US*)
Ba Da Bing Records & Management (*US*)
Black Dahlia Music (*US*)
Blackheart Records Group (*US*)
Bloo Coo Records (*UK*)
Blue Canoe Records (*US*)
Blue Elan Records (*US*)
Bluesky Pie Records (*UK*)
Brash Music (*US*)
Brushfire Records (*US*)
Burnside Distribution (*US*)
Cherry Red Records (*UK*)
Cherrytree Records (*US*)
Circuit Records (*UK*)
Columbia Records (*UK*)
Columbia Records (*US*)
Come Play With Me (*UK*)
Communion Records US (*US*)
Cooking Vinyl (*UK*)
Cruise International Records (*UK*)
Daemon Records (*US*)
Daptone Records (*US*)
DCD2 Records (*US*)

Decca Records (*UK*)
Deek Recordings (*UK*)
Droma Records (*UK*)
Electric Honey Music (*UK*)
Elton Audio Records (*US*)
EMI Records (*UK*)
Erased Tapes Records (*UK*)
Estrus Records (*US*)
Fantasy Records (*US*)
Fat Hippy Records (*UK*)
FatCat Records UK (*UK*)
Fever Records (*US*)
Fiction Records (*UK*)
First Access Entertainment (FAE) (*US*)
Flowers in the Dustbin (*UK*)
Gerry Loves Records (*UK*)
Green Pepper Junction (*UK*)
Handsome Dad Records (*UK*)
Island Records (*UK*)
Jeepster Recordings Ltd (*UK*)
Jungle Records (*UK*)
Kemado Media Group (*US*)
Kobalt Music (*US*)
Kranky (*US*)
Lazy Bones Recordings (*US*)
Lazy S.O.B. Recordings (*US*)
Learn Fear (*UK*)
Limbo Records (*UK*)
Measured Records (*UK*)
Mexican Summer (*US*)

MRG Recordings (*US*)
MTS Records (*US*)
National Anthem (*UK*)
Noisy Poet Records (*US*)
Nutopia Music (*UK*)
One Little Independent Records (*UK*)
The Orchard (*US*)
Ostereo (*UK*)
Parlophone Records (*UK*)
Play It Again Sam (*UK*)
Polydor Records (*UK*)
Purple Worm Records (*UK*)
Ramp Records (*US*)
Raven Black Music (*UK*)
RCA Label Group UK (*UK*)
Real World Ltd (*UK*)
Republic Records (*US*)
Rose Coloured Records (*UK*)
The Royalty Network, Inc. (*US*)
Sacred Bones Records (*US*)
Scruff of the Neck (SOTN) (*UK*)
Sick House Entertainment (*US*)
Silver Blue Productions / Joel Diamond
Entertainment (*US*)
Small Pond Record Label (*UK*)
Sonic Images Records (*US*)
Sony Music Entertainment UK Ltd (*UK*)
Sony Music Entertainment (*US*)
Sotones Music Co-Operative (*UK*)
Soulection (*US*)
Sphere Music (*Can*)
Stef Angel Music (*US*)
Stones Throw Records (*US*)
Sumerian Records (*US*)
Sunbird Records (*UK*)
Symbiotic Records (*US*)
Team Love Records (*US*)
Teide Records (*UK*)
Third Man Records (*US*)
37 Records & Management (*US*)
300 Entertainment (*US*)
Tontena Music (*UK*)
Topshelf Records (*US*)
Toucan Cove Entertainment (*US*)
Tough Love Records (*UK*)
Traffic Cone Records (*UK*)
True Panther Sounds (*US*)
Unfun Records (*US*)
Union Entertainment Group (UEG), Inc.
(*US*)
Universal Music UK (*UK*)
UniversalCMG World Entertainment 1954
(*US*)
Vagrant Records (*US*)
Wagg Records (*UK*)

Warner Music Group (WMG) (*US*)
Warner Records (*US*)
Wichita Recordings (*UK*)
Young Poet Records (*UK*)
Acid
Do As You Please (*UK*)
Dorado Music (*UK*)
Futurist Recordings (*UK*)
Acoustic
Accidental Entertainment (*US*)
Acoustic Disc (*US*)
Arctic Siren Records (*US*)
ATO Records (*US*)
Bohemian Jukebox (*UK*)
Cowboy Rockstar Records (*US*)
Just Music (*UK*)
Lab Records (*UK*)
Nettwerk Records (*UK*)
So Ridiculous Music Group (*US*)
SoundScapes Media Group (*US*)
Spiritual Records (*UK*)
Staylittle Music (*UK*)
Tonotopic Records (*UK*)
Wah Wah 45s (*UK*)
ZTT Records (*UK*)
Alternative
A&M Records (*US*)
Accidental Entertainment (*US*)
The Adult Teeth Recording Company
(*UK*)
American Laundromat Records (*US*)
AnalogueTrash Ltd (*UK*)
Asthmatic Kitty Records (*US*)
Astralwerks Records (*US*)
ATO Records (*US*)
BackWords Recordings (*US*)
Bad Bat Records (*UK*)
Bar/None Records (*US*)
Beggars Group (US) (*US*)
Beggars Group Canada (*Can*)
Bohemian Jukebox (*UK*)
Bread Records (*UK*)
Burnt Toast Vinyl (*US*)
Buzz Records (*UK*)
Carpark Records (*US*)
Cascine (*US*)
CCT Records (*UK*)
Chalkpit Records Ltd (*UK*)
Chemikal Underground Records (*UK*)
Clue Records (*UK*)
Compass Records (*US*)
Cowboy Rockstar Records (*US*)
Dangerbird Records (*US*)
Dead by Mono Records (*UK*)
Demon Music Group (*UK*)

Dirty Bingo Records (*UK*)
Dirty Hit (*UK*)
Dissention Records (*UK*)
Doing Life Records (*UK*)
Domino Recording Company (*UK*)
Drag City (*US*)
Drongo Records (*UK*)
Drum With Our Hands (*UK*)
Easy Life Records (*UK*)
Engineer Records (*UK*)
Esoteric Recordings (*UK*)
Fantastic Plastic (*UK*)
Fast Static (*UK*)
Flat50 Records (*UK*)
Fox Records (*UK*)
Freaks R Us (*UK*)
Frontier Records (*US*)
Glasstone Records (*UK*)
Graphite Records (*UK*)
Hassle Records (*UK*)
Heavenly Recordings (*UK*)
Hit And Run Records (*UK*)
Ignition Records (*UK*)
Iron Man Records (*UK*)
Lab Records (*UK*)
The Leaf Label Ltd (*UK*)
Lewis Recordings (*UK*)
Lex Records Ltd (*UK*)
Loose Music (*UK*)
Manifesto Records, Inc. (*US*)
Marshall Records (*UK*)
Memphis Industries (*UK*)
MNRK Music Group (*US*)
Moksha Recordings Ltd (*UK*)
Mook Records (*UK*)
Mute Records (*UK*)
No Dancing Records (*UK*)
Phantasy Sound Ltd (*UK*)
Pravda Records (*US*)
Public Pressure (*UK*)
Relentless Records (*UK*)
Rock Action Records (*UK*)
Schnitzel Records Ltd (*UK*)
Shangri-La Projects, Inc. (*US*)
Side One Dummy Records (*US*)
Skate Mountain Records (*US*)
Snapper Music (*UK*)
So Recordings (*UK*)
Sound of Pop Inc. (*Can*)
Sparks Music (*Can*)
Spiritual Records (*UK*)
Stolen Recordings (*UK*)
Strange Music Inc. (*US*)
Sunday Best Recordings (*UK*)
Supersonic Media (*UK*)

Superstar Destroyer Records (*UK*)
Three Galleys Records (*UK*)
Tommy Boy (*US*)
TommyBoy Entertainment LLC (*US*)
Tonotopic Records (*UK*)
Tooth & Nail Records (*US*)
Triple Crown Records (*US*)
Urband & Lazar (*US*)
Warp Records (*UK*)
WW Records (*UK*)
XL Recordings (*UK*)
ZTT Records (*UK*)
Ambient
The Adult Teeth Recording Company (*UK*)
Bad Bat Records (*UK*)
Blindsight Records (*UK*)
Brain Bomb Productions (BBP) (*UK*)
Burning Shed Limited (*UK*)
CCT Records (*UK*)
Celestial Harmonies (*US*)
Cold Spring (*UK*)
Drum With Our Hands (*UK*)
Enhanced Music (*UK*)
Just Music (*UK*)
RareNoiseRecords (*UK*)
Six Degrees Records (*US*)
ThrillerTracks (*US*)
Van Richter (*US*)
Warp Records (*UK*)
Waveform Records (*US*)
Americana
Alligator Records (*US*)
Carnival Music (*US*)
Compass Records (*US*)
Cowboy Rockstar Records (*US*)
Dualtone Records (*US*)
Loose Music (*UK*)
MNRK Music Group (*US*)
Quarto Valley Records (*US*)
Rounder Records (*US*)
Signature Sound Recordings (*US*)
Skate Mountain Records (*US*)
Sub Pop Records (*US*)
Sugar Hill Records (*US*)
Avant-Garde
BackWords Recordings (*US*)
Tonotopic Records (*UK*)
Black Metal
Century Media Records (US) (*US*)
Cowboy Rockstar Records (*US*)
Blues
Acoustic Disc (*US*)
Alligator Records (*US*)
The Birdman Recording Group, Inc. (*US*)

Blind Pig Records (*US*)
Buzz Records (*UK*)
CMH Records (*US*)
Compass Records (*US*)
Concord Music Group (*US*)
Cowboy Rockstar Records (*US*)
Dead by Mono Records (*UK*)
Delmark Records (*US*)
Flat50 Records (*UK*)
Malaco Music Group (*US*)
Mega Truth Records (*US*)
NorthernBlues Music Inc. (*Can*)
Perry Road Records Ltd (*UK*)
Public Pressure (*UK*)
Quarto Valley Records (*US*)
Rounder Records (*US*)
SCI Fidelity Records (*US*)
Shanachie Entertainment (*US*)
Shrapnel Records (*US*)
Skaggs Family Records (*US*)
Skate Mountain Records (*US*)
SoundScapes Media Group (*US*)
Spiritual Records (*UK*)
Stackhouse & BluEsoterica (*US*)
Stony Plain Records (*Can*)
Stryker Records, Inc. (*US*)
Sugar Hill Records (*US*)
Summit Records, Inc (*US*)
Sunnyside Records (*US*)
Talking Elephant (*UK*)
Terminus Records (*US*)
Valley Entertainment (*US*)
Wild Records (*US*)
Yep Roc Records (*US*)
Break Beat
Botchit & Scarper Records (*UK*)
Brain Bomb Productions (BBP) (*UK*)
Do As You Please (*UK*)
Finger Lickin' Records (*UK*)
Ninja Tune (*UK*)
Celtic
Compass Records (*US*)
Greentrax Recordings (*UK*)
Linn Records (*UK*)
Lismor Recordings (*UK*)
Valley Entertainment (*US*)
Vertical Records (*UK*)
Chill
Brain Bomb Productions (BBP) (*UK*)
Enhanced Music (*UK*)
Just Music (*UK*)
Needwant (*UK*)
Release / Sustain (*UK*)
So Ridiculous Music Group (*US*)
Waveform Records (*US*)

Christian
Black River Entertainment (*US*)
Capitol Christian Music Group (*US*)
Celestial Harmonies (*US*)
Cowboy Rockstar Records (*US*)
Curb Records (*US*)
Fair Trade (*US*)
Primarily A Cappella (*US*)
Rockzion Records (*US*)
Skaggs Family Records (*US*)
Vineyard Worship (*US*)
Word Records (*US*)
Classic
Drum With Our Hands (*UK*)
Esoteric Recordings (*UK*)
Frontier Records (*US*)
Kufe Records Ltd (*UK*)
1-2-3-4 Go! Records (*US*)
Skate Mountain Records (*US*)
SoundScapes Media Group (*US*)
Stony Plain Records (*Can*)
Talking Elephant (*UK*)
Classical
Acoustic Disc (*US*)
API Records (*US*)
Arabesque Recordings (*US*)
BackWords Recordings (*US*)
The Birdman Recording Group, Inc. (*US*)
Cantaloupe Music (*US*)
Caritas Records (*UK*)
Celestial Harmonies (*US*)
Chandos Records Ltd (*UK*)
Chesky Records (*US*)
Concord Music Group (*US*)
CRD Records Limited (*UK*)
Delos (*US*)
Divine Art Record Company (*UK*)
Linn Records (*UK*)
Parma Recordings (*US*)
Signum Records (*UK*)
Six Degrees Records (*US*)
SOMM Recordings (*UK*)
SoundScapes Media Group (*US*)
Summit Records, Inc (*US*)
Trestle Records (*UK*)
Club
Throne of Blood Records (*US*)
Commercial
Amathus Music (*US*)
BEC Recordings (*US*)
First Run Records (*UK*)
Skate Mountain Records (*US*)
Contemporary
Appleseed Recordings (*US*)
Island Records (US) (*US*)

MadTech Records (*UK*)
Mountain Apple Company (*US*)
Primarily A Cappella (*US*)
Silver Wave Records (*US*)
Six Degrees Records (*US*)
SLAM Productions (*UK*)
Surfdog Records (*US*)
Trestle Records (*UK*)
Verve Label Group (*US*)
Word Records (*US*)
Country
Alternative Tentacles Records (*US*)
Average Joes Entertainment (*US*)
Big Loud Records (*US*)
The Birdman Recording Group, Inc. (*US*)
Black River Entertainment (*US*)
Buzz Records (*UK*)
Capitol Records Nashville (*US*)
Carnival Music (*US*)
CMH Records (*US*)
Cowboy Rockstar Records (*US*)
Curb Records (*US*)
Flat50 Records (*UK*)
Heavenly Recordings (*UK*)
Kufe Records Ltd (*UK*)
Loose Music (*UK*)
My-Zeal Productions, Co. (*US*)
New Pants Publishing (*US*)
1-2-3-4 Go! Records (*US*)
Perry Road Records Ltd (*UK*)
Pravda Records (*US*)
Saddle Creek (*US*)
Shanachie Entertainment (*US*)
Shrapnel Records (*US*)
Skaggs Family Records (*US*)
Skate Mountain Records (*US*)
So Ridiculous Music Group (*US*)
Sony Music Nashville (*US*)
Stony Plain Records (*Can*)
Stryker Records, Inc. (*US*)
Valley Entertainment (*US*)
Warner Music Nashville (*US*)
Word Records (*US*)
Yep Roc Records (*US*)
Dance
Amathus Music (*US*)
Astralwerks Records (*US*)
Axtone (*UK*)
Bad Bat Records (*UK*)
Beggars Group (US) (*US*)
Big Beat (*US*)
Black Butter Records (*UK*)
Capitol Music Group (*US*)
Chocolate Fireguard Music Ltd (*UK*)

Cr2 Records (*UK*)
Craniality Sounds (*US*)
Critical Music (*UK*)
Dauman Music (*US*)
Defected (*UK*)
Finger Lickin' Records (*UK*)
Fired Up Records (*UK*)
Hope Recordings (*UK*)
Innerground Records (*UK*)
Needwant (*UK*)
New State Music (*UK*)
Paradise Palms Records (*UK*)
Phantasy Sound Ltd (*UK*)
Positiva Records (*UK*)
R&S Records (*US*)
Saint Productions (*UK*)
Six Degrees Records (*US*)
Southern Fried Records (*UK*)
Spiral Galaxy Entertainment (*US*)
Subliminal Records (*US*)
Supersonic Media (*UK*)
37 Adventures (*UK*)
Thump Records (*US*)
Tommy Boy (*US*)
TommyBoy Entertainment LLC (*US*)
Ultra Music (*US*)
Warp Records (*UK*)
WW Records (*UK*)
Xploded (*UK*)
Deep Funk
Cowboy Rockstar Records (*US*)
Disco
Axtone (*UK*)
Coloursounds (*UK*)
PAPERecordings (*UK*)
Throne of Blood Records (*US*)
Doom
Cold Spring (*UK*)
Downtempo
Brain Bomb Productions (BBP) (*UK*)
Just Music (*UK*)
Ninja Tune (*UK*)
Waveform Records (*US*)
Drum and Bass
Brain Bomb Productions (BBP) (*UK*)
Critical Music (*UK*)
Dorado Music (*UK*)
Elevate Records (*UK*)
Hospital Records (*UK*)
Infidelity Records (*UK*)
Innerground Records (*UK*)
Ram Records (*UK*)
Saving Grace Music (*UK*)
So Ridiculous Music Group (*US*)

Supersonic Media (*UK*)
Dub
Pumpkin Records (*UK*)
RareNoiseRecords (*UK*)
Wah Wah 45s (*UK*)
Dubstep
Axtone (*UK*)
CCT Records (*UK*)
Lewis Recordings (*UK*)
NoFace Records (*US*)
Saving Grace Music (*UK*)
So Ridiculous Music Group (*US*)
Southpoint (*UK*)
Electronic
Accidental Entertainment (*US*)
The Adult Teeth Recording Company
(*UK*)
Akira (*UK*)
Alias Records (*US*)
Amathus Music (*US*)
Aphagia Recordings (*US*)
Astralwerks Records (*US*)
Axtone (*UK*)
Babygrande Records, Inc. (*US*)
BackWords Recordings (*US*)
Bad Bat Records (*UK*)
Beggars Group (US) (*US*)
Big Beat (*US*)
Blindsight Records (*UK*)
Border Community (*UK*)
Burning Shed Limited (*UK*)
Cantaloupe Music (*US*)
Cascine (*US*)
CCT Records (*UK*)
Chocolate Fireguard Music Ltd (*UK*)
Circus Records (*UK*)
Cleopatra Records (*US*)
Cold Spring (*UK*)
Coloursounds (*UK*)
Cr2 Records (*UK*)
Critical Music (*UK*)
Dirty Bingo Records (*UK*)
Dorado Music (*UK*)
Double Denim Records (*UK*)
Drum With Our Hands (*UK*)
Enhanced Music (*UK*)
Esoteric Recordings (*UK*)
Far Out Recordings (*UK*)
Finger Lickin' Records (*UK*)
Freaks R Us (*UK*)
Glasstone Records (*UK*)
Houndstooth (*UK*)
InTime Records (*UK*)
Just Music (*UK*)
JW Music Limited (*UK*)

Lewis Recordings (*UK*)
MadTech Records (*UK*)
Milan Records (*US*)
MNRK Music Group (*US*)
Moksha Recordings Ltd (*UK*)
Mute Records (*UK*)
Needwant (*UK*)
Ninja Tune (*UK*)
NoFace Records (*US*)
One Inch Badge (OIB) Records (*UK*)
101BPM (*UK*)
Paradise Palms Records (*UK*)
Phantasy Sound Ltd (*UK*)
Pinball Records (*UK*)
Public Pressure (*UK*)
R&S Records (*US*)
Ramber Records (*UK*)
Rock Action Records (*UK*)
Saddle Creek (*US*)
Saved Records (*UK*)
SCI Fidelity Records (*US*)
Shanachie Entertainment (*US*)
Six Degrees Records (*US*)
So Ridiculous Music Group (*US*)
Sonic Cathedral (*UK*)
Soundplate (*UK*)
Southern Fried Records (*UK*)
Sub Pop Records (*US*)
Subliminal Records (*US*)
Sunday Best Recordings (*UK*)
37 Adventures (*UK*)
ThrillerTracks (*US*)
Throne of Blood Records (*US*)
Thump Records (*US*)
Tommy Boy (*US*)
TommyBoy Entertainment LLC (*US*)
Tonotopic Records (*UK*)
Trestle Records (*UK*)
Ultra Music (*US*)
Voltage Records (*UK*)
Wah Wah 45s (*UK*)
Warp Records (*UK*)
Waveform Records (*US*)
WW Records (*UK*)
XL Recordings (*UK*)
ZTT Records (*UK*)
Emo
Bullet Tooth (*US*)
Deep Elm Records (*US*)
Dine Alone Records (*Can*)
Disconnect Disconnect Records (*UK*)
Doing Life Records (*UK*)
Engineer Records (*UK*)
Hassle Records (*UK*)
Pinky Swear Records (*UK*)

Revelation Records (*US*)
Ethnic
Sonic Safari Music (*US*)
Experimental
The Adult Teeth Recording Company (*UK*)
Aphagia Recordings (*US*)
Bad Bat Records (*UK*)
Biscornus Records (*Can*)
Bohemian Jukebox (*UK*)
Cold Spring (*UK*)
Dance To The Radio (*UK*)
Drag City (*US*)
Fire Records (*UK*)
Freaks R Us (*UK*)
Futurist Recordings (*UK*)
The Leaf Label Ltd (*UK*)
SLAM Productions (*UK*)
T&R Recordings (*US*)
Tonotopic Records (*UK*)
Warp Records (*UK*)
Extreme
Cowboy Rockstar Records (*US*)
Rotten Records (*US*)
Folk
Acoustic Disc (*US*)
Akira (*UK*)
American Laundromat Records (*US*)
Appleseed Recordings (*US*)
Bohemian Jukebox (*UK*)
Bread Records (*UK*)
Breakfast Records LLP (*UK*)
Buzz Records (*UK*)
Compass Records (*US*)
Cowboy Rockstar Records (*US*)
Drum With Our Hands (*UK*)
Dualtone Records (*US*)
Fellside Recordings (*UK*)
Fika Recordings (*UK*)
Flat50 Records (*UK*)
Folkroom Records (*UK*)
JohnJohn Records (*UK*)
Lab Records (*UK*)
Nettwerk Records (*UK*)
New Pants Publishing (*US*)
Oh Boy Records (*US*)
One Inch Badge (OIB) Records (*UK*)
Park Records (*UK*)
Quatre Femmes Records (*UK*)
Rounder Records (*US*)
Saving Grace Music (*UK*)
Shanachie Entertainment (*US*)
Signature Sound Recordings (*US*)
Six Degrees Records (*US*)
Spiritual Records (*UK*)

Staylittle Music (*UK*)
Stony Plain Records (*Can*)
Sub Pop Records (*US*)
Surfdog Records (*US*)
Talking Elephant (*UK*)
Three Galleys Records (*UK*)
Yep Roc Records (*US*)
Funk
Chalkpit Records Ltd (*UK*)
Cowboy Rockstar Records (*US*)
Mello Music Group (*US*)
1-2-3-4 Go! Records (*US*)
Wah Wah 45s (*UK*)
Funky
Cowboy Rockstar Records (*US*)
Craniality Sounds (*US*)
Stryker Records, Inc. (*US*)
Fusion
Celestial Harmonies (*US*)
Moksha Recordings Ltd (*UK*)
Garage
The Birdman Recording Group, Inc. (*US*)
Bomp Records (*US*)
Breakfast Records LLP (*UK*)
Champion Records (*UK*)
Dead by Mono Records (*UK*)
Do As You Please (*UK*)
Fuzzkill Records (*UK*)
1-2-3-4 Go! Records (*US*)
Pumpkin Records (*UK*)
Ramber Records (*UK*)
Rare Vitamin Records (*UK*)
Saving Grace Music (*UK*)
Skate Mountain Records (*US*)
Southpoint (*UK*)
Vallance Records (*UK*)
Wicked Cool Records (*US*)
Wild Records (*US*)
Glam
Cowboy Rockstar Records (*US*)
Glitch
Aphagia Recordings (*US*)
Gospel
Capitol Christian Music Group (*US*)
CMH Records (*US*)
Hacienda Records (*US*)
Malaco Music Group (*US*)
My-Zeal Productions, Co. (*US*)
NorthernBlues Music Inc. (*Can*)
Shanachie Entertainment (*US*)
Spiral Galaxy Entertainment (*US*)
Gothic
Century Media Records (US) (*US*)
Cleopatra Records (*US*)
Invisible Records (*US*)

Van Richter (*US*)
Grime
  Saving Grace Music (*UK*)
  Southpoint (*UK*)
Guitar based
  BackWords Recordings (*US*)
  Breakfast Records LLP (*UK*)
  Cowboy Rockstar Records (*US*)
  Fantastic Plastic (*UK*)
  Fika Recordings (*UK*)
  G² Records & Publishing (*US*)
  I'm Not From London (*UK*)
  Marshall Records (*UK*)
  Shrapnel Records (*US*)
  Voltage Records (*UK*)
  Warp Records (*UK*)
Hard
  A389 Recordings (*US*)
  Century Media Records (US) (*US*)
  Cowboy Rockstar Records (*US*)
  Drag City (*US*)
  Fired Up Records (*UK*)
  Leviathan Records (*US*)
  Shrapnel Records (*US*)
  Southern Lord Recordings (*US*)
  Spinefarm Records (*US*)
  Stryker Records, Inc. (*US*)
  Suburban Noize Records (*US*)
  T&R Recordings (*US*)
Hardcore
  Alternative Tentacles Records (*US*)
  Blindsight Records (*UK*)
  Boslevan Records (*UK*)
  Bridge Nine Records (*US*)
  Bullet Tooth (*US*)
  Century Media Records (US) (*US*)
  Cowboy Rockstar Records (*US*)
  Dine Alone Records (*Can*)
  Disconnect Disconnect Records (*UK*)
  Dog Knights Productions (*UK*)
  Engineer Records (*UK*)
  Hassle Records (*UK*)
  Killing Moon Records (*UK*)
  1-2-3-4 Go! Records (*US*)
  Pinky Swear Records (*UK*)
  Revelation Records (*US*)
  Rotten Records (*US*)
  Side One Dummy Records (*US*)
  Speedowax (*UK*)
  Supersonic Media (*UK*)
  T&R Recordings (*US*)
  Victory Records (*US*)
Heavy
  Cowboy Rockstar Records (*US*)
  Leviathan Records (*US*)

MNRK Music Group (*US*)
  Public Pressure (*UK*)
  Shrapnel Records (*US*)
  T&R Recordings (*US*)
Hip-Hop
  0207 Def Jam Recordings (*UK*)
  Babygrande Records, Inc. (*US*)
  Barbarian Productions (*US*)
  Big Beat (*US*)
  Black Butter Records (*UK*)
  Cash Money Records (*US*)
  CCT Records (*UK*)
  Chocolate Fireguard Music Ltd (*UK*)
  Cleopatra Records (*US*)
  Closed Sessions (*US*)
  Def Jam Recordings (*US*)
  Dine Alone Records (*Can*)
  Dorado Music (*UK*)
  Finger Lickin' Records (*UK*)
  Island Records (US) (*US*)
  Kudos Records Limited (*UK*)
  Lab Records (*UK*)
  Lewis Recordings (*UK*)
  Mello Music Group (*US*)
  MNRK Music Group (*US*)
  Ninja Tune (*UK*)
  1-2-3-4 Go! Records (*US*)
  Public Pressure (*UK*)
  Rhymesayers Entertainment (*US*)
  Sapien Records Limited (*UK*)
  Saving Grace Music (*UK*)
  Shady Records (*US*)
  Skate Mountain Records (*US*)
  Slip-N-Slide Records (*US*)
  So Ridiculous Music Group (*US*)
  Spiral Galaxy Entertainment (*US*)
  Stryker Records, Inc. (*US*)
  Suburban Noize Records (*US*)
  Surfdog Records (*US*)
  Thump Records (*US*)
  Tommy Boy (*US*)
  TommyBoy Entertainment LLC (*US*)
  Ultra Music (*US*)
  Viper Records (*US*)
  Waxploitation Records (*US*)
  Word Records (*US*)
Horror
  Cowboy Rockstar Records (*US*)
  Dead by Mono Records (*UK*)
House
  Amathus Music (*US*)
  Axtone (*UK*)
  Big Beat (*US*)
  Brain Bomb Productions (BBP) (*UK*)
  Champion Records (*UK*)

Circus Recordings (*UK*)
Coloursounds (*UK*)
Cr2 Records (*UK*)
Craniality Sounds (*US*)
Defected (*UK*)
Do As You Please (*UK*)
Futurist Recordings (*UK*)
Gruuv (*UK*)
JW Music Limited (*UK*)
Kudos Records Limited (*UK*)
Needwant (*UK*)
NoFace Records (*US*)
PAPERecordings (*UK*)
Pinball Records (*UK*)
Release / Sustain (*UK*)
Saved Records (*UK*)
Saving Grace Music (*UK*)
Shabby Doll Records (*UK*)
Soundplate (*UK*)
Strictly Rhythm (*US*)
Subliminal Records (*US*)
Supersonic Media (*UK*)
Throne of Blood Records (*US*)
Toolroom Records (*UK*)
House
Amathus Music (*US*)
Axtone (*UK*)
Big Beat (*US*)
Brain Bomb Productions (BBP) (*UK*)
Champion Records (*UK*)
Circus Recordings (*UK*)
Coloursounds (*UK*)
Cr2 Records (*UK*)
Craniality Sounds (*US*)
Defected (*UK*)
Do As You Please (*UK*)
Futurist Recordings (*UK*)
Gruuv (*UK*)
JW Music Limited (*UK*)
Kudos Records Limited (*UK*)
Needwant (*UK*)
NoFace Records (*US*)
PAPERecordings (*UK*)
Pinball Records (*UK*)
Release / Sustain (*UK*)
Saved Records (*UK*)
Saving Grace Music (*UK*)
Shabby Doll Records (*UK*)
Soundplate (*UK*)
Strictly Rhythm (*US*)
Subliminal Records (*US*)
Supersonic Media (*UK*)
Throne of Blood Records (*US*)
Toolroom Records (*UK*)

Indie
4AD (*US*)
A&M Records (*US*)
Accidental Entertainment (*US*)
The Adult Teeth Recording Company (*UK*)
Akira (*UK*)
Alias Records (*US*)
Alternative Tentacles Records (*US*)
American Laundromat Records (*US*)
Anti (*US*)
ATO Records (*US*)
Babygrande Records, Inc. (*US*)
BackWords Recordings (*US*)
Bar/None Records (*US*)
Barsuk Records (*US*)
Beggars Group (US) (*US*)
Bomp Records (*US*)
Boslevan Records (*UK*)
Bread Records (*UK*)
Breakfast Records LLP (*UK*)
Capitol Music Group (*US*)
Carnival Music (*US*)
Chalkpit Records Ltd (*UK*)
Clue Records (*UK*)
Coloursounds (*UK*)
Cowboy Rockstar Records (*US*)
Dance To The Radio (*UK*)
Dangerbird Records (*US*)
Deep Elm Records (*US*)
Demon Music Group (*UK*)
Dine Alone Records (*Can*)
Dirty Bingo Records (*UK*)
Doing Life Records (*UK*)
Donut Records (*UK*)
Dualtone Records (*US*)
Engineer Records (*UK*)
Fierce Panda Records (*UK*)
Fika Recordings (*UK*)
Fire Tower Entertainment (*US*)
First Run Records (*UK*)
Flat50 Records (*UK*)
Glasstone Records (*UK*)
Hand in Hive (*UK*)
Hassle Records (*UK*)
Heavenly Recordings (*UK*)
Infinite Hive (*UK*)
InTime Records (*UK*)
Island Records (US) (*US*)
Killing Moon Records (*UK*)
Manifesto Records, Inc. (*US*)
Marshall Records (*UK*)
Memphis Industries (*UK*)
Mook Records (*UK*)

No Dancing Records (*UK*)
1-2-3-4 Go! Records (*US*)
Paradise Palms Records (*UK*)
Perry Road Records Ltd (*UK*)
Philophobia Music (*UK*)
Quatre Femmes Records (*UK*)
Reach Out International Records (ROIR) (*US*)
Relapse Records (*US*)
Rock Action Records (*UK*)
Rough Trade Records (*UK*)
Saddle Creek (*US*)
Saving Grace Music (*UK*)
Signature Sound Recordings (*US*)
Slumberland Records (*US*)
So Recordings (*UK*)
Speedowax (*UK*)
Staylittle Music (*UK*)
Stolen Recordings (*UK*)
Stryker Records, Inc. (*US*)
Sub Pop Records (*US*)
Sunday Best Recordings (*UK*)
Surfdog Records (*US*)
Tee Pee Records (*US*)
37 Adventures (*UK*)
Urband & Lazar (*US*)
Vallance Records (*UK*)
Victory Records (*US*)
ZTT Records (*UK*)
Industrial
Aphagia Recordings (*US*)
Cleopatra Records (*US*)
Cold Spring (*UK*)
Cowboy Rockstar Records (*US*)
Van Richter (*US*)
Instrumental
Aphagia Recordings (*US*)
Babygrande Records, Inc. (*US*)
BackWords Recordings (*US*)
Biscornus Records (*Can*)
CMH Records (*US*)
Dead by Mono Records (*UK*)
ThrillerTracks (*US*)
Trestle Records (*UK*)
Valley Entertainment (*US*)
Jazz
Acoustic Disc (*US*)
Arabesque Recordings (*US*)
The Birdman Recording Group, Inc. (*US*)
Blue Note Label Group (*US*)
Bolero Records (*US*)
Cantaloupe Music (*US*)
Chesky Records (*US*)
Cleopatra Records (*US*)
Compass Records (*US*)

Concord Music Group (*US*)
Delmark Records (*US*)
Dorado Music (*UK*)
G² Records & Publishing (*US*)
JohnJohn Records (*UK*)
Kudos Records Limited (*UK*)
Linn Records (*UK*)
Mack Avenue (*US*)
Malaco Music Group (*US*)
Mello Music Group (*US*)
My-Zeal Productions, Co. (*US*)
Ninja Tune (*UK*)
1-2-3-4 Go! Records (*US*)
Posi-Tone (*US*)
Primarily A Cappella (*US*)
Quarto Valley Records (*US*)
RareNoiseRecords (*UK*)
Revolver Records (*UK*)
Rounder Records (*US*)
Shanachie Entertainment (*US*)
Shrapnel Records (*US*)
SLAM Productions (*UK*)
SoundScapes Media Group (*US*)
Spiral Galaxy Entertainment (*US*)
Summit Records, Inc (*US*)
Sunnyside Records (*US*)
Upbeat Recordings (*UK*)
Valley Entertainment (*US*)
Verve Label Group (*US*)
Wah Wah 45s (*UK*)
Latin
Accidental Entertainment (*US*)
Acoustic Disc (*US*)
Bolero Records (*US*)
Concord Music Group (*US*)
Hacienda Records (*US*)
Six Degrees Records (*US*)
So Ridiculous Music Group (*US*)
SoundScapes Media Group (*US*)
Thump Records (*US*)
Tommy Boy (*US*)
Tumi Music Ltd (*UK*)
Leftfield
Bohemian Jukebox (*UK*)
Kudos Records Limited (*UK*)
Ninja Tune (*UK*)
No Dancing Records (*UK*)
PAPERecordings (*UK*)
Sunday Best Recordings (*UK*)
Lo-fi
Fuzzkill Records (*UK*)
Slumberland Records (*US*)
So Ridiculous Music Group (*US*)
Mainstream
Skate Mountain Records (*US*)

So Ridiculous Music Group (*US*)
Melodic
BackWords Recordings (*US*)
So Ridiculous Music Group (*US*)
Stryker Records, Inc. (*US*)
Tonotopic Records (*UK*)
Metal
A389 Recordings (*US*)
Alternative Tentacles Records (*US*)
Blindsight Records (*UK*)
Bullet Tooth (*US*)
Candlelight Records (*UK*)
Century Media Records (US) (*US*)
Cleopatra Records (*US*)
Cowboy Rockstar Records (*US*)
Earache London (*UK*)
Glasstone Records (*UK*)
Graphite Records (*UK*)
Hassle Records (*UK*)
Infinite Hive (*UK*)
Invisible Records (*US*)
Iron Man Records (*UK*)
Island Records (US) (*US*)
Leviathan Records (*US*)
Marshall Records (*UK*)
MNRK Music Group (*US*)
Public Pressure (*UK*)
Relapse Records (*US*)
Revolver Records (*UK*)
Roadrunner Records (*UK*)
Rotten Records (*US*)
Sapien Records Limited (*UK*)
Shrapnel Records (*US*)
Snapper Music (*UK*)
So Ridiculous Music Group (*US*)
Southern Lord Recordings (*US*)
Spinefarm Records (*US*)
Sub Pop Records (*US*)
T&R Recordings (*US*)
Tee Pee Records (*US*)
Venn Records (*UK*)
Victory Records (*US*)
Modern
The Birdman Recording Group, Inc. (*US*)
Celestial Harmonies (*US*)
Cowboy Rockstar Records (*US*)
Signature Sound Recordings (*US*)
Terminus Records (*US*)
Mystical
BackWords Recordings (*US*)
New Age
Bolero Records (*US*)
Cantaloupe Music (*US*)
Silver Wave Records (*US*)
Valley Entertainment (*US*)

New Wave
Bomp Records (*US*)
Cowboy Rockstar Records (*US*)
Dead by Mono Records (*UK*)
Fire Records (*UK*)
So Ridiculous Music Group (*US*)
Noise Core
Cold Spring (*UK*)
T&R Recordings (*US*)
Non-Commercial
Cowboy Rockstar Records (*US*)
Nostalgia
Cowboy Rockstar Records (*US*)
Pop
825 Records (*US*)
A&M Records (*US*)
Accidental Entertainment (*US*)
The Adult Teeth Recording Company (*UK*)
Alternative Tentacles Records (*US*)
American Laundromat Records (*US*)
API Records (*US*)
Asthmatic Kitty Records (*US*)
ATO Records (*US*)
Barbarian Productions (*US*)
BEC Recordings (*US*)
Beggars Group Canada (*Can*)
Blue Note Label Group (*US*)
Bomp Records (*US*)
Capitol Music Group (*US*)
Carnival Music (*US*)
Cascine (*US*)
Cash Money Records (*US*)
Chalkpit Records Ltd (*UK*)
Cleopatra Records (*US*)
CMH Records (*US*)
Coloursounds (*UK*)
Compass Records (*US*)
Concord Music Group (*US*)
Curb Records (*US*)
Dirty Bingo Records (*UK*)
Disconnect Disconnect Records (*UK*)
Double Denim Records (*UK*)
Drag City (*US*)
Drum With Our Hands (*UK*)
Esoteric Recordings (*UK*)
Fire Tower Entertainment (*US*)
First Run Records (*UK*)
Flair Records (*UK*)
Hand in Hive (*UK*)
Hassle Records (*UK*)
Heavenly Recordings (*UK*)
Hit And Run Records (*UK*)
InTime Records (*UK*)
Island Records (US) (*US*)

JW Music Limited (*UK*)
Killing Moon Records (*UK*)
Lab Records (*UK*)
Manifesto Records, Inc. (*US*)
My-Zeal Productions, Co. (*US*)
New Pants Publishing (*US*)
One Inch Badge (OIB) Records (*UK*)
Philophobia Music (*UK*)
Pinky Swear Records (*UK*)
Pravda Records (*US*)
Quatre Femmes Records (*UK*)
Ramber Records (*UK*)
Saint Productions (*UK*)
Sapien Records Limited (*UK*)
Saving Grace Music (*UK*)
Schoolboy Records (*US*)
Signature Sound Recordings (*US*)
Six Degrees Records (*US*)
Skate Mountain Records (*US*)
Slip-N-Slide Records (*US*)
Slumberland Records (*US*)
So Ridiculous Music Group (*US*)
Sound of Pop Inc. (*Can*)
SoundScapes Media Group (*US*)
Sparks Music (*Can*)
Spiral Galaxy Entertainment (*US*)
Stryker Records, Inc. (*US*)
Sub Pop Records (*US*)
Surfdog Records (*US*)
T&R Recordings (*US*)
37 Adventures (*UK*)
Thump Records (*US*)
Tommy Boy (*US*)
TommyBoy Entertainment LLC (*US*)
Trestle Records (*UK*)
Ultra Music (*US*)
Verve Label Group (*US*)
Wax Records Inc. (*US*)
Xploded (*UK*)
Yep Roc Records (*US*)
Post
Biscornus Records (*Can*)
Blindsight Records (*UK*)
Bohemian Jukebox (*UK*)
Deep Elm Records (*US*)
Dine Alone Records (*Can*)
Disconnect Disconnect Records (*UK*)
Fire Records (*UK*)
Freaks R Us (*UK*)
Killing Moon Records (*UK*)
Kscope (*UK*)
Rare Vitamin Records (*UK*)
Slumberland Records (*US*)
Snapper Music (*UK*)
Speedowax (*UK*)

Supersonic Media (*UK*)
Superstar Destroyer Records (*UK*)
Power
Bomp Records (*US*)
Cold Spring (*UK*)
Cowboy Rockstar Records (*US*)
Progressive
Aphagia Recordings (*US*)
Burning Shed Limited (*UK*)
Cowboy Rockstar Records (*US*)
Esoteric Recordings (*UK*)
Kscope (*UK*)
Public Pressure (*UK*)
RareNoiseRecords (*UK*)
Shrapnel Records (*US*)
Snapper Music (*UK*)
So Ridiculous Music Group (*US*)
Stryker Records, Inc. (*US*)
Superstar Destroyer Records (*UK*)
Psychebilly
Cowboy Rockstar Records (*US*)
Dead by Mono Records (*UK*)
Nervous Records (*UK*)
Pumpkin Records (*UK*)
Psychedelic
BackWords Recordings (*US*)
Bohemian Jukebox (*UK*)
Dead by Mono Records (*UK*)
Donut Records (*UK*)
Esoteric Recordings (*UK*)
Fire Records (*UK*)
Fuzzkill Records (*UK*)
Public Pressure (*UK*)
Quatre Femmes Records (*UK*)
Ramber Records (*UK*)
Rare Vitamin Records (*UK*)
So Ridiculous Music Group (*US*)
Sonic Cathedral (*UK*)
Vallance Records (*UK*)
Punk
Alternative Tentacles Records (*US*)
Beggars Group (US) (*US*)
Bomber Music Ltd (*UK*)
Bomp Records (*US*)
Boslevan Records (*UK*)
Breakfast Records LLP (*UK*)
Bullet Tooth (*US*)
Cantaloupe Music (*US*)
Cleopatra Records (*US*)
Cowboy Rockstar Records (*US*)
Dead by Mono Records (*UK*)
Deep Elm Records (*US*)
Dine Alone Records (*Can*)
Disconnect Disconnect Records (*UK*)
Dissention Records (*UK*)

Dog Knights Productions (*UK*)
Engineer Records (*UK*)
Fire Records (*UK*)
Flat50 Records (*UK*)
Freaks R Us (*UK*)
Frontier Records (*US*)
Glasstone Records (*UK*)
Hassle Records (*UK*)
Hit And Run Records (*UK*)
Infinite Hive (*UK*)
Iron Man Records (*UK*)
Island Records (US) (*US*)
Manifesto Records, Inc. (*US*)
Marshall Records (*UK*)
Mook Records (*UK*)
No Front Teeth (*UK*)
1-2-3-4 Go! Records (*US*)
Pinky Swear Records (*UK*)
Pumpkin Records (*UK*)
Rare Vitamin Records (*UK*)
Reach Out International Records (ROIR) (*US*)
Revelation Records (*US*)
Rotten Records (*US*)
Sapien Records Limited (*UK*)
Side One Dummy Records (*US*)
Skate Mountain Records (*US*)
Slumberland Records (*US*)
So Ridiculous Music Group (*US*)
Speedowax (*UK*)
Sub Pop Records (*US*)
Suburban Noize Records (*US*)
Surfdog Records (*US*)
T&R Recordings (*US*)
Tee Pee Records (*US*)
Vallance Records (*UK*)
Venn Records (*UK*)
Victory Records (*US*)
Ragga
So Ridiculous Music Group (*US*)
R&B
0207 Def Jam Recordings (*UK*)
825 Records (*US*)
A&M Records (*US*)
Alternative Tentacles Records (*US*)
Barbarian Productions (*US*)
Blue Note Label Group (*US*)
Concord Music Group (*US*)
Def Jam Recordings (*US*)
Island Records (US) (*US*)
JW Music Limited (*UK*)
Kufe Records Ltd (*UK*)
Malaco Music Group (*US*)
My-Zeal Productions, Co. (*US*)

New Pants Publishing (*US*)
1-2-3-4 Go! Records (*US*)
Pravda Records (*US*)
Sapien Records Limited (*UK*)
Shanachie Entertainment (*US*)
Skate Mountain Records (*US*)
Slip-N-Slide Records (*US*)
So Ridiculous Music Group (*US*)
Soul II Soul (*UK*)
Spiral Galaxy Entertainment (*US*)
Stony Plain Records (*Can*)
Surfdog Records (*US*)
Thump Records (*US*)
Verve Label Group (*US*)
Rap
Cleopatra Records (*US*)
Def Jam Recordings (*US*)
Island Records (US) (*US*)
Lewis Recordings (*UK*)
New Pants Publishing (*US*)
Shady Records (*US*)
Skate Mountain Records (*US*)
Slip-N-Slide Records (*US*)
So Ridiculous Music Group (*US*)
Soul II Soul (*UK*)
Stryker Records, Inc. (*US*)
Surfdog Records (*US*)
Thump Records (*US*)
Ultra Music (*US*)
Viper Records (*US*)
Word Records (*US*)
Reggae
Bomber Music Ltd (*UK*)
Kufe Records Ltd (*UK*)
Lab Records (*UK*)
1-2-3-4 Go! Records (*US*)
Reach Out International Records (ROIR) (*US*)
Shanachie Entertainment (*US*)
Side One Dummy Records (*US*)
Slip-N-Slide Records (*US*)
Surfdog Records (*US*)
Ultra Music (*US*)
VP Records (*US*)
Wah Wah 45s (*UK*)
Reggaeton
Cleopatra Records (*US*)
Regional
Canyon (*US*)
Far Out Recordings (*UK*)
Greentrax Recordings (*UK*)
Lismor Recordings (*UK*)
Mountain Apple Company (*US*)
Scotdisc (*UK*)

Silver Wave Records (*US*)
Rhythm and Blues
Dead by Mono Records (*UK*)
Heavenly Recordings (*UK*)
So Ridiculous Music Group (*US*)
Rock and Roll
Bomber Music Ltd (*UK*)
Cowboy Rockstar Records (*US*)
Dead by Mono Records (*UK*)
Donut Records (*UK*)
Fury Records (*UK*)
Fuzzkill Records (*UK*)
Nervous Records (*UK*)
Skate Mountain Records (*US*)
Stony Plain Records (*Can*)
Stryker Records, Inc. (*US*)
Wicked Cool Records (*US*)
Rock
4AD (*US*)
825 Records (*US*)
A&M Records (*US*)
A389 Recordings (*US*)
Accidental Entertainment (*US*)
The Adult Teeth Recording Company
(*UK*)
Akira (*UK*)
Alias Records (*US*)
Alive Naturalsound (*US*)
Alternative Tentacles Records (*US*)
American Laundromat Records (*US*)
Anti (*US*)
Aphagia Recordings (*US*)
API Records (*US*)
ATO Records (*US*)
Babygrande Records, Inc. (*US*)
BackWords Recordings (*US*)
Bar/None Records (*US*)
Barsuk Records (*US*)
Beggars Group (US) (*US*)
Beggars Group Canada (*Can*)
Blindsight Records (*UK*)
Bomp Records (*US*)
Boslevan Records (*UK*)
Bread Records (*UK*)
Breakfast Records LLP (*UK*)
Bright Antenna Records (*US*)
Bullet Tooth (*US*)
Burning Shed Limited (*UK*)
Cantaloupe Music (*US*)
Capitol Music Group (*US*)
Carnival Music (*US*)
Carpark Records (*US*)
Century Media Records (US) (*US*)
Chocolate Fireguard Music Ltd (*UK*)
Clue Records (*UK*)

CMH Records (*US*)
Concord Music Group (*US*)
Cowboy Rockstar Records (*US*)
Curb Records (*US*)
Dangerbird Records (*US*)
Dead by Mono Records (*UK*)
Deep Elm Records (*US*)
Dine Alone Records (*Can*)
Disconnect Disconnect Records (*UK*)
Doing Life Records (*UK*)
Donut Records (*UK*)
Drag City (*US*)
Drongo Records (*UK*)
Dualtone Records (*US*)
Esoteric Recordings (*UK*)
Fierce Panda Records (*UK*)
Fire Records (*UK*)
Flat50 Records (*UK*)
Frontier Records (*US*)
Fuzzkill Records (*UK*)
Glasstone Records (*UK*)
Graphite Records (*UK*)
Hassle Records (*UK*)
Hit And Run Records (*UK*)
Ignition Records (*UK*)
Infinite Hive (*UK*)
InTime Records (*UK*)
Invisible Records (*US*)
Iron Man Records (*UK*)
Island Records (US) (*US*)
Killing Moon Records (*UK*)
Kscope (*UK*)
Lab Records (*UK*)
Leviathan Records (*US*)
Manifesto Records, Inc. (*US*)
Marshall Records (*UK*)
Mega Truth Records (*US*)
MNRK Music Group (*US*)
New Pants Publishing (*US*)
No Dancing Records (*UK*)
No Front Teeth (*UK*)
One Inch Badge (OIB) Records (*UK*)
1-2-3-4 Go! Records (*US*)
Perry Road Records Ltd (*UK*)
Pravda Records (*US*)
Quarto Valley Records (*US*)
Quatre Femmes Records (*UK*)
Ramber Records (*UK*)
Rare Vitamin Records (*UK*)
Reach Out International Records (ROIR)
(*US*)
Relapse Records (*US*)
Revelation Records (*US*)
Revolver Records (*UK*)
Roadrunner Records (*UK*)

Rock Action Records (*UK*)
Rockzion Records (*US*)
Rough Trade Records (*UK*)
Rounder Records (*US*)
Saddle Creek (*US*)
Sapien Records Limited (*UK*)
Saving Grace Music (*UK*)
Schnitzel Records Ltd (*UK*)
SCI Fidelity Records (*US*)
Shangri-La Projects, Inc. (*US*)
Shrapnel Records (*US*)
Signature Sound Recordings (*US*)
Six Degrees Records (*US*)
Skate Mountain Records (*US*)
Slush Fund Recordings (*US*)
Snapper Music (*UK*)
So Recordings (*UK*)
Sonic Cathedral (*UK*)
SoundScapes Media Group (*US*)
Southern Lord Recordings (*US*)
Sparks Music (*Can*)
Speedowax (*UK*)
Spinefarm Records (*US*)
Spiritual Records (*UK*)
Stryker Records, Inc. (*US*)
Sub Pop Records (*US*)
Suburban Noize Records (*US*)
Superstar Destroyer Records (*UK*)
Surfdog Records (*US*)
T&R Recordings (*US*)
Talking Elephant (*UK*)
Tee Pee Records (*US*)
Terminus Records (*US*)
Tooth & Nail Records (*US*)
Triple Crown Records (*US*)
Urband & Lazar (*US*)
Vallance Records (*UK*)
Valley Entertainment (*US*)
Venn Records (*UK*)
Victory Records (*US*)
Wax Records Inc. (*US*)
Wicked Cool Records (*US*)
Word Records (*US*)
Yep Roc Records (*US*)
Rockabilly
Bomber Music Ltd (*UK*)
Cowboy Rockstar Records (*US*)
Dead by Mono Records (*UK*)
Fury Records (*UK*)
Nervous Records (*UK*)
Pravda Records (*US*)
Pumpkin Records (*UK*)
Wild Records (*US*)

Roots
Acoustic Disc (*US*)
Alligator Records (*US*)
Appleseed Recordings (*US*)
Blind Pig Records (*US*)
Buzz Records (*UK*)
Compass Records (*US*)
Fellside Recordings (*UK*)
Mountain Home Music Company (*US*)
NorthernBlues Music Inc. (*Can*)
Oh Boy Records (*US*)
Round Hill Music (*US*)
Rounder Records (*US*)
Signature Sound Recordings (*US*)
Skaggs Family Records (*US*)
Skate Mountain Records (*US*)
Stony Plain Records (*Can*)
Sugar Hill Records (*US*)
Vertical Records (*UK*)
Yep Roc Records (*US*)
Shoegaze
Slumberland Records (*US*)
Sonic Cathedral (*UK*)
Superstar Destroyer Records (*UK*)
Warp Records (*UK*)
Singer-Songwriter
825 Records (*US*)
A&M Records (*US*)
Alias Records (*US*)
American Laundromat Records (*US*)
BackWords Recordings (*US*)
Barbarian Productions (*US*)
Beggars Group (US) (*US*)
Birdland Records (*UK*)
Bohemian Jukebox (*UK*)
Burning Shed Limited (*UK*)
Burnt Toast Vinyl (*US*)
Champion Records (*UK*)
Cowboy Rockstar Records (*US*)
Doing Life Records (*UK*)
Dualtone Records (*US*)
Nettwerk Records (*UK*)
SCI Fidelity Records (*US*)
Shanachie Entertainment (*US*)
Signature Sound Recordings (*US*)
Skate Mountain Records (*US*)
So Ridiculous Music Group (*US*)
Spiritual Records (*UK*)
Sub Pop Records (*US*)
Surfdog Records (*US*)
Urband & Lazar (*US*)
Ska
Bomber Music Ltd (*UK*)

1-2-3-4 Go! Records (*US*)
Pumpkin Records (*UK*)
Side One Dummy Records (*US*)
Soul
0207 Def Jam Recordings (*UK*)
Alive Naturalsound (*US*)
Big Crown Records (*US*)
Chalkpit Records Ltd (*UK*)
Concord Music Group (*US*)
Dorado Music (*UK*)
Malaco Music Group (*US*)
Mello Music Group (*US*)
My-Zeal Productions, Co. (*US*)
1-2-3-4 Go! Records (*US*)
Pravda Records (*US*)
Saving Grace Music (*UK*)
Skate Mountain Records (*US*)
Slapped Up Soul Records (*UK*)
So Ridiculous Music Group (*US*)
Wah Wah 45s (*UK*)
Wild Records (*US*)
Soulful
Skate Mountain Records (*US*)
So Ridiculous Music Group (*US*)
Soundtracks
Aphagia Recordings (*US*)
Barbarian Productions (*US*)
Biscornus Records (*Can*)
Cold Spring (*UK*)
Cowboy Rockstar Records (*US*)
First Night Records (*UK*)
Milan Records (*US*)
Skate Mountain Records (*US*)
So Ridiculous Music Group (*US*)
ThrillerTracks (*US*)
Watertower Music (*US*)
Spoken Word
BackWords Recordings (*US*)
So Ridiculous Music Group (*US*)
Surf
Dead by Mono Records (*UK*)
Wild Records (*US*)
Synthpop
Van Richter (*US*)
Techno
Astralwerks Records (*US*)
Axtone (*UK*)
Brain Bomb Productions (BBP) (*UK*)
CCT Records (*UK*)
Circus Recordings (*UK*)
Cr2 Records (*UK*)
Do As You Please (*UK*)
Futurist Recordings (*UK*)
Gruuv (*UK*)
Kudos Records Limited (*UK*)

Needwant (*UK*)
Neighbourhood (*UK*)
NoFace Records (*US*)
R&S Records (*US*)
Release / Sustain (*UK*)
Saved Records (*UK*)
So Ridiculous Music Group (*US*)
Subliminal Records (*US*)
Thrash
Cowboy Rockstar Records (*US*)
Speedowax (*UK*)
Traditional
BackWords Recordings (*US*)
Bomp Records (*US*)
Century Media Records (US) (*US*)
Fellside Recordings (*UK*)
Greentrax Recordings (*UK*)
Linn Records (*UK*)
Lismor Recordings (*UK*)
Mountain Apple Company (*US*)
Sonic Safari Music (*US*)
Trance
Amathus Music (*US*)
Axtone (*UK*)
Brain Bomb Productions (BBP) (*UK*)
Enhanced Music (*UK*)
New State Music (*UK*)
NoFace Records (*US*)
So Ridiculous Music Group (*US*)
Tribal
Brain Bomb Productions (BBP) (*UK*)
Trip Hop
Biscornus Records (*Can*)
So Ridiculous Music Group (*US*)
Underground
Amathus Music (*US*)
The Birdman Recording Group, Inc. (*US*)
Bomber Music Ltd (*UK*)
Craniality Sounds (*US*)
Futurist Recordings (*UK*)
Heavenly Recordings (*UK*)
Release / Sustain (*UK*)
Shabby Doll Records (*UK*)
Suburban Noize Records (*US*)
Urban
0207 Def Jam Recordings (*UK*)
Affluent Records (*US*)
Black Butter Records (*UK*)
Capitol Music Group (*US*)
Cash Money Records (*US*)
Def Jam Recordings (*US*)
Island Records (US) (*US*)
JW Music Limited (*UK*)
101BPM (*UK*)
Shady Records (*US*)

Slip-N-Slide Records (*US*)
So Ridiculous Music Group (*US*)
Soul II Soul (*UK*)
Surfdog Records (*US*)
Thump Records (*US*)
Visionary Music Group (*US*)
World
Acoustic Disc (*US*)
Beggars Group (US) (*US*)
Bolero Records (*US*)
Cantaloupe Music (*US*)
Canyon (*US*)
Celestial Harmonies (*US*)
Chesky Records (*US*)
Compass Records (*US*)
Concord Music Group (*US*)

JohnJohn Records (*UK*)
Lab Records (*UK*)
Luaka Bop (*US*)
Milan Records (*US*)
NorthernBlues Music Inc. (*Can*)
Primarily A Cappella (*US*)
Shanachie Entertainment (*US*)
Silver Wave Records (*US*)
Six Degrees Records (*US*)
Sonic Safari Music (*US*)
Stackhouse & BluEsoterica (*US*)
Sunnyside Records (*US*)
Tumi Music Ltd (*UK*)
Ultra Music (*US*)
Valley Entertainment (*US*)

US Managers

For the most up-to-date listings of these and hundreds of other managers, visit https://www.musicsocket.com/managers

To claim your free access to the site, please see the back of this book.

21st Century Artists, Inc.
32 W 22nd St, Fl 3
New York, NY 10010
Email: info@21stca.com
Website: https://www.21stca.com

Represents: Artists/Bands

Genres: Folk; Rock; Roots

New York based management company representing artists dealing in folk music, rock, and roots.

25 Artist Agency
25 Music Square West
Nashville, TN 37203
Fax: +1 (615) 687-6699
Email: david@25ent.com
Email: dara@25ent.com
Website: https://www.25ccm.com/
Website: https://www.instagram.com/25artistagency/

Represents: Artists/Bands

Genres: Christian

Contact: David Breen; Dara Easterday; Todd Thomas

Christian record label, based in Nashville, Tennessee.

ACA Music & Entertainment
705 Larry Court
Waukesha, WI 53186
Fax: +1 (262) 790-9149
Email: info@acaentertainment.com
Website: http://acaentertainment.com
Website: https://www.facebook.com/AcaMusicEntertainment/

Represents: Artists/Bands; DJs; Tribute Acts

Genres: All types of music

Describes itself as the oldest and largest provider of live entertainment in the Midwest.

Act 1 Entertainment
28 Price Street
Patchogue, NY 11772
Email: info@act1entertainment.net
Email: karl@act1entertainment.net
Website: http://act1entertainment.net
Website: https://www.facebook.com/Act1Inc/

Represents: Artists/Bands; Comedians; DJs; Tribute Acts

Genres: Jazz; R&B; Soul; Blues; Swing; Roots; Rockabilly; Country; Reggae; Classic Rock

Contact: Karl BD Reamer

Management company based in Patchogue, New York.

Advanced Alternative Media (AAM)

New York / Los Angeles
Email: info@aaminc.com
Website: http://www.aaminc.com
Website: https://www.facebook.com/ AdvancedAlternativeMedia

Represents: Artists/Bands; Producers; Songwriters; Sound Engineers

Genres: Alternative; Pop; Rock; Indie

Management company with offices in New York, London, and Los Angeles.

Aesthetic V

Website: https://www.vickyhamilton.com
Website: https://www.facebook.com/ aestheticv

Represents: Artists/Bands

Genres: All types of music

Contact: Vicky Hamilton

Management by long time Grammy Award-Winning music industry executive and personal manager, responsible for developing or managing such acts as Guns 'N' Roses, Mötley Crüe, Poison, Faster Pussycat and many others. Also offers consultancy service.

Allure Media Entertainment Group

Website: http://indiemusicpublicity.com
Website: https://www.facebook.com/ alluremediaent

Represents: Artists/Bands

Genres: Hip-Hop; Pop; Rock; R&B; Alternative Rock

Contact: Ken Cavalier

Provides publicity and marketing solutions for indie artists and labels. Send links to music online via online submission form.

American Artists Entertainment Group

29 Royal Palm Pointe Suite 5
Vero Beach, Florida 32960
Email: online@aaeg.com
Website: https://aaeg.com
Website: https://aaeg.com/submission/form. php
Website: https://www.facebook.com/ aaegcom/

Represents: Artists/Bands

Genres: Country; Pop; R&B; Rock

Management company with offices in Vero Beach, Florida, New York, and Hollywood. Has a 45-year history in the performing arts, and today serves over 16 countries and over 100 cities worldwide. Approach via online submission form.

American International Artists, Inc.

356 Pine Valley Road
Hoosick Falls, NY 12090
Fax: +1 (518) 686-1960
Email: cynthia@aiartists.com
Website: https://aiartists.com
Website: https://www.instagram.com/ aiartists/

Represents: Artists/Bands; Film / TV Composers

Genres: Classical; Jazz

Contact: Cynthia Herbst

Management company based in Hoosick Falls, NY. Devoted to the building and development of international careers of its world-class composers and jazz and classical performers, and to the development and co-ordination of special projects.

AMW Group Inc.

Website: https://www.amworldgroup.com
Website: https://facebook.com/amwgrp

Represents: Artists/Bands

Genres: All types of music

We have worked with promoting music for over 24 years. We work with different clients including major and independent labels, artists and producers. If you're looking for modern and effective ways to promote your music you have come to the right place.

APA (Agency for the Performing Arts)
10585 Santa Monica Blvd.
Los Angeles, CA 90025
Website: https://www.apa-agency.com

Represents: Artists/Bands

Genres: All types of music

Management company with offices in Los Angeles, Nashville, New York, Atlanta, Toronto, and London.

Arslanian & Associates, Inc.
5419 Hollywood Boulevard, Suite C717
Hollywood, CA 90027
Email: oscar@discoverhollywood.com
Email: nyla@discoverhollywood.com
Website: http://www.arslanianassociates.com

Represents: Artists/Bands

Genres: Classic Rock

Contact: Oscar Arslanian; Nyla Arslanian

Management company based in Hollywood, California.

Artist Representation and Management (ARM) Entertainment
Email: info@armentertainment.com
Website: https://armentertainment.com

Represents: Artists/Bands

Genres: Blues; Country; Classic Rock; Metal

Entertainment business with a focus on 70s, 80s, and 90s rock.

Backer Entertainment
Email: info@backerentertainment.com
Website: https://backerentertainment.com

Represents: Artists/Bands; Tribute Acts

Genres: All types of music

Manages mainly tribute acts for events.

Backstage Entertainment
Nashville, TN 37220
Email: staff@backstageentertainment.net
Website: https://backstageentertainment.net
Website: https://www.facebook.com/BackstageEntertainment

Represents: Artists/Bands

Genres: All types of music

Contact: Paul Loggins

Artist management/marketing firm which specialises in working with independent artists, and aims to bridge the gap between radio, print and social media.

BBA Management & Booking
Email: info@bbabooking.com
Website: https://www.bbabooking.com
Website: https://www.facebook.com/bbabooking

Represents: Artists/Bands

Genres: Jazz; Classical; Rock; Latin

Contact: Michael Mordecai; Laura Mordecai

Management and booking for jazz, classical, and versatile party bands in Central Texas.

Big Beat Productions, Inc.
1515 University Drive, Suite 106
Coral Springs, FL 33071
Fax: +1 (954) 755-8733
Email: talent@bigbeatproductions.com
Website: http://www.bigbeatproductions.com
Website: https://www.facebook.com/bigbeatproductions/

Represents: Artists/Bands; Comedians; DJs

Genres: Contemporary; Classic Rock; R&B; Disco; Regional; Jazz; Country

Contact: Richard Lloyd; Gary Ladka; Elissa Solomon

Management company based in Coral Springs, Florida.

Big Hassle Management
New York and Los Angeles
Email: weinstein@bighassle.com
Email: jim@bighassle.com
Website: https://www.bighassle.com
Website: https://www.facebook.com/
bighasslemedia/

Represents: Artists/Bands

Genres: Indie; Pop; Rock; Alternative

Contact: Ken Weinstein

Management company with offices in New
York and Los Angeles.

Big Noise
11 South Angell Street, Suite 336
Providence, RI 02906
Email: al.bignoise@gmail.com
Website: http://www.bignoisenow.com

Represents: Artists/Bands

Genres: All types of music

Contact: Al Gomes; Connie Watrous

Award-winning Music Firm specialising in
artist development, project management,
career strategies, and promotion and
publicity. Based in Providence, Rhode
Island. Looking for artists who are unique,
talented, professional, and ready to launch.
Considers all genres. Query by phone or
email in first instance. Must be at least 18.

Bill Silva Management
Website: https://www.
billsilvaentertainment.com

Represents: Artists/Bands; Songwriters

Genres: All types of music

Contact: Bill Silva

Management company, including music
management, model management, and music
publishing.

Bitchin' Entertainment
1750 Collard Valley Road
Cedartown, GA 30125
Email: Ty@BitchinEntertainment.com

Email: Rodney@BitchinEntertainment.com
Website: http://www.
bitchinentertainment.com

Represents: Artists/Bands; Tribute Acts

Genres: Rock; Pop; R&B; Funk; Urban;
Hip-Hop; Rap; Instrumental; Jazz; Classical;
Ambient; World; Experimental; House;
Trance; Electronic; Techno; Alternative;
Metal; Punk; Gothic; Country; Americana;
Blues; Folk; Singer-Songwriter; Spoken
Word

Management company based in Cedartown,
Georgia. Send query by email with link to
your music online. See website for full
submission guidelines, and details of who to
approach regarding specific genres. For
unsolicited demos, a submission code must
be obtained before submitting.

Blind Ambition Management, Ltd
Atlanta, GA 30307
Email: info@blindambitionmgt.com
Website: http://www.blindambitionmgt.com
Website: https://www.facebook.com/
BlindAmbitionManagement

Represents: Artists/Bands; Film / TV
Composers; Songwriters

Genres: Blues; Gospel; Roots; Folk; Singer-
Songwriter

Management company based in Atlanta,
Georgia, providing career management,
business management, creative guidance,
publicity, legal, and marketing services for
recording artists and music-related
businesses.

Booking Entertainment
Two Park Avenue 20th Floor
New York, NY 10016
Email: agents@bookingentertainment.com
Website: https://www.
bookingentertainment.com
Website: https://www.facebook.com/profile.
php?id=100057634982148

Represents: Artists/Bands

Genres: Pop; Rock; Jazz; R&B;
Contemporary

Books big name entertainment for private parties, public concerts, corporate events, and fundraisers.

Brick Wall Management
39 West 32nd Street, Suite 1403
New York, NY 10001
Website: https://www.brickwallmgmt.com

Represents: Artists/Bands; Producers

Genres: Country; Pop; Rock; Singer-Songwriter

Contact: Michael Solomon; Rishon Blumberg

Management company based in New York.

Brilliant Corners Artist Management
2069 Mission Street, Suite A
San Francisco, CA 94110

SEATTLE OFFICE:
1434-C Elliott Ave W
Seattle, WA 98119
Email: info@brilliantcorners.com
Website: https://brilliantcorners.com
Website: https://www.facebook.com/brilliantcornersmgmt

Represents: Artists/Bands

Genres: Indie; Rock; Singer-Songwriter

Management company with offices in San Francisco and Seattle. Not actively seeking unsolicited demos and strongly discourages sending physical copies. If approaching by email send only to the email address above; do not attach anything; and do not follow up.

Brilliant Productions
Email: npegel@att.net
Website: https://brilliant-productions.com
Website: https://www.youtube.com/user/itsbrilliant

Represents: Artists/Bands

Genres: Blues; Regional; Roots; Americana

Contact: Nancy Lewis-Pegel

Music booking and management for roots / blues / Southern / jam / Americana music.

Bsquared MGMT
Email: bsquaredmgmt@gmail.com
Website: https://www.bsquaredmgmt.com
Website: http://facebook.com/bsquaredmgmt1

Represents: Artists/Bands

Genres: All types of music

Artist Branding, Artist Development, Booking, Playlisting, Social Media MGMT and More...

Bulletproof Artist Management
241 Main Street
Easthampton, MA 01027
Email: patty@bulletproofartists.com
Website: https://bulletproofartists.com
Website: https://twitter.com/bproofmgmt

Represents: Artists/Bands; Producers

Genres: Country; Pop; Rock; Folk

Contact: Patty Romanoff

Management company based in Easthampton, Massachusetts.

Burgess World Co.
PO Box 646
Mayo, MD 21106-0646
Email: info@burgessworldco.com
Website: http://www.burgessworldco.com

Represents: Artists/Bands; Producers; Sound Engineers

Genres: Alternative; Blues; Jazz; Rock; Singer-Songwriter

Management company based in Mayo, Maryland. Originally founded to manage producers and engineers, but in the nineties expanded into artist management.

C Management
Email: info@studioexpresso.com
Website: http://www.studioexpresso.com/CHome.htm

Represents: Artists/Bands; Film / TV Composers; Producers; Songwriters; Sound Engineers; Studio Technicians; Supervisors

Genres: All types of music

Management company representing producers, mixers, engineers, songwriters, arrangers, magicians, and musicians.

Cantaloupe Music Productions, Inc.
157 West 79 Street
New York, NY 10024-6415
Email: ellenazorin@gmail.com
Website: https://www.cantaloupeproductions.com
Website: https://www.facebook.com/CantaloupeMusicProductions

Represents: Artists/Bands

Genres: Regional; Latin; World; Jazz; Blues; Swing

Contact: Ellen Azorin, President

Handles Brazilian music, Argentine tango, and other Latin-American music.

Celebrity Enterprises (CE) Inc.
137 Saddle Spur Trail
Tijeras, NM 87059
Email: info@worldstageevents.com
Email: sales@ent123.com
Website: https://www.ent123.com

Represents: Artists/Bands

Genres: All types of music

Provides acts for corporate events and fundraisers, performing arts centres and casinos, and other special events.

Celebrity Talent Agency Inc.
111 East 14th Street Suite 249
New York, NY 10003
Fax: +1 (201) 837-9011
Email: markg@celebritytalentagency.com
Email: alinak@celebritytalentagency.com
Website: https://www.celebritytalentagency.com
Website: https://www.facebook.com/CelebrityTalentAgency/

Represents: Artists/Bands; Comedians; DJs

Genres: Dance; Hip-Hop; R&B; Latin; Reggae; Jazz; Gospel

Contact: Mark Green; Alina Kim

Talent agency with offices in New York and London.

Century Artists Management Agency, LLC
711 West End Avenue, Suite 3CS
New York, New York 10025
Email: centuryartists@gmail.com
Website: https://www.camatalent.com
Website: https://twitter.com/centuryartists

Represents: Artists/Bands; Producers; Songwriters

Genres: All types of music

Contact: Paul E. Horton, President

Offers strategic brand management for artists in music, television, film, and the performing arts. Seeking established and new talent.

Chaney Gig Affairs (CGA)
California
Email: ChaneyGigAffairs@gmail.com
Website: https://www.chaneygigaffairs.com
Website: https://www.facebook.com/ChaneyGigAffairs/

Represents: Artists/Bands

Genres: Jazz; R&B; Soul

Provides Music and Artist Management Services; Web Design, EPKs and Video/Media Content Creation; and Event Management.

Chapman & Co. Management
Fax: +1 (818) 788-9525
Email: info@chapmanmanagement.com
Email: steve@chapmanmanagement.com
Website: https://www.chapmanmanagement.com

Represents: Artists/Bands

Genres: Contemporary Jazz

Contact: Steve Chapman

Management company concentrating on smooth, contemporary jazz.

Ciulla Management, Inc.
Email: mail@ciullamgmt.com
Website: https://ciullamgmt.com

Represents: Artists/Bands

Genres: Rock; Metal

Management company handling rock/metal artists.

Collin Artists
1099 N. Mar Vista Ave
Pasadena, CA 91104
Email: collinartists@gmail.com
Website: http://www.collinartists.com

Represents: Artists/Bands

Genres: Instrumental Jazz; Latin; World; Blues; R&B; Swing; Contemporary Jazz

Contact: Barbara Collin

Management company based in Pasadena, California.

Columbia Artists Music LLC (CAMI Music)
1180 Avenue of the Americas, 8th Floor
New York, NY 10036
Fax: +1 (212) 841-9581
Email: info@camimusic.com
Website: https://www.camimusic.com

Represents: Artists/Bands; Film / TV Composers; Lyricists; Variety Artists

Genres: Classical; Instrumental; Jazz; World

Represents classical, jazz, and popular musicians; orchestras, ensembles, etc.

Concerted Efforts
PO Box 440326
Somerville MA, 02144
Fax: +1 (617) 209-1300
Email: concerted@concertedefforts.com
Website: https://concertedefforts.com

Represents: Artists/Bands

Genres: Blues; Folk; Jazz; Gospel; Soul; Singer-Songwriter; Rock; World

Music booking agency based in Somerville, Massachusetts.

Creative Artists Agency (CAA)
2000 Avenue of the Stars
Los Angeles, CA 90067
Fax: +1 (424) 288-2900
Website: https://www.caa.com
Website: https://www.instagram.com/creativeartistsagency/

Represents: Artists/Bands

Genres: All types of music

Talent agency with offices across the US, as well as in the UK, China, and Europe.

Crush Music Media Management
Email: info@crushmusic.com
Website: https://www.crushmusic.com

Represents: Artists/Bands; Producers; Songwriters

Genres: All types of music

Full service music company based in New York and Los Angeles

Culler Talent Management
Los Angeles
Website: https://www.linkedin.com/in/chandler-culler-913972a8

Represents: Artists/Bands

Genres: All types of music

Contact: Chandler Culler

Provides talent management and event booking for all types of entertainers from all over.

D. Bailey Management, Inc.
17815 Gunn Hwy Suite 5
Odessa, FL 33556
Fax: +1 (813) 960-4662
Email: dennis@dbaileyemanagement.com

Website:
https://www.dbaileymanagement.com
Website: https://www.facebook.com/
dbaileymanagement

Represents: Artists/Bands

Genres: Pop; R&B; Rock

Contact: Dennis Bailey

Live entertainment, event management, and artist management, based in Odessa, Florida.

DAS Communications Ltd
83 Riverside Drive
New York, NY 10024
Website: https://www.bloomberg.com/
profile/company/0835448D:US

Represents: Artists/Bands; Producers; Songwriters

Genres: Hip-Hop; Pop; Rock

Management company based in New York.

Dave Kaplan Management
1126 South Coast Highway 101
Encinitas, CA 92024
Fax: +1 (760) 944-7808
Email: demo@surfdog.com
Website: https://surfdog.com
Website: https://www.facebook.com/
surfdogrecords/

Represents: Artists/Bands

Genres: Rock

Contact: Dave Kaplan; Scott Seine

Management company based in Encinitas, California. Also runs associated record label. Accepts submissions by post, marked for the attention of A&R, but prefers links by email (no MP3 attachments).

David Belenzon Management, Inc.
PO Box 5000 PMB 67,
Rancho Santa Fe, CA 92067

Fax: +1 (858) 832-8381
Email: David@Belenzon.com
Website: https://www.belenzon.com

Represents: Artists/Bands; Variety Artists

Genres: Contemporary; Pop; Rock; R&B

Contact: David Belenzon

Management company based in Rancho Santa Fe, California, representing artists, variety artists, plus theatrical and production shows.

Dawn Elder Management
Email: deworldmusic@aol.com
Website: https://dawnelderworldentertainment.com
Website: https://www.facebook.com/
DawnElderWorldEntertainment/

Represents: Artists/Bands

Genres: Classical; Jazz; Pop; Rock; Roots; Traditional; World

Have managed, represented and organised international tours for some of the most highly regarded international artists today.

DCA Productions
302A 12th Street, # 330
New York, NY 10014
Email: info@dcaproductions.com
Website: https://dcaproductions.com
Website: https://www.facebook.com/
dcaproductionsplus/

Represents: Artists/Bands; Comedians; Variety Artists

Genres: Pop; Rock; Folk

Contact: Daniel C. Abrahmsen, President; Gerri Abrahamsen, Vice President

Management company founded in 1983, specialising in variety performers, comedians, musical performers, theatre productions, and producing live events.

DDB Productions
Email: ddbprods@gmail.com
Website: https://www.ddbprods.com/
Website: http://www.deedeebridgewater.com

Represents: Artists/Bands; Lyricists; Producers; Songwriters; Studio Vocalists

Genres: Jazz; World; Alternative

Contact: Dee Dee Bridgewater

A boutique record label, music production company and talent management firm, based in Los Angeles, CA and New Orleans, LA. Founded by triple Grammy and Tony award winning Jazz artist.

Deep South Artist Management
RALEIGH
PO Box 17737
Raleigh, NC 27619

NASHVILLE
PO Box 121975
Nashville, TN 37212
Email: hello@deepsouthentertainment.com
Website: https://www.deepsouthentertainment.com
Website: https://www.facebook.com/deepsouthent

Represents: Artists/Bands

Genres: Alternative; Country; Pop; Rock; Americana; Christian

Record label, artist management firm, talent agency, and concert production company based in Raleigh, North Carolina, with offices in both Raleigh and Nashville, Tennessee.

Def Ro Inc.
33 Prospect Street, Suite 1r
Bloomfield, NJ 07003
Email: defroinc@msn.com
Website: http://sirro.tripod.com/index.html
Website: http://defroinc.blogspot.co.uk

Represents: Artists/Bands

Genres: Hip-Hop; Pop; R&B

Contact: Will Strickland

Management company based in Bloomfield, New Jersey. Send up to three tracks by mail only.

Direct Management Group (DMG)
8332 Melrose Ave, Top Floor
Los Angeles, CA 90069
Website: https://directmanagement.com

Represents: Artists/Bands

Genres: Pop

Contact: Martin Kirkup; Bradford Cobb; Steven Jensen

Management company based in West Hollywood, California. Founded in April 1985. Describes itself as an internationally oriented entertainment company with broad-based success in the representation of musical artists.

Dog & Pony Industries
Email: info@dogandponyindustries.com
Website: http://www.dogandponyindustries.com

Represents: Artists/Bands

Genres: All types of music

Specializing in talent management and the coordinating of concert tours and special projects in the Music, TV & Film industries. Contact by email.

Domo Music Group Management
11022 Santa Monica Blvd. #300
Los Angeles, CA 90025
Email: dino@domomusicgroup.com
Website: https://www.domomusicgroup.com
Website: https://www.facebook.com/officialdomomusicgroup

Represents: Artists/Bands; DJs; Film / TV Composers; Producers; Songwriters; Studio Musicians

Genres: Contemporary; Classical; Folk; Indie; New Age; Pop; Rock; Singer-Songwriter; World; Ethnic

Management company based in Los Angeles, California, handling Japanese artists. Prefers links to music online by email or via submission form on website, or send CD by post marked for the attention of A&R.

East Coast Entertainment (ECE)

Email: info@bookece.com
Website: https://www.bookece.com
Website: https://www.facebook.com/EastCoastEntertainment/

Represents: Artists/Bands; Comedians; DJs

Genres: All types of music

Describes itself as the largest full-service entertainment agency in the country.

Elevation Group Inc.

Email: kent@elevationgroup.net
Website: https://www.elevationgroup.net

Represents: Artists/Bands

Genres: All types of music

Contact: Kent Sorrell

Management company based in California.

Emcee Artist Management

Website: https://www.emceeartist.com

Represents: Artists/Bands

Genres: Jazz; Blues; Rock

Contact: Liz Penta

Management company representing jazz, blues, and rock artists. No hip-hop.

Enlight Entertainment, Inc.

Website: http://www.enlight-ent.com
Website: https://www.facebook.com/tashia.l.stafford

Represents: Artists/Bands; Producers; Songwriters

Genres: R&B; Gospel; Rap

Contact: Tashia Stafford

Offers the following services:

- Producer and Personal Management
- Independent Publishing Company Consulting
- Administrative Assistant Services
- A & R Consulting and Administration
- Personal Assistants
- Song Writing Clinics

Entertainment Services International

1819 South Harlan Circle
Lakewood, CO 80232
Fax: +1 (303) 936-0069
Email: randy@esientertainment.com
Website: http://www.esientertainment.com

Represents: Artists/Bands

Genres: Rock; Classic Rock

Contact: Randy Erwin

Manager based in Lakewood, Colorado.

Entourage Talent Associates, Ltd

Email: info@entouragetalent.com
Website: https://www.entouragetalent.com
Website: https://www.facebook.com/EntourageTalentAssociates

Represents: Artists/Bands

Genres: Pop; Rock; Singer-Songwriter; Jazz

Not currently seeking new acts for representation. However, you can submit your music and information for consideration for support/packaging with one of the existing clients for an upcoming tour. Send submissions by email, or via form on website.

Fat City Artists

1906 Chet Atkins Place, Suite 502 Nashville, TN 37212
Fax: +1 (615) 321-5382
Website: http://fatcityartists.com

Represents: Artists/Bands

Genres: Acoustic; Blues; R&B; Celtic; Country; Folk; Funk; Gospel; Jazz; Pop; Reggae; Rockabilly; Rock and Roll; Ska; Swing; World

Artists management based in Nashville, Tennessee. Not signing new artists as at November 2022.

Fire Tower Entertainment
Los Angeles, CA
Email: artists@firetowerent.com
Email: info@firetowerent.com
Website: https://firetowerent.com
Website: https://www.facebook.com/firetowerent

Represents: Artists/Bands

Genres: Indie; Pop; Singer-Songwriter

Entertainment startup located in Los Angeles focused on artist management and A&R services.

First Access Entertainment
Website: https://www.facebook.com/firstaccessent

Represents: Artists/Bands

Genres: Pop; Rap; R&B; Hip-Hop

Management Company, Record Label, Music Publisher.

First Artists Management
4764 Park Granada, Suite 110
Calabasas, CA 91302
Fax: +1 (818) 377-7760
Email: info@firstartistsmgmt.com
Website: https://www.firstartistsmanagement.com

Represents: Film / TV Composers; Supervisors

Genres: Soundtracks

Management company based in Calabasas, California, specialising in the representation of composers, music supervisors, and music editors for film and television.

5B Artist Management
Email: info@5bam.com
Website: https://5bam.com
Website: https://twitter.com/5Bartistsmedia

Represents: Artists/Bands

Genres: Alternative; Metal; Rock

Management and events company with offices in New York, Los Angeles, and the UK.

Fleming Artists
2232 S. Main St, Ste 372
Ann Arbor, MI 48103
Email: jim@flemingartists.com
Email: cynthia@flemingartists.com
Website: https://www.flemingartists.com
Website: https://www.facebook.com/flemingartists/

Represents: Artists/Bands

Genres: Contemporary Roots Rock; Blues; Folk; Pop; Rock

Management company with a mission to "represent a high quality, diverse roster of performing artists by providing them with a unique, thoughtful and individualized approach to concert booking."

Fresh Flava Entertainment
2705 12th Street NE
Washington, DC 20018
Email: freshflava17@gmail.com
Website: http://www.freshflava.com

Represents: Artists/Bands

Genres: Hip-Hop; Jazz; Gospel; R&B; Rock

Management company based in Washington DC.

Funzalo Music / Mike's Artist Management
PO Box 2518
Agoura Hills, CA 91376
Email: mike@mikesmanagement.com
Website: https://funzalorecords.com
Website: https://www.facebook.com/funzalorecords

Represents: Artists/Bands; Producers

Genres: All types of music

Contact: Mike Lembo

Record label and management company based in Agoura Hills, California.

Gary Stamler Management

PO Box 34575
Los Angeles, CA 90034
Email: garystamler@me.com
Email: nancysefton@gsmgmt.net
Website: https://www.gsmgmt.net

Represents: Artists/Bands; Producers

Genres: All types of music

Contact: Gary Stamler; Nancy Sefton

Management company based in Los
Angeles.

Gayle Enterprises, Inc.

51 Music Square East
Nashville, TN 37203
Email: info@crystalgayle.com
Website: https://crystalgayle.com
Website: https://www.facebook.com/
236343614779

Represents: Artists/Bands

Genres: All types of music

Contact: Bill Gatzimos

Management company based in Nashville,
Tennessee, dedicated to representing one
artist only. No submissions or queries.

Gold Mountain Entertainment

LOS ANGELES

12400 Ventura Blvd., Suite 444
Studio City, CA 91604

NASHVILLE

11 Music Square East, Suite 103
Nashville, TN 37203
Fax: +1 (615) 255-9001
Email: info@gmemusic.com
Website: http://www.gmemusic.com

Represents: Artists/Bands

Genres: Contemporary; Blues; Folk; Indie;
Pop; Punk; Reggae; Rock; Singer-
Songwriter; World

Management company with offices in Los
Angeles, Nasville, and Montreal.

Good Guy Entertainment

Email: aa@goodguyent.com
Website: https://www.facebook.com/
GoodGuyEntertainment

Represents: Artists/Bands

Genres: Pop; Urban

Management company specialising in artist
and project development, mass media
marketing and promotion, independent
record promotion, and television production.

The Gorfaine/Schwartz Agency, Inc.

4111 West Alameda Avenue, Suite 509
Burbank, CA 91505
Website: https://www.gsamusic.com
Website: https://www.facebook.com/
gorfaineschwartz

Represents: Artists/Bands; Producers

Genres: All types of music

Represents the film industry's top
composers, music producers, songwriters,
music supervisors and music editors.

Grassy Hill Entertainment

303 West 42nd Street, Suite 614
New York, NY 10036
Fax: +1 (212) 977-1069
Email: managers@grassyhill.net
Email: margo.parks@
grassyhillentertainment.com
Website: http://www.
grassyhillentertainment.com

Represents: Artists/Bands

Genres: Roots; Americana; Folk; Singer-
Songwriter

Contact: Margo Parks; Julia Reinhart

A full service management company based
in New York, describing itself as a "talent
incubator" for independent artists in the roots
/ americana genres.

Hard Head Management

PO Box 651
New York, NY 10014

Email: info@hardhead.com
Website: https://www.hardhead.com

Represents: Artists/Bands

Genres: Americana; Electronic; Rock

Contact: Stefani Scamardo

Management company based in New York.

Hardin Entertainment
Email: info@hardinentertainment.com
Website: http://www.hardinentertainment.com
Website: https://www.facebook.com/hardinbourke/

Represents: Artists/Bands; Film / TV Composers; Lyricists; Producers; Songwriters; Studio Vocalists; Supervisors

Genres: Contemporary; Alternative; Americana; Blues; Christian; Country; Dance; Electronic; Folk; Hardcore; Indie; Latin; Pop; Rock; Roots; Singer-Songwriter; World

Management company with offices in Los Angeles and New York.

HardKnockLife Entertainment
Website: https://hardknocklifeent.com
Website: https://www.instagram.com/hardknocklifeent/

Represents: Artists/Bands

Genres: Acoustic; Hip-Hop; Pop; R&B; Rap

Contact via form on website, including links to your music online.

Harmony Artists
20501 Ventura Blvd Suite 289
Woodland Hills, CA 91364
Fax: +1 (323) 655-5154
Email: contact_us@harmonyartists.com
Website: https://www.harmonyartists.com
Website: https://www.facebook.com/HarmonyArtistsLA/

Represents: Artists/Bands; Tribute Acts

Genres: Blues; Latin; Jazz; Swing

Specialises in providing top national headline and regional entertainment for venues throughout the world.

Headline Talent Agency
New York, NY
Website: http://headlinetalent.net
Website: https://www.instagram.com/headlinetalentagency/

Represents: Artists/Bands

Genres: All types of music

Represents award-winning creatives in Film, Television, and Theater in New York City, Los Angeles, and around the globe. Does not accept cold submissions of any kind. All referrals must be sent directly from the industry professional giving the referral.

Hello! Booking, Inc.
Email: info@hellobooking.com
Website: https://www.hellobooking.com
Website: https://www.facebook.com/hellobookingusa

Represents: Artists/Bands; Tribute Acts

Genres: Country; Folk; Indie; Jazz; Hip-Hop; Acoustic; Rockabilly; Rock; Pop

Show booking company based in Minneapolis.

Hoffman Entertainment
21301 S. Tamiami Trl. STE 320-151
Estero, FL 33928
Email: info@ilovehoffman.com
Email: wayne@ilovehoffman.com
Website: https://ilovehoffman.com/
Website: https://www.facebook.com/ilovehoffman

Represents: Artists/Bands; Comedians; Variety Artists

Genres: All types of music

Contact: Wayne Hoffman

Provides a range of talent for events, including music, celebrities, comedy, variety, and speakers.

Hornblow Group USA, Inc.
Email: info@hornblowgroup.com
Website: https://www.hornblowgroup.com
Website: https://www.facebook.com/
hornblowmusic/

Represents: Artists/Bands; Film / TV
Composers; Lyricists; Producers;
Songwriters; Studio Musicians

Genres: Indie; Pop; Rock; Alternative;
Singer-Songwriter

Full-service artist management firm,
independent record label, purveyors of cool
t-shirts and bumper stickers.

Howard Rosen Promotion, Inc.
Email: info@howiewood.com
Email: Howie@howiewood.com
Website: https://howiewood.com/
Website: https://myspace.com/howardrosen

Represents: Artists/Bands

Genres: All types of music

Contact: Howard Rosen; Alex Louton

Full service radio promotion company based
in Ojai, California. Submit music using
online submissions system on website.

IMC Entertainment Group
19360 Rinaldi Street # 217
Porter Ranch, CA 91326
Website: http://www.imcentertainment.com

Represents: Artists/Bands

Genres: Pop; R&B

Entertainment company based in Porter
Ranch, California, providing entertainment
and production services worldwide.
Specialises in music performance,
production, publishing and supervision
services.

IMG Artists
Pleiades House
7 West 54th Street
New York, NY 10019
Fax: +1 (212) 994-3550

Email: artistsny@imgartists.com
Website: https://imgartists.com
Website: https://twitter.com/imgartistsny

Represents: Artists/Bands

Genres: Classic; Folk; Gospel; Jazz; World;
Latin; Singer-Songwriter

Describes itself as the global leader in the
arts management business, with offices in
New York, London, Paris, Hanover, and
Seoul.

Impact Artist Management
Kingston, NY 12401
Email: info@impactartist.com
Website: http://www.impactartist.com
Website: https://www.facebook.com/
impactartistmanagement

Represents: Artists/Bands; Film / TV
Composers; Songwriters; Supervisors

Genres: Contemporary; Blues; Folk; Indie;
Jazz; Latin; R&B; Rock; Roots; Singer-
Songwriter; World; Alternative; Alternative
Country

Management company based in Kingston,
New York.

In De Goot Entertainment
Fax: +1 (212) 924-3242
Website: https://www.indegoot.com
Website: https://www.facebook.com/
Indegoot/

Represents: Artists/Bands

Genres: Indie; Metal; Pop; Rock;
Underground

Management company based in New York,
with offices in London and Nashville.

In Touch Entertainment
309 W 55th St
New York, NY 10019
Email: info@intouchent.com
Website: https://intouchent.com
Website: https://www.facebook.com/
intouchentertainment

Represents: Artists/Bands

Genres: All types of music

A worldwide entertainment organisation that manages both established and up-and-coming recording artists, books talent into venues, oversees music recording, and promotes and produces concerts and films. Send electronic press kit by email, including bio, audio, video, tour history, and contact info. Response only if interested.

Ina Dittke & Associates

6538 Collins Avenue, Suite 295,
Miami Beach, FL 33141
Email: ina@inadittke.com
Email: gina@inadittke.com
Website: https://inadittke.com
Website: https://www.facebook.com/inadittkeassociates/

Represents: Artists/Bands

Genres: Jazz; Latin; World

Music agency based in Miami, Florida, representing a varied and international roster of artists.

Invasion Group, Ltd

Email: info@invasiongroup.com
Website: https://www.invasiongroup.com
Website: https://facebook.com/invasiongroupltd

Represents: Artists/Bands; Film / TV Composers; Lyricists; Producers; Songwriters; Sound Engineers; Studio Musicians; Studio Technicians; Studio Vocalists; Supervisors

Genres: All types of music

A boutique management company serving career artists, labels and special projects.

James Joseph Music Management LA

3229 Rambla Pacifico Street
Malibu, CA 90265
Email: jj3@jamesjoseph.co.uk
Website: http://www.jamesjoseph.co.uk

Represents: Artists/Bands

Genres: All types of music

Management company with offices in Los Angeles, California, and London, UK.

Jampol Artist Management

8033 W. Sunset Blvd., Suite 3250
West Hollywood, CA 90046
Email: assistant@jamincla.com
Website: https://wemanagelegends.com
Website: https://www.facebook.com/jjampol

Represents: Artists/Bands

Genres: All types of music

Manages great legacy artists. Dedicated to the re-introduction of timeless art through modern means, and helps iconic artist legacies make the transition to the digital age with integrity. Does not manage new artists. If you are a legacy artist looking to extend your reach, use new technologies, or place your legacy in a modern context, send query by email.

Jay Anthony's Next Level Booking and Entertainment Agency, LLC

Las Vegas, NV
Email: Jayanthony@nextlevelbookingandentertainment.com
Email: Nextlevelbookingagency@gmail.com
Website: https://www.nextlevelbookingandentertainment.com
Website: https://www.facebook.com/JayAnthonysnextlevel/

Represents: Artists/Bands; Tribute Acts

Genres: All types of music

Always looking for exceptional talent to add to their roster. Looking for: experienced artists that believe in perfecting their craft; acts with great EPK's (no demo sites); and tributes acts that sound and look like the original act.

Jeff Roberts & Associates

Hendersonville, TN 37075
Email: info@jeffroberts.com
Website: https://jeffroberts.com
Website: https://www.facebook.com/jrabooking

Represents: Artists/Bands

Genres: Christian

We are a Christian music booking agency celebrating over 34 years in ministry-driven artist representation. We are committed to Christian music artists who use their platform and talent to reach communities all over the world for Christ.

Kari Estrin Management & Consulting
PO Box 60232
Nashville, TN 37206
Email: kari@kariestrin.com
Website: https://www.kariestrin.com
Website: https://www.facebook.com/kariestrinmanagement/

Represents: Artists/Bands

Genres: Americana; Folk; Roots; Acoustic

Based in Nashville, Tennessee. Offers artist management and consulting.

KBH Entertainment
Los Angeles, CA
Email: support@kbhentertainment.com
Website: https://kbhentertainment.com
Website: https://www.facebook.com/KBHEntertainment

Represents: Artists/Bands; Film / TV Composers; Producers; Studio Musicians; Studio Vocalists

Genres: All types of music

Contact: Brent Harvey

Talent booking, event production, artist development, career strategy, entertainment consulting and marketing company based in Los Angeles, California.

Kraft-Engel Management
3349 Cahuenga Blvd. West
Los Angeles, CA 90068
Email: info@Kraft-Engel.com
Website: https://kraft-engel.com

Represents: Film / TV Composers; Songwriters; Supervisors

Genres: Soundtracks

Management company based in Los Angeles, California, specialising in representing film and theatre composers, songwriters and music supervisors.

Kuper Personal Management
515 Bomar Street
Houston, TX 77006
Email: info@kupergroup.com
Website: http://www.kupergroup.com

Represents: Artists/Bands

Genres: Alternative; Americana; Folk; Roots Rock

Management company based in Houston, Texas, offering personal management and artist development.

The Kurland Agency
173 Brighton Avenue
Boston, MA 02134-2003
Email: agents@thekurlandagency.com
Website: https://www.thekurlandagency.com

Represents: Artists/Bands

Genres: Jazz; Blues

Contact: Ted Kurland

Management company based in Boston, best known for representing jazz artists.

LA Personal Development
Email: Glebe99@yahoo.com
Website: https://www.lapersdev.com
Website: https://www.facebook.com/lapersonaldevelopment/

Represents: Artists/Bands

Genres: All types of music

Contact: Mike Gormley

A management/consulting company started in 1983.

Laffitte Management Group
Email: hello@lmg.me
Website: https://lmg.me

Website: https://www.instagram.com/laffittemgmt/

Represents: Artists/Bands; Producers; Songwriters

Genres: Pop; R&B; Rock

Management company representing over 45 artists, songwriters, and producers.

Lake Transfer Artist & Tour Management
Studio City, CA
Website: http://laketransfermgmt.com
Website: https://twitter.com/LTMusicMgmt

Represents: Artists/Bands

Genres: All types of music

Artist and tour management based in Studio City, California.

Larro Media
Email: steven@larromedia.com
Website: https://larromedia.com
Website: https://www.facebook.com/steven.rosen.969

Represents: Artists/Bands

Genres: All types of music

Contact: Steven Rosen

A full-service music, film and TV, and talent development company specializing in artist synch representation, music supervision and music clearance, talent/brand management, and TV and film production.

Len Weisman Personal Management
357 S. Fairfax Ave. #430
Los Angeles, CA 90036
Fax: +1 (323) 653-7670
Email: persmanmnt@aol.com
Website: https://persmanmnt.com

Represents: Artists/Bands

Genres: R&B; Gospel; Hip-Hop

Represents professional and experienced R&B Artists; Gospel Artists and HipHop

Artists to meet promotional, trade show, or corporate event needs.

Leonard Business Management
5777 W. Century Blvd, Suite 1600
Los Angeles, CA 90045
Fax: +1 (310) 458-8862
Email: info@lbmgt.com
Website: http://leonardbusinessmanagement.com
Website: https://www.facebook.com/pages/Leonard-Business-Management/665044716881370

Represents: Artists/Bands

Genres: All types of music

Provides business management services to the entertainment industry, including business management, tour accounting, royalty services, etc.

Lippman Entertainment
Fax: +1 (805) 686-5866
Email: music@lippmanent.com
Email: info@lippmanent.com
Website: http://www.lippmanent.com
Website: https://www.facebook.com/lippmanent
Website: http://www.myspace.com/lippmanentertainment

Represents: Artists/Bands; Film / TV Composers; Producers; Sound Engineers; Studio Technicians

Genres: Pop; R&B; Rap; Hip-Hop; Rock; Singer-Songwriter; Urban

Contact: Michael Lippman; Nick Lippman

Management company based in California. Not accepting submissions as at September 2024.

Madison House Inc.
1401 Walnut St, Suite 500
Boulder, CO 80302
Email: info@madison-house.com
Website: https://madisonhouseinc.com
Website: https://www.facebook.com/MadisonHouseInc

Represents: Artists/Bands

Genres: All types of music

Management company based in Boulder, Colorado.

Magus Entertainment Inc.
268 Water St
New York, NY 10038
Email: info@magusentertainment.com
Website: https://magusentertainment.com
Website: https://www.facebook.com/
MagusEntertainment/

Represents: Artists/Bands; Lyricists;
Producers; Songwriters; Sound Engineers;
Studio Musicians; Studio Technicians;
Studio Vocalists

Genres: Contemporary; Electronic; Indie;
Latin; Pop; Punk; R&B; Rap; Hip-Hop;
Rock; Urban; Singer-Songwriter

A New-York-based, full-service
management company, representing both
high profile recording artists and a number of
mixers and producers.

Maine Road Management
PO Box 1412
Woodstock, NY 12498
Email: mailbox@
maineroadmanagement.com
Website: https://maineroadmanagement.com
Website: https://www.facebook.com/
maineroadmanagement

Represents: Artists/Bands; Producers

Genres: Country; Folk; Indie; Jazz; Rock

Contact: David Whitehead

New York-based management company.

Major Bob Music, Inc.
Website: https://www.majorbob.com
Website: https://www.facebook.com/
majorbobmusic

Represents: Songwriters

Genres: Country; R&B; Soul; Pop

Contact: Bob Doyle

Management and publishing company based
in Nashville, Tennessee.

The Major Group
33117 Woodward Ave., Suite 331,
Birmingham, MI 48009
Email: contact@themajorgroup.com
Email: bmajor@themajorgroup.com
Website: http://www.themajorgroup.com
Website: https://www.facebook.com/
tmgmajorproductions

Represents: Artists/Bands

Genres: Jazz; Rap; Techno; Rock; Pop;
R&B

Contact: Brian Major

Management company based in Michigan.
Accepts unsolicited material. Submit via
online form.

The Management Ark, Inc.
Edward C. Arrendell, II
3 Bethesda Metro Center, Suite 700
Bethesda, MD 20814

Vernon H. Hammond III, CFP
116 Villiage Boulevard, Suite 200
Princeton, NJ 08540
Email: ed@managementark.pro
Email: vernon@managementark.com
Website: http://www.managementark.com

Represents: Artists/Bands

Genres: Jazz

Contact: Edward C. Arrendell, II; Vernon H.
Hammond III, CFP

Jazz management company with offices in
Bethesda, Maryland, and Princeton, New
Jersey.

Mars Jazz Booking
1006 Ashby Place
Charlottesville, VA 22901-4006
Fax: +1 (434) 979-6179
Email: reggie@marsjazz.com
Website: https://marsjazz.com

Represents: Artists/Bands

Genres: Jazz

Contact: Reggie Marshall

Jazz booking agency. Not currently accepting new clients or press kits, but happy to receive CDs and contact details and may contact further down the line if interested.

Mascioli Entertainment
Email: Mascioli319@gmail.com
Website: https://masciolientertainment.com

Represents: Artists/Bands

Genres: Country; Jazz; R&B; Swing; Rock

Contact: Paul Mascioli

Full-service entertainment company based in Orlando, Florida, offering artists management and booking for conventions, casinos, arenas, theaters, night clubs, fairs, festivals, and special events.

Mauldin Brand Agency
Email: info@mauldinbrand.com
Website: https://www.mauldinbrandinc.com

Represents: Artists/Bands; Producers; Songwriters

Genres: Hip-Hop; R&B; Rap; Pop

Contact: Michael Mauldin

Your Black American Entertainment Connection with more than 40 years experience in music leadership, management, branding, and marketing. Creates partnerships and enhances branded assets within the consumer marketplace with special focus on teens, young adults, legacy, and the future.

Max Bernard Management
Email: myron@maxbernard.com
Website: https://maxbernard.com
Website: https://www.facebook.com/maxbernardmanagement/

Represents: Artists/Bands; Producers; Songwriters; Studio Musicians; Studio Vocalists

Genres: Urban Indie Jazz R&B Soul Singer-Songwriter; Soundtracks Blues Mainstream Soulful

Contact: Myron Bernard

We, pride ourselves on this blueprint that we specialize in creating a backdrop of musical ambiance featuring the world's finest and unique talent while servicing your entertainment needs.

We actively commit to find quality entertainment and entertainer's that suit your local and international demographic areas and taste.

Offers personal consulting services in all areas of artist development, live entertainment and social media and online network marketing.

Media/PR services are outsourced additions provided to clients. Special event(s) implementation and tour management services are available upon request.

MBK Entertainment
519 8th Ave, 19th Floor
New York, NY 10018
Fax: +1 (212) 629-0035
Email: info@mbkentertainment.com
Website: https://www.mbkentertainment.com

Represents: Artists/Bands; Film / TV Composers; Lyricists; Producers; Songwriters; Studio Musicians; Studio Vocalists

Genres: Contemporary; Gospel; Pop; R&B; Rap; Hip-Hop; Reggae; Urban

Contact: Jeff Robinson

Management company based in New York.

McDonough Management LLC
Email: frank@mcdman.com
Website: http://www.mcdman.com
Website: https://www.facebook.com/mcdmanagement

Represents: Producers; Songwriters; Sound Engineers

Genres: Rock

Contact: Frank McDonough

Management company representing record producers, engineers and mixers.

McGhee Entertainment
Los Angeles, CA
Email: info@mcgheela.com
Website: https://www.mcgheela.com
Website: https://www.facebook.com/
McGheeEntertainment

Represents: Artists/Bands; Songwriters

Genres: Country; Metal; Rock; Singer-Songwriter; World

Management company with offices in Los Angeles and Nashville.

Media Five Entertainment
PO BOX 21300
Lehigh Valley, PA 18002
Email: submissions@medafiveent.com
Email: david.sestak@mediafiveent.com
Website: http://www.mediafiveent.com

Represents: Artists/Bands; Sound Engineers; Studio Musicians; Studio Technicians

Genres: Indie; Punk; Rock

Contact: David Sestak; Patty Condiotti

Approach by email or through contact form on website. Response only if interested.

Michael Anthony's Electric Events
Post Office Box 280848
Lakewood, CO 80228
Email: info2@electricevents.com
Website: http://www.electricevents.com

Represents: Artists/Bands; Tribute Acts; Variety Artists

Genres: Country; Pop; Dance; Classic Rock

Contact: Michael A Tolerico

Music entertainment booking agency based in Lakewood, Colorado.

Michael Hausman Artist Management Inc.
Email: info@michaelhausman.com
Website: https://michaelhausman.com

Represents: Artists/Bands

Genres: Contemporary; Pop; Rock; Singer-Songwriter

Management company based in New York.

Mike's Artist Management
PO Box 2518
Agoura Hills, CA 91376
Email: mike@mikesmanagement.com
Website: https://funzalorecords.com/mikes-artist-management/
Website: https://www.facebook.com/funzalorecords

Represents: Artists/Bands

Genres: Americana; Pop; Rock; Indie; Folk

Contact: Mike Lembo

Record label and artist management based in Agoura Hills, California.

MM Music Agency
10000 Washington Blvd
Culver City, CA 90232
Fax: +1 (305) 831-4472
Email: info@mmmusicagency.com
Website: https://www.mmmusicagency.com
Website: https://www.facebook.com/mmmusicagency

Represents: Artists/Bands

Genres: Jazz; Regional; Contemporary

Contact: Maurice Montoya

Music agency based in Florida, handling jazz, Afro-Caribbean, Brazilian and contemporary music.

MOB Agency
6404 Wilshire Blvd
Los Angeles, CA 90048
Fax: +1 (323) 653-0428
Email: Mitch@mobagency.com
Email: joy@mobagency.com
Website: http://www.mobagency.com

Website: https://www.yellowpages.com/los-angeles-ca/mip/mob-agency-471004016

Represents: Artists/Bands

Genres: Alternative; Rock

Agency based in Los Angeles.

Modern Management
Email: info@modmgmt.com
Website: https://www.modmgmt.com
Website: https://www.facebook.com/modernmgmt

Represents: Artists/Bands

Genres: Country

Country management company.

Moksha Entertainment and Music Management (US)
Los Angeles
Email: MyInfoAtMoksha@gmail.com
Email: MokshaMusicManagement@gmail.com
Website: https://www.mokshaentertainment.com/

Represents: Artists/Bands

Genres: Pop; Punk Rock; Psychedelic Punk; Rock

Entertainment, Film, Music Management, Tour Services, and Recording Company, with offices in LA and London. Strives to embolden and embody the human spirit through entertainment, music and film.

Monqui Presents
PO Box 5908
Portland, OR 97228
Email: web@monqui.com
Website: https://monqui.com
Website: https://www.facebook.com/monquipresents

Represents: Artists/Bands

Genres: Alternative; Indie; Rock; Country; Pop

"Importers of fine live music", serving the Northwest since 1983.

Morris Higham Management
2001 Blair Blvd
Nashville, TN 37212
Website: https://morrishigham.com
Website: https://www.facebook.com/morrishighammanagement/

Represents: Artists/Bands

Genres: Country

Management company based in Nashville. Does not accept unsolicited material.

MTS Management
Email: michael@mtsmanagementgroup.com
Website: https://www.mtsmanagementgroup.com

Represents: Artists/Bands

Genres: Commercial Christian Hard Glam Melodic Progressive Power Country Guitar based Metal Pop Rock

Contact: Michael Stover

Full Service Artist Management, Publicity and promotions firm. Reasonable packages with the Indie Artist in Mind. National and International chart success, appearances, press and touring.

Murphy to Manteo (MTM) Music Management
Email: MarkZenow@MTMfirm.com
Website: http://www.mtmfirm.com

Represents: Artists/Bands; Producers; Songwriters

Genres: All types of music

Management company with its roots in Columbia, South Carolina. Contact by phone or by email.

Music + Art Management
15 W. Walnut St. Suite 202
Asheville, NC 28801
Website: https://musicandart.net
Website: https://www.facebook.com/Music-and-Art-Management-163558147005567/

Represents: Artists/Bands

Genres: Electronic; World; Experimental; Rock; Jazz

Full service management and production company specialising in the careers of performing and recording artists. Based in Asheville, North Carolina.

Music City Artists
7104 Peach Ct.
Brentwood, TN 37027
Email: charles.ray@action-ent.com
Website: http://musiccityartists.com
Website: https://twitter.com/mcartists

Represents: Artists/Bands

Genres: All types of music

Contact: Charles Ray, President / Agent

Full service booking agency representing nationally known artists for performing arts centers, casinos, and corporate entertainment.

Music Gallery International
Email: musicgallerymanagement@gmail.com
Website: https://musicgalleryinternational.com

Represents: Artists/Bands; Studio Musicians

Genres: Alternative Hard Heavy Industrial Mainstream Power Americana Emo Garage Gothic Hardcore Metal Punk Rock

Contact: Jamie Moore

Offers management and consulting for a fixed fee (not a percentage). Approach via online form on website, providing links to your music, your social media profiles, and any press your band may have received.

Music Group Entertainment Worldwide, LLC
Email: musicgroupceo@gmail.com
Website: https://themusicgroupworld.com
Website: https://www.facebook.com/musicgroupworldwide

Represents: Artists/Bands

Genres: All types of music

Celebrity Booking Agency / Independent international Placement / Artist Development.

MusicBizMentors
Email: musicbizmentors@gmail.com
Website: https://musicbizmentors.com
Website: https://www.facebook.com/MusicBizMntrs

Represents: Artists/Bands

Genres: All types of music

Contact: Chris Fletcher

Offers music industry mentoring and coaching.

Myriad Artists
PO BOX 550
Carrboro, NC 27510
Email: trish@myriadartists.com
Email: booking@myriadartists.com
Website: https://www.myriadartists.com
Website: https://www.facebook.com/myriadartists/

Represents: Artists/Bands

Genres: Blues; Folk; Jazz; Americana

Contact: Trish Galfano

Management company based in Carrboro, North Carolina.

Nashville Records, LLC
Nashville, TN
Email: music@nashvillerecordsusa.com
Website: https://nashvillerecordsusa.com

Represents: Artists/Bands; Songwriters

Genres: Christian Acoustic Americana Country Pop Gospel; Americana

Contact: Lincoln Plowman

A full-service Artist Management and Record Label company. If you are serious about your career, so are we.

Females and minorities encouraged to apply.

Nettwerk Management

3900 West Alameda Ave, Suite 850
Burbank, CA 91505

NEW YORK
263 S. 4th St. P.O. Box 110649 Brooklyn,
NY 11211
Fax: +1 (747) 477-1093
Website: https://nettwerk.com
Website: https://www.facebook.com/
nettwerkmusicgroup

Represents: Artists/Bands; Film / TV
Composers; Producers; Songwriters; Sound
Engineers; Studio Technicians

Genres: Contemporary; Christian;
Electronic; Folk; Indie; Latin; Pop; Punk;
Rap; Rock; Hip-Hop; Dance; Singer-
Songwriter; World

Media company with offices in New York,
London, Vancouver, and Germany. Also
label and music publishing company.

New Heights Entertainment

Email: info@newheightsent.com
Website: http://www.newheightsent.com

Represents: Artists/Bands; Producers;
Songwriters

Genres: All types of music

Contact: Alan Melina

Privately held personal management and
consulting firm, with its core business
focusing on Music Producers, Songwriters,
Record Label Management, Music
Publishing, Brand Development and
Strategic Guidance for Entertainment
Content and IP Creators. No unsolicited
materials.

Nexus Artist Management

Email: info@nexusartists.com
Website: https://www.nexusartists.com
Website: https://www.facebook.com/Nexus.
Artist.Management/

Represents: Artists/Bands; DJs

Genres: Hip-Hop; Funk; Reggae; Dubstep;
Electronic; House; Techno; Progressive;
Break Beat

US management company handling
electronic artists.

Nice Management

Email: steve@nicemgmt.com
Website: https://nicemgmt.com
Website: https://www.facebook.com/
nicemgmt/

Represents: Artists/Bands; Film / TV
Composers; Producers; Songwriters

Genres: Rock

Contact: Steve Nice

Management company representing bands,
composers, producers, songwriters, and
mixers.

Nightside Entertainment, Inc.

Email: nightsideentertainment@gmail.com
Website: https://www.facebook.com/
nightsideentertainment

Represents: Artists/Bands

Genres: All types of music

Full service music booking agency.

NSI Management

2 Threadneedle Alley
Newburyport, MA
Email: contact@newsoundmgmt.com
Website: https://www.newsoundmgmt.com
Website: http://facebook.com/
danrussellmusic

Represents: Artists/Bands

Genres: Folk; Indie; Rock; Singer-
Songwriter

Contact: Dan Russell

Management company based in
Newburyport, Massachusetts.

Once 11 Entertainment

Email: javier@once11ent.com
Website: https://www.once11ent.com
Website: https://www.facebook.com/
Once11Ent/

Represents: Artists/Bands

Genres: Latin; World

Arts and entertainment consulting and personal management firm representing all kinds of Latin and World music.

Open All Nite Entertainment
9636 McLennan Avenue
Northridge, CA 91413
Email: info@openallnite.com
Website: https://www.openallnite.com
Website: https://www.facebook.com/openallnite

Represents: Artists/Bands

Genres: All types of music

Contact: Steve Belkin

Consultant for indie/emerging artists and labels in development of all aspects of career and business.

Opus 3 Artists
470 Park Avenue South
9th Floor North
New York, NY 10016
Email: info@opus3artists.com
Website: https://www.opus3artists.com
Website: https://www.facebook.com/opus3artists

Represents: Artists/Bands

Genres: Classical; Jazz

Represents classical and jazz performing artists. Offices in New York and Berlin.

Outrider Music, LLC
Charlottesville, VA
Email: anne@outridermusic.com
Website: http://www.outridermusic.com
Website: https://www.facebook.com/Outridermusic/

Represents: Artists/Bands; Lyricists; Songwriters

Genres: Post Rock; Progressive Rock; Post Metal; Hard Rock; Heavy Rock; Melodic Hardcore; Rock; Punk; Pop Rock; Pop Punk; Electronic Rock; Atmospheric Rock; Alternative; Alternative Rock; Acoustic Rock; Instrumental; Indie; Hardcore; Indie

Rock; Ambient; Ambient Rock; Emo; Post Emo

Contact: Anne McGinnis-Townsend

I was born and raised in Charlottesville, and I became obsessed with music at an early age. I spent my early teenage years playing guitar in various pop-punk and alternative rock bands, but it soon became clear to me that I enjoyed the behind-the-scenes work just as much, if not more, than actually playing. After graduating from Charlottesville High School, I got my degree in Music Business from New York University. While at NYU, I spent two semesters interning for Warner Music Group and I had the opportunity to meet and learn from some incredible people. I realized that what I really wanted to do was to help upcoming artists navigate the early stages of their careers. Growing up in Charlottesville, I saw too many of our "hometown heroes" get signed to bad record deals and wash out, and I wanted to help prevent that. I started Outrider Music because I wanted to be an advocate for local bands, to help them navigate both the fun stuff (branding, marketing, touring, booking) and the not-so-fun stuff (contracts, PROs, insurance, taxes). I want to be a part of your team.

Pacific Talent
Email: andy@pacifictalent.com
Website: http://www.pacifictalent.com
Website: https://www.instagram.com/pacifictalentpdx/

Represents: Artists/Bands

Genres: All types of music

Contact: Andy Gilbert

Management company based in Oregon.

Paradigm Talent Agency
700 N San Vicente Blvd, Suite G820
West Hollywood, CA 90069
Website: https://www.paradigmagency.com

Represents: Artists/Bands

Genres: All types of music

Talent agency with offices in Los Angeles and New York.

Paradise Artists
108 E Matilija St.
Ojai, CA 93023

NEW YORK:
P.O. Box 20088
New York, NY 10011
Email: info@paradiseartists.com
Website: https://www.paradiseartists.com
Website: https://www.facebook.com/ParadiseArtists

Represents: Artists/Bands

Genres: Rock; Rock and Roll; Pop

Management company with offices in New York and California.

Persistent Management
Los Angeles, CA
Email: pm@persistentmanagement.com
Website: https://www.persistentmanagement.com
Website: https://www.facebook.com/persistentmanagement

Represents: Artists/Bands; Producers

Genres: All types of music

Management company based in Los Angeles. Submit your details through online Artist Submissions form, including links to music online. No postal submissions or phone calls.

Pinnacle Arts Management, Inc.
801 West 181st Street
Apartment 20
New York, NY 10033
Fax: +1 (212) 795-3060
Website: https://www.pinnaclearts.com

Represents: Artists/Bands

Genres: Classical

Provides artists' management, production, and consulting services for performing artists and arts organizations worldwide, with

offices in New York, U.S.A. and in Munich, Germany. Its primary scope of activities is in the world of opera, where one hundred and twenty-five of its clients have appeared with seventy-five opera companies during the past season. In addition, its clients appear on a regular basis with many major symphony orchestras in the U.S. and Canada.

Platinum Star Management
Beverly Hills, CA
Website: https://platinumstarmgmt.com
Website: https://www.facebook.com/platinumstarmanagement

Represents: Artists/Bands

Genres: All types of music

Been in the music and entertainment industry for over twenty years, whether it was working for Madonna's record label, Maverick Records (now part of Warner Bros Records) or slogging it out working for larger management firms, entertainment and digital marketing companies or movie studios like Sony Pictures. If you truly believe you or your band has the songs, the drive, the fans and magic to make it to the top then send a query by email.

Position Music
Los Angeles
Email: submissions@positionmusic.com
Email: contact@positionmusic.com
Website: https://www.positionmusic.com
Website: https://soundcloud.com/position_music

Represents: Artists/Bands; Film / TV Composers

Genres: Rap; Hip-Hop; Rock; Alternative; Dance; Electronic; Hardcore; Metal; Pop; R&B; Singer-Songwriter; Urban; World

An independent publisher, record label and management firm. Send streaming links only by email.

PRA [Patrick Rains & Associates]

Email: pra@prarecords.com
Website: https://www.prarecords.com
Website: https://twitter.com/prarecords

Represents: Artists/Bands

Genres: Jazz; Pop; Rock

Contact: Patrick Rains; Stephanie Pappas

Management company based in New York. No unsolicited material.

Primary Wave

NEW YORK
116 East 16th Street, 9th Floor
New York, NY 10003

LOS ANGELES
10850 Wilshire Blvd., Suite #600
Los Angeles, CA 90024
Email: info@primarywave.com
Website: https://primarywave.com
Website: https://www.facebook.com/ PrimaryWave/

Represents: Artists/Bands; Producers; Songwriters

Genres: All types of music

Offers talent management, music publishing, television and film production, and brand marketing.

Prodigal Son Entertainment

Website: https://www.prodigalson-entertainment.com
Website: https://www.facebook.com/ ScottWilliamsPSE
Website: https://myspace.com/ prodigalsonentertainment

Represents: Artists/Bands

Genres: Alternative; Country; Christian; Instrumental; Rock; Hard Rock

Contact: Scott Williams

Artist management and career consultancy services.

Progressive Global Agency (PGA)

PO Box 50294
Nashville, TN 37205
Fax: +1 (615) 354-9101
Email: info@pgamusic.com
Website: https://pgamusic.com
Website: https://www.facebook.com/ progressiveglobalagency

Represents: Artists/Bands

Genres: Pop; Rock; World

Contact: Buck Williams

Management company based in Nashville, Tennessee.

Proper Management

1114 West Main Street
Franklin, TN 37064
Website: http://www.propermgmt.com

Represents: Artists/Bands

Genres: Christian

Christian music management company based in Nashville, Tennessee. Not accepting submissions as at June 2023. Check website for current status.

Pyramid Entertainment Group

377 Rector Place, Suite 21A
New York, NY 10280
Fax: +1 (212) 242-6932
Website: https://pyramid-ent.com

Represents: Artists/Bands

Genres: Gospel; Jazz; Funk; Hip-Hop; R&B; Urban

Contact: Sal Michaels

Management company based in New York.

Q Management

Fax: +1 (615) 599-1235
Website: https://qmanagementgroup.com

Represents: Artists/Bands

Genres: Rock

Rock manager based in Franklin, Tennessee.

Q Prime Management, Inc.
Email: newyork@qprime.com
Email: nashville@qprime.com
Website: https://qprime.com

Represents: Artists/Bands; Producers

Genres: Blues; Folk; Metal; Pop; Rock; Alternative; Singer-Songwriter

Contact: Cliff Burnstein; Peter Mensch

Management company with offices in New York, Nashville and London.

Rainmaker Artists
PO Box 342229
Austin, TX 78734
Fax: +1 (512) 843-7500
Website: https://www.rainmakerartists.com
Website: https://open.spotify.com/playlist/6bgMwK0DD5mlJStc3MaKBo

Represents: Artists/Bands

Genres: Pop; Rock

Management company based in Austin, Texas.

RAM Talent Group
Fort Lee, NJ
Email: ruben@rubenrodriguezentertainment.net
Website: http://ramtalentgroup.com
Website: https://www.facebook.com/RAMTalentGroup/

Represents: Artists/Bands

Genres: Gospel; Latin; Urban

Contact: Ruben Rodriguez

A full service music and entertainment management company with diverse talents.

Red Light Management (RLM)
Charlottesville; New York; Nashville; Los Angeles; Atlanta; Seattle
Website: https://www.redlightmanagement.com
Website: http://twitter.com/redlightmgmt

Represents: Artists/Bands; Film / TV Composers; Songwriters; Studio Musicians

Genres: Blues; Christian; Country; Dance; Electronic; Hardcore; Indie; Latin; Metal; Pop; Rap; Hip-Hop; Rock; Singer-Songwriter; World

Management company with offices in Charlottesville, New York, Nashville, Los Angeles, London, Bristol, Atlanta, and Seattle.

Regime Seventy-Two
Email: info@regimeinc.com
Website: https://www.regime72.com

Represents: Artists/Bands

Genres: All types of music

A company based in Art, Music, Fashion and Business.

Riot Artists
Email: staff@riotartists.com
Website: https://www.riotartists.com
Website: https://www.facebook.com/RiotArtists

Represents: Artists/Bands

Genres: World; Traditional; Contemporary

Management company specialising in World music reflecting traditional culture, and incorporating contemporary sounds to varying degrees. Books artists from around the world, with an emphasis on Canada, the US, Mexico, Brazil, and Europe.

Ron Rainey Management Inc.
8500 Wilshire Boulevard, Suite 525
Beverly Hills, CA 90211
Fax: +1 (310) 557-8421
Website: http://www.ronrainey.com

Represents: Artists/Bands

Genres: Contemporary; Blues; Pop; Country; Rock

Management company based in Beverly Hills, California.

RPM Music Productions
420 West 14th Street, Suite 6NW
New York, NY 10014

Email: info@rpm-productions.com
Website: http://rpm-productions.com

Represents: Artists/Bands

Genres: Jazz; Pop

Contact: Danny Bennett

Management company based in New York.

Russell Carter Artist Management

Website: https://www.facebook.com/pages/
Russell-Carter-Artist-Management/
174050332290?pnref=about.overview
Website: https://twitter.com/RCAM_mgnt
Website: https://myspace.com/rcam

Represents: Artists/Bands

Genres: Contemporary; Alternative;
Americana; Blues; Folk; Indie; Jazz; Singer-
Songwriter; Pop; Rock

Management company based in Atlanta,
Georgia.

Selak Entertainment, Inc.

466 Foothill Blvd. #184
La Canada, CA 91011
Fax: +1 (626)584-8122
Email: steve@selakentertainment.com
Website: https://selakentertainment.com
Website: https://www.facebook.com/
selakentertainment/

Represents: Artists/Bands; Comedians;
Tribute Acts

Genres: All types of music

Management company based in La Canada,
California.

Self Group

Portland, OR
Email: info@selfgroup.org
Website: https://www.selfgroup.org
Website: https://www.facebook.com/
selfgroup

Represents: Artists/Bands

Genres: All types of music

An anarcho-syndicalist creative collective.
The means of production, control and
ownership of rights, royalties and all else
governing each individuals artists' career is
theirs alone. We come together to form a
structure and outlet to present those creations
and achieve a communal method through
solidarity to carve a more unified means of
navigating an industry and world still under
the shadow of capitalism where the means of
production remains in the hands of the few
acting as dictatorial authoritarian governors
making overarching decisions as to the
welfare of the many. Exclusive and specific
to the music community in Portland, Oregon.

Semaphore Mgmt & Consulting

Website: https://www.semaphoremgmt.com
Website: https://www.instagram.com/
semaphoremgmt

Represents: Artists/Bands

Genres: Alternative Atmospheric Avant-
Garde Electronic Experimental Glam
Industrial Heavy Hard Kraut Leftfield New
Wave Non-Commercial Post Psychedelic
Thrash Underground

Full scale artist management and consulting
agency. We offer a la carte consulting and
retainer services to bands and labels alike.

September Management (US)

New York / Los Angeles
Email: info@sept.com
Website: https://sept.com

Represents: Artists/Bands; Producers; Sound
Engineers

Genres: All types of music

Represents a roster of internationally
renowned recording artists, producers and
mix engineers who have collectively
amassed 44 Grammys, 12 Brit Awards, 2
Oscars, 2 Golden Globes and sold over 100
million albums worldwide. The company has
offices in London, New York and Los
Angeles.

Sherrod Artist Management
Morehead City, NC
Email: infosherrodartistmanagement@
mail.com
Email: sherrodimprove79@gmail.com
Website: http://www.
sherrodartistmanagement.com
Website: https://www.facebook.com/
sherrodartistmanagement/

Represents: Artists/Bands

Genres: All types of music

Artist Management / Consultant / Artist
Development / Music Manager / A&R.
Charges $25 to submit.

Silva Artist Management (SAM)
Email: info@sammusicbiz.com
Website: http://www.sammusicbiz.com

Represents: Artists/Bands

Genres: Alternative; Indie; Metal; Pop;
Punk; Rock

Management company managing major
international rock/indie bands.

Singerman Entertainment
Los Angeles, CA
Email: info@SingermanEnt.com
Website: https://singermanent.com

Represents: Artists/Bands

Genres: Heavy Metal; Thrash; Rock;
Hardcore; Rock and Roll

Management company with offices in Los
Angeles, California. No unsolicited
materials.

SKH Music
540 President Street
Brooklyn, NY 11215
Email: skaras@skhmusic.com
Website: https://skhmusic.com

Represents: Artists/Bands; Lyricists;
Producers

Genres: All types of music

Contact: Steve Karas

Management company formed in June 2009.

SMC Artists
Website: https://www.smcartists.com

Represents: Film / TV Composers;
Songwriters

Genres: All types of music

Management company representing film and
TV composers and songwriters.

Solid Music Company
Email: david@solidmusic.net
Website: https://www.solidmusic.net
Website: https://www.facebook.com/profile.
php?id=100070887527477

Represents: Artists/Bands; Songwriters

Genres: All types of music

Contact: David Surnow

A management company for musicians and
songwriters.

Sound Management, Inc.
1525 South Winchester Boulevard
San Jose, California 95128
Fax: +1 (408) 741-5824
Email: robert@soundmgt.com
Email: ron@soundmgt.com
Website: https://www.soundmgt.com/
Website: https://www.facebook.com/
SoundMgtRecords

Represents: Artists/Bands

Genres: Pop; Rock

Full-Service Artist Management Company
based in San Jose, California, navigating the
careers of a diverse roster including Multi-
Platinum, Grammy Nominated, and
Internationally Acclaimed Artists.

Soundtrack Music Associates (SMA)
1601 North Sepulveda Boulevard #579
Manhattan Beach, CA 90266

Email: info@soundtrk.com
Website: https://soundtrk.com

Represents: Film / TV Composers;
Supervisors

Genres: Soundtracks

Contact: John Tempereau; Koyo Sonae;
Isabel Pappani

Represents award-winning composers, music
supervisors and music editors for film,
television and all media.

Sparks Entertainment Management Co.

PO Box 531973
Livonia, MI 48153
Email: sparksentertainment78@gmail.com
Website: https://www.facebook.com/
BSparksEntertainment
Website: https://www.instagram.com/
SparksEntertainment78

Represents: Artists/Bands

Genres: All types of music

Contact: Brian Sparks

Management company based in Livonia,
Michigan.

Spectrum Talent Agency

1650 Broadway
New York, NY 10019
Email: gage@spectrumtalentagency.com
Email: jan@spectrumtalentagency.com
Website: https://www.
spectrumtalentagency.com
Website: https://www.facebook.com/
SpectrumTalentAgency

Represents: Artists/Bands

Genres: Dance; Hip-Hop; Pop; R&B; House

Full service global booking agency.

Spinning Plates

Nashville, TN
Email: Debbie@spinningplatesmgmt.com
Website: https://spinningplatesmgmt.com/

Represents: Artists/Bands; Tribute Acts

Genres: Country; Rock

A boutique management, marketing, and
production company based in Nashville,
Tennessee, focusing on "making deals
happen".

Starkravin' Management

McLane & Wong
11135 Weddington Street, Suite #424
North Hollywood, CA 91601
Fax: +1 (818) 587-6802
Email: bcmclane@aol.com
Website: http://www.benmclane.com

Represents: Artists/Bands; Producers;
Songwriters

Genres: Pop; R&B; Rock

Contact: Ben McLane

Management and entertainment law
company based in North Hollywood.
Provides personal management and legal
services.

Sterling Artist Management

Email: mark@sterlingartist.com
Website: http://www.sterlingartist.com

Represents: Artists/Bands; Producers;
Songwriters; Studio Musicians

Genres: Blues; Jazz; Singer-Songwriter

Contact: Mark Sterling

Devoted to managing artists whose talent,
dedication and drive position them for
success in today's music industry.

Steven Scharf Entertainment (SSE)

Website: http://www.stevenscharf.com

Represents: Artists/Bands; Film / TV
Composers; Producers; Songwriters;
Supervisors

Genres: Alternative; Americana; Blues;
Folk; Indie; Jazz; Metal; Pop; Rap; Hip-Hop;
Rock; Roots; Singer-Songwriter; World;
Soundtracks

Contact: Steven Scharf

Management company handling artists, composers, and producers.

Stiefel Entertainment
21650 Oxnard St # 1925
Woodland Hills, CA 91364
Email: contact@StiefelEnt.com
Website: http://www.stiefelent.com
Website: https://www.linkedin.com/company/stiefel-entertainment

Represents: Artists/Bands

Genres: Contemporary; Dance; Indie; Pop; Rock; Singer-Songwriter

Contact: Arnold Stiefel

Management company based in Woodland Hills, California.

Stiletto Entertainment
Website: https://www.stilettoentertainment.com
Website: https://www.facebook.com/stilettoentertainment

Represents: Artists/Bands; Producers; Songwriters

Genres: All types of music

Broadcasting and media production company.

Street Smart Management
Los Angeles, CA
Website: https://www.facebook.com/streetsmartmanagement
Website: https://twitter.com/streetsmartmgmt

Represents: Artists/Bands

Genres: Indie; Rock; Metal; Pop

Management company based in Los Angeles, California.

Suncoast Music Management
Email: suncoastbooking@aol.com
Email: suncoastoh@hotmail.com
Website: http://www.suncoastentertainment.biz

Represents: Artists/Bands; Tribute Acts

Genres: Disco; Classic Rock; Rock

Contact: Al Spohn; Quinton Coontz; Andy Bowman; Daniel Nathan

Management company specialising in tribute acts.

Sweet! Music Management
Email: ssweet@sweetmusicmanagement.com
Website: https://www.sweetmusicmanagement.com

Represents: Artists/Bands

Genres: Alternative Funky Hard Mainstream Modern Americana Blues Country Deep Funk Folk Fusion Funk Indie Pop Punk Rock Rock and Roll Singer-Songwriter Soul

Contact: Sean Sweet

Represents new Artists/Bands to develop and promote them. Located in Chicago, IL. Please send inquiries by email or phone.

TAC Music Management
Website: https://tacmusicmanagement.com

Represents: Artists/Bands; Songwriters; Studio Musicians; Tribute Acts

Genres: Acoustic; Classic; Hard; Traditional; Regional; Soulful; Heavy; Funky; Commercial; Alternative; Americana; Blues; Country; Folk; Fusion; Funk; Guitar based; Indie; Jazz; Metal; R&B; Rock; Rock and Roll; Roots; Rhythm and Blues; Singer-Songwriter; Rockabilly

Services include artist management, booking, promotion and marketing to both local and national artists. Genres include blues, rock, Americana, bluegrass, folk, country, and tributes.

Take Out Management
Email: AlexTakeOutManagement@gmail.com
Website: https://howiewood.com/take-out-management/
Website: https://www.facebook.com/HowardRosenPromotion/

Represents: Artists/Bands; Producers

Genres: All types of music

Contact: Howard Rosen

Has managed independent acts as well as acts signed to Columbia, Curb, Atlantic, etc. Currently focused on working with producers for upcoming major and independent releases. Contact by phone or by email.

Talent Source
The Mill at Nyack
15 North Mill Street
Nyack, NY 10960
Fax: +1 (845) 359-4609
Email: info@talentsourcemanagement.com
Website: http://www.talentsourcemanagement.com
Website: https://www.facebook.com/BoDiddleyOfficial

Represents: Artists/Bands; Variety Artists

Genres: All types of music

Contact: Margo Lewis; Faith Fusillo

Management company based in Nyack, New York.

Tenth Street Entertainment
113 North San Vicente Blvd, 2nd Floor, Suite 241
Beverly Hills, CA 90211

1115 Broadway, 12th Floor
New York, NY 10010
Email: info@10thst.com
Website: http://www.10thst.com

Represents: Artists/Bands; Producers

Genres: All types of music

International company with offices in LA, London, and New York.

That's Entertainment International Inc. (TEI Entertainment)
3820 E. La Palma Ave
Anaheim, CA 92807
Email: thomas@teientertainment.com

Email: jmcentee@teientertainment.com
Website: http://www.teientertainment.com

Represents: Artists/Bands

Genres: All types of music

Contact: John D. McEntee, President

Celebrity Entertainment Resource Company based in Anaheim, California.

Third Coast Talent
PO Box 170
Chapmansboro, TN 37035
Fax: +1 (615) 685-3332
Email: carrie@thirdcoasttalent.com
Website: https://www.thirdcoasttalent.com
Website: https://www.facebook.com/ThirdCoastTalent

Represents: Artists/Bands

Genres: Country

Contact: Carrie Moore-Reed

Management company based in Chapmansboro, Tennessee.

Thirty Tigers
611 Merritt Avenue
Nashville, TN 37203
Website: https://www.thirtytigers.com/
Website: https://www.facebook.com/thirtytigers/

Represents: Artists/Bands

Genres: Indie; Rock; Urban

Contact: David Macias

Management company based in Nashville, Tennessee, with offices in Los Angeles, New York, North Carolina and London.

This Day And Age Management
301 South Perimeter Drive
Nashville, TN 37211
Website: https://www.thisdayandagemanagement.com
Website: https://www.instagram.com/thisdayandagemanagement/

Represents: Artists/Bands

Genres: Pop R&B Rap

Contact: David Patrick Small

We are a management and artist development company located in Nashville, TN. We focus on label pitches, booking and sync licensing pitches.

Threee
Website: https://www.threee.com
Website: https://twitter.com/threee_ent

Represents: Film / TV Composers; Producers; Songwriters

Genres: All types of music

Management company based in Los Angeles, California, representing producers, mixers, songwriters, and composers.

TKO Artist Management
Website: http://www.tkoartistmanagement.com
Website: https://www.facebook.com/TKOArtistMgmt/

Represents: Artists/Bands

Genres: Country

Management company based in Nashville Tennessee.

Tom Callahan & Associates (TCA)
Email: tc@tomcallahan.com
Website: https://www.tomcallahan.com
Website: https://www.linkedin.com/in/tom-callahan-771294/

Represents: Artists/Bands

Genres: All types of music

Full service music consulting company based in Boulder, Colorado, offering record promotion, publicity, internet marketing, production, and more.

A Train Entertainment
PO Box 29242
Oakland, CA 94604
Email: postmaster@a-train.com

Website: http://a-train.com
Website: https://www.facebook.com/ATrainEnt/

Represents: Artists/Bands

Genres: All types of music

Entertainment services, including publishing administration, artist management, physical and digital distribution, international sales and more.

True Talent Entertainment
Email: TRUETALENTENTER@GMAIL.com
Website: http://www.truetalententer.com
Website: https://www.youtube.com/channel/UCXh-_1hDdqYly92TorFfu7A

Represents: Artists/Bands; Film / TV Composers; Lyricists; Producers

Genres: R&B

Management, promotion, and production company. No unsolicited submissions.

Trunk Bass Entertainment
Email: info@trunkbassent.com
Website: https://www.trunkbassent.com
Website: https://www.facebook.com/TrunkBASSent/

Represents: Artists/Bands

Genres: Alternative; Hip-Hop; Pop; R&B

Offers a range of services, including Podcast Editing, Artist Booking, Music Consultancy, Artist Development, Music Supervision, EPK Building, Campaign Management, Video Production, Tour Management, and Content Creation.

Tsunami Entertainment
1600 E. Desert Inn Road
Las Vegas, NV 89169
Email: Info@tsunamient.com
Website: https://www.tsunamient.com

Represents: Artists/Bands; Producers

Genres: All types of music

A creative and business solutions Company operating in the music, entertainment and media space, providing brand strategy, business development, marketing services, operational support systems and financial management.

Tuscan Sun Music
Nashville, TN
Email: mgmt@angelica.org
Website: http://www.tuscansunmusic.com
Website: http://www.angelica.org

Represents: Artists/Bands

Genres: Ambient; New Age; Pop

Management company based in Nashville, Tennessee.

Uncle Booking
5438 Winding Way Drive
Houston, TX 77091
Email: erik@unclebooking.com
Website: http://www.unclebooking.com

Represents: Artists/Bands

Genres: All types of music

Booking agency based in Texas.

Union Entertainment Group
Email: info@ueginc.com
Website: http://www.ueginc.com

Represents: Artists/Bands

Genres: Rock; Alternative; Blues; Country; Pop; Rap; Hip-Hop

Music management company.

United Talent Agency
9336 Civic Center Drive
Beverly Hills, CA 90210
Website: https://www.unitedtalent.com
Website: https://www.facebook.com/UnitedTalent/

Represents: Artists/Bands

Genres: All types of music

International talent agency with offices in Atlanta, Chicago, London, Los Angeles, New York, and Nashville.

Universal Attractions Agency
NEW YORK
15 West 36th Street, 8th Floor
New York, NY 10018

LOS ANGELES
21650 W. Oxnard St., Suite 1460
Woodland Hills, CA 91367

Fax: +1 (212) 333-4508 / +1 (646) 304-5178
Email: info@universalattractions.com
Website: https://universalattractions.com
Website: https://www.facebook.com/UAAtalent/

Represents: Artists/Bands

Genres: All types of music

Talent agency with offices in New York and Los Angeles.

Universal Tone Management
Email: fanclub@santana.com
Email: merch@santana.com
Website: https://www.santana.com/universal-tone-management-contact-us/

Represents: Artists/Bands; Songwriters

Genres: Blues; Latin; Pop; Rock

Management company based in San Rafael, California.

Val's Artist Management (VAM)
Email: info@vamnation.com
Website: http://www.vamnation.com
Website: https://www.facebook.com/VAMNation-Entertainment-108496975907793/

Represents: Artists/Bands

Genres: Contemporary; Blues; Classical; Country; Dance; Folk; Indie; Jazz; Latin; Pop; Punk; R&B; Rap; Hip-Hop; Rock; Roots; Urban; World

Contact: Valerie Wilson Morris

Aims to identify and cultivate the most elite talent in the entertainment industry. Describes itself as having "a keen understanding of the many facets of the industry gleaned through personal experience and proven professional success".

Variety Artists International
Email: John@varietyart.com
Email: Lloyd@varietyart.com
Website: https://varietyart.com

Represents: Artists/Bands

Genres: Folk; Jazz; Pop; Rap; Rock

Management company providing tour booking services.

Vector Management
Nashville, New York and Los Angeles
Website: https://vectormgmt.com

Represents: Artists/Bands; Songwriters

Genres: Contemporary; Alternative; Americana; Country; Folk; Gospel; Metal; Pop; Rock; Singer-Songwriter

Management company with offices in Nashville, New York, Toronto, and Los Angeles.

Velvet Hammer Music & Management Group
Website: https://velvethammer.net
Website: https://www.facebook.com/velvethammermusicandmanagementgroup

Represents: Artists/Bands

Genres: All types of music

Contact: David Benveniste (Beno); Mark Wakefield; Samantha Waterman; Taryn Mazza; Kristin Van Trieste; Sara Pacheco; Samantha Surtida; Lauren Horne; Max Kane

Prides itself on identifying quality talent. Submit demos through online submission system.

Walker Entertainment Group
PO Box 7926
Houston, TX 77270
Website: http://www.walkerentertainmentgroup.com

Website: https://facebook.com/walkerentertainmentgrouptx

Represents: Artists/Bands

Genres: All types of music

Global provider of event management, production, and entertainment services.

Waxploitation
Email: artists@waxploitation.com
Website: http://www.waxploitation.com
Website: https://www.facebook.com/WaxploitationRecords/

Represents: Artists/Bands

Genres: Electronic; Indie; Hip-Hop; Rap; Reggae; Rock

Management company based in Los Angeles, California.

Westwood Music Group
2740 Kalsted Street, Suite 200
North Port, FL 34288
Email: westwoodgrp3@gmail.com
Website: https://www.westwoodmusicgroup.com

Represents: Artists/Bands; Film / TV Composers; Songwriters

Genres: Pop; Rock; Country; Blues; Jazz; R&B; Latin; Gospel; Instrumental

Contact: Victor Kaply

Established in 1985, and currently based in North Port, Florida.

Whiplash PR and Management
398 Columbus Ave,
PMB #183,
Boston, MA 02116
Email: Rockergirl363@aol.com
Website: https://www.whiplashprandmanagement.com

Represents: Artists/Bands

Genres: All types of music

An independent PR, brand and marketing agency that services bands, musicians, indie labels and music service companies internationally. Send music by email.

William Morris Endeavor (WME)

BEVERLY HILLS:
9560 Wilshire Blvd
Beverly Hills, CA 90210

9601 Wilshire Blvd
Beverly Hills, CA 90210

131 S Rodeo, 2nd Floor
Beverly Hills, CA 90212

NASHVILLE:
1201 Demonbreun
Nashville, TN 37203

NEW YORK:
11 Madison Avenue
New York, NY 10010
Website: https://wmeagency.com

Represents: Artists/Bands

Genres: All types of music

The world's longest running talent agency, representing music artists, authors, comedians, actors, sportspeople, etc. Has represented iconic names such as Charlie Chaplin, Marilyn Monroe, and Elvis Presley.

Wolfson Entertainment, Inc.

2659 Townsgate Road, Suite 119
Westlake Village, CA 91361
Website: https://www.wolfsonent.com/
Website: https://www.facebook.com/
wolfsonentinc

Represents: Artists/Bands

Genres: All types of music

Contact: Jonathan Wolfson

Management company based in Westlake Village, California.

Worldsound, LLC

Seattle, WA 98148
Website: https://www.worldsound.com
Website: https://www.facebook.com/
worldsoundllc

Represents: Artists/Bands

Genres: Celtic; Folk; Pop; Rock; World; Rock and Roll

Management company founded in Southern California in 1992, now based in Seattle, Washington.

Wright Entertainment Group (WEG)

Website: https://www.wegmusic.com
Website: https://www.facebook.com/
wegmusic

Represents: Artists/Bands

Genres: Hip-Hop; Pop; R&B; Rap; Rock; Singer-Songwriter

Contact: Johnny Wright

Artist management company. Develops and assembles aspiring musical talent and also represents a roster of veteran entertainers.

Yellow Couch Management

Website: https://www.
yellowcouchstudio.com
Website: https://www.facebook.com/steven.
foxbury

Represents: Artists/Bands

Genres: All types of music

Contact: Steven Foxbury

A boutique artist management company providing comprehensive and creative strategies for those we serve. Our goal is to help shape enduring careers that are both personally and professionally fulfilling.

UK Managers

For the most up-to-date listings of these and hundreds of other managers, visit https://www.musicsocket.com/managers

*To claim your **free** access to the site, please see the back of this book.*

!K7
217 Chester House
Kennington Park
1-3 Brixton Road
London
SW9 6DE
Email: artist-mgmt@k7.com
Website: http://k7.com
Website: https://twitter.com/K7MusicHQ

Represents: Artists/Bands

Genres: All types of music

Represents a varied roster of artists from a wide range of genres.

1 2 One Entertainment
Email: paul@12one.net
Website: https://www.12one.com
Website: https://www.facebook.com/12OneEntertainment/

Represents: Artists/Bands

Genres: Dance; Pop; Urban

Contact: Paul Kennedy

For general music submissions use the form on the website, adding music links to external websites like SoundCloud, Songspace, or Wetransfer.

2-Tone Entertainment (2TE)
91 Peterborough Road
London
SW6 3BU
Email: info@2tone-entertainment.com
Website: https://www.instagram.com/2tone_ent/
Website: https://www.facebook.com/2tone.entertainment

Represents: Artists/Bands

Genres: Dance; Urban; Pop

Record label and talent management based in London.

2k Management
Email: info@2kmngt.com
Website: https://twitter.com/2K_Management
Website: https://www.instagram.com/2k.management

Represents: Artists/Bands

Genres: All types of music

Open to all types of music, but particularly interested in Afro, rap, and hip-hop.

360 Artist Development
42 Western Avenue
Birstall
WF17 0PF

Email: info@360artistdevelopment.com
Website: https://www.
360artistdevelopment.com
Website: https://www.facebook.com/
360artistdevelopment

Represents: Artists/Bands

Genres: All types of music

Management / consultancy company based
in Wakefield. Submit demos via contact
form on website.

4 Tunes Ltd
Website: http://4-tunes.com

Represents: Artists/Bands

Genres: All types of music

Contact: Andy Murray

Now retired, no longer has any management
clients or plans for any – but doesn't rule out
the possibility completely.

7pm Management
Email: seven@7pmmanagement.com
Email: wolfie@7pmmanagement.com
Website: https://7pmmanagement.com/
Website: https://twitter.com/
7pmmanagement

Represents: Artists/Bands; DJs; Producers

Genres: All types of music

Works with music but is not genre specific.
In simplest terms if we love it and if we can
help make it as a business make money then
we work with it.

Also acts as a consultant to top companies
within the global industry.

A&R Factory
Email: info@anrfactory.com
Website: https://www.anrfactory.com
Website: https://www.facebook.com/
anrfactory

Represents: Artists/Bands

Genres: All types of music

Independent music blog that also offers an
artist development program. Send demos
through online submission form on website.

A2E – Artists 2 Events
PO Box 64
Ammanford
Carmarthenshire
SA18 9AB
Email: mike@artists2events.co.uk
Email: rob@artists2events.co.uk
Website: http://www.artists2events.co.uk

Represents: Artists/Bands

Genres: Acoustic; Blues; Celtic

Contact: Mike / Rob

Management company based in Ammanford,
Carmarthenshire.

Aguia Music
Email: luana@aguiamusic.com
Website: https://www.facebook.com/
AguiaMusic
Website: https://linktr.ee/aguiamusic

Represents: Artists/Bands

Genres: Americana; Country; Folk; Hip-
Hop; R&B; Rap

All about the Vision – we understand the
importance of having a coherent plan and
supporting our artists in their professional
and personal lives, always with the creative
vision and approach making sure that every
step counts to our future.

AJM
Email: juste@ajmofficial.co.uk
Website: https://www.ajmofficial.co.uk
Website: https://www.facebook.com/ajm.
mgmt

Represents: Artists/Bands

Genres: Electronic; Pop

Send query by email with links to music
online, bio, links to press shots (Dropbox or
similar), your biggest achievements so far,
and your goals and ambitions for the next 12
months.

Amber Artists
Email: management@amberartists.com
Email: info@amberartists.com
Website: http://www.amberartists.com

Represents: Artists/Bands

Genres: All types of music

Provides PR and management.

American Artiste (UK)
Cambridge
Email: information@americanartiste.com
Website: https://www.americanartiste.com
Website: https://www.facebook.com/americanartisteltd

Represents: Artists/Bands

Genres: All types of music

Management company with offices in Cambridge, UK, and Hollywood, USA. Send links to music online through online contact form.

Amour:Music
London
Email: info@amourmusic.co.uk
Website: https://amourmusic.co.uk
Website: https://www.facebook.com/AmourMusicUK/

Represents: Artists/Bands

Genres: All types of music

Artist Management and Career Guidance company based in London. Send submissions by email.

Amour:Music
Email: info@amourmusic.co.uk
Website: https://amourmusic.co.uk
Website: https://soundcloud.com/amourmusicuk

Represents: Artists/Bands

Genres: Contemporary; Singer-Songwriter

Send query by email with links to streaming music online. No attachments or download links.

Anger Management
Email: info@angermanagementlive.co.uk
Website: https://www.angermanagementlive.co.uk
Website: https://www.facebook.com/AngerManagement100

Represents: Artists/Bands

Genres: All types of music

Provides artist and tour management services.

The Animal Farm
4th Floor, Block A
The Biscuit Factory
100 Clements Road
London
SE16 4DG
Email: info@theanimalfarm.co.uk
Website: http://www.theanimalfarm.co.uk
Website: https://www.facebook.com/theanimalfarmmusic

Represents: Artists/Bands

Genres: All types of music

Send query by email or through online form giving link to website where you can be seen and your music heard. Include reason for approach. No MP3 attachments by email. Do not expect feedback.

AprilSeven Music
London
Email: aprilsevenmusic@gmail.com
Email: mail@aprilsevenmusic.com
Website: https://www.aprilsevenmusic.com

Represents: Artists/Bands; Producers

Genres: Jazz; Electronic; Soul

Music consultancy based in London, with expertise in marketing, PR, international and local distribution, and management.

Artistes International Representation (AIR) Ltd
AIR House
Spennymoor
County Durham
DL16 7SE

Fax: +44 (0) 1388 812445
Email: info@airagency.com
Website: http://www.airagency.com

Represents: Artists/Bands; Comedians;
Tribute Acts

Genres: All types of music

Management company based in County
Durham.

Askonas Holt Ltd
15 Fetter Lane
London
EC4A 1BW
Email: info@askonasholt.co.uk
Website: https://www.askonasholt.com
Website: https://www.facebook.com/
askonasholt/

Represents: Artists/Bands

Genres: Classical

Formed in 1998 through an amalgamation of
two long-established artist management
companies, both based in London but with
international connections.

ASM Talent
Email: albert@asmtalent.co.uk
Email: assistant@asmtalent.co.uk
Website: https://www.asmtalent.com

Represents: Artists/Bands

Genres: All types of music

Contact: Albert Samuel

A well-established London-based talent
agency with a combination of over 50 years
of talent management experience.

Aspire Music Management
Email: mel@aspiremusicmanagement.co.uk
Website: https://www.
aspiremusicmanagement.co.uk
Website: https://www.facebook.com/
AspireMusicManagement.co.uk/

Represents: Artists/Bands; Songwriters

Genres: Melodic Rock; Pop Rock; Acoustic

Contact: Melanie Perrett

Management company based in northern
England, representing unsigned and indie
artists and songwriters. Handles a wide range
of genres, but particularly interested in
Melodic Rock, Pop Rock, and Acoustic. Will
consider other genres, however.

Associated London Management
London
Email: martin@
associatedlondonmanagement.com
Email: jason@
associatedlondonmanagement.com
Website: http://www.
associatedlondonmanagement.com
Website: https://facebook.com/ALMgmt

Represents: Artists/Bands

Genres: Alternative

Management company based in London.

ATC Management
The Hat Factory
166-168 Camden Street
London
NW1 9PT
Email: info@atcmanagement.com
Website: https://www.atcmanagement.com
Website: https://www.facebook.com/
atcmanagement/

Represents: Artists/Bands

Genres: All types of music

London based management company with
offices in Los Angeles, New York, and
Copenhagen.

AuthorityMGMT
Second Floor
Unit 14 Tileyard Studios
Tileyard Road
London
N7 9AH
Website: https://www.authoritymgmt.com
Website: http://soundcloud.com/
authoritymgmt

Represents: Artists/Bands; Songwriters

Genres: Dance; Pop; Singer-Songwriter

Music management company based in London, with a global outlook. Represents artists and songwriters at all levels. Extensive experience in management, A&R, records, publishing and brands deals.

Autonomy Music Group
Autonomy Management
6a Tileyard Studios
Tileyard Road
London
N7 9AH
Email: hi@autonomymusicgroup.com
Email: jobs@autonomymusicgroup.com
Website: https://autonomymusicgroup.com

Represents: Artists/Bands; DJs; Producers; Songwriters

Genres: All types of music

Provides bespoke artist and campaign services to artists, bands, producers, record labels and DJs. Send query via email.

Avenoir Records
Email: martin@avenoir.org
Website: https://avenoir.org
Website: https://www.facebook.com/avenoirrecords

Represents: Artists/Bands

Genres: All types of music

Offers various music and entertainment industry consultancy packages that range from advice, simple online marketing and branding through to full musical production, development and managerial services at a cost to suit any budget.

B.H. Hopper Management Ltd.
Shepherds Building – Unit G7
Rockley Road
London
W14 0DA
Email: hopper@hoppermanagement.com
Website: http://www.hoppermanagement.com

Represents: Artists/Bands

Genres: Jazz

Management company based in London handling Jazz artists only.

Bad Apple Music Group
Email: hello@badapplemusic.group
Website: https://www.badapplemusic.group
Website: https://www.facebook.com/badapplemusicgroup

Represents: Artists/Bands

Genres: Alternative; Indie; Rock

With strong experience in the ever-changing industry, we are proud to offer artist management and development, release plan assistance, and more to help you to take the right next steps in your music career.

Big Bear Music
PO Box 944
Birmingham
B16 8UT
Email: admin@bigbearmusic.com
Website: https://www.bigbearmusic.com
Website: https://www.facebook.com/Bigbearmusic/

Represents: Artists/Bands

Genres: Blues; Jazz; Swing

Contact: Jim Simpson

Represents and tours jazz, blue and swing attractions of the highest quality, mostly those signed to the Record label. We also oranise events and jazz festivals, including a midlands jazz festival established in 1985.

Big Hug Management
Email: jeff@bighugmanagement.com
Website: http://www.bighugmanagement.com
Website: https://www.facebook.com/bighugmanagement

Represents: Artists/Bands

Genres: All types of music

Contact: Jeff Powell

One-man music management company. Home to Artists, Songwriters and Creatives. It's about raw talent and the long haul. No quick fixes. Artist Integrity is at the forefront.

Big Life Management
67-69 Chalton Street
London
NW1 1HY
Email: reception@biglifemanagement.com
Website: https://www.biglifemanagement.com

Represents: Artists/Bands; Producers

Genres: All types of music

Management company based in London, representing bands, solo artists, and producers. Send query by email with links to music online.

BiGiAM Promotions & Management
Email: info@bigiam.co.uk
Website: https://bigiam.co.uk
Website: https://www.facebook.com/BiGiAMPR/

Represents: Artists/Bands

Genres: All types of music

We promote, advise and manage businesses, events and personal creativity linked to music and the arts. Our portfolio is relatively wide and relatively varied; we play a significant role in the development, project management, marketing/promotions and sponsorship of a number of Brighton area based events.

If you think we can help your company/band/event etc, please approach us for a no obligation chat; we may well be less expensive than you think. Our aim is to provide unrivalled value and excellence in everything we do.

Blinding Talent
Website: https://www.blindingtalent.com/
Website: https://www.facebook.com/blindingtalent

Represents: Artists/Bands

Genres: All types of music

Provides digital marketing campaigns for independent artists, starting at £600.

BLOCS
Email: info@blocshq.com
Website: https://blocshq.com
Website: https://www.facebook.com/BLOCSHQ/

Represents: Artists/Bands

Genres: All types of music

A new model new music company with bases in Cardiff, Carmarthen, Swansea and Wrexham, and working with artists across the areas of management, live, and releases, with each working relationship tailored to meet the particular needs of each artist project.

Blue Raincoat Music
Unit G2
1 Leonard Circus
64 Paul Street
EC2A 4DQ
Email: info@blueraincoatmusic.com
Email: artists@blueraincoatmusic.com
Website: https://www.blueraincoatmusic.com
Website: https://www.facebook.com/WeAreBRM

Represents: Artists/Bands

Genres: All types of music

Management company based in London.

Bold Management
85 Bold Street
Liverpool
L1 4HF
Fax: +44 (0) 1517 091895
Email: martin@bold-management.com
Website: https://www.bold-management.com
Website: https://www.facebook.com/boldmanagement

Represents: Artists/Bands; Producers; Songwriters

Genres: Pop; Rock; Indie

Develops and manages the careers of a large and varied number of clients including TV personalities, music artists, songwriters and sports people.

Brian Yeates Associates Ltd
Website: https://www.yeatesentertainment.co.uk
Website: https://www.facebook.com/yeatesentertainment

Represents: Artists/Bands; Comedians; DJs; Tribute Acts

Genres: All types of music

Contact: Ashley Yeates

Management company based in the Midlands, with 30 years experience representing a variety of acts.

Brighthelmstone Promotions
Email: brighthelmstonepromotions@gmail.com
Email: james@brighthelmstonepromotions.co.uk
Website: https://www.brighthelmstonepromotions.co.uk
Website: https://www.facebook.com/brighthelmstonepromotions/

Represents: Artists/Bands

Genres: Americana; Folk; Indie

Management company based in Brighton, specialising in Americana and Roots.

BrightonsFinest
Email: theteam@brightonsfinest.com
Email: frank@brightonsfinest.com
Website: https://brightonsfinest.com
Website: https://twitter.com/brightonsfinest

Represents: Artists/Bands

Genres: All types of music

Artist management, live events, and sessions.

Brum Media Group
Birmingham
Email: letschat@bmguk.com
Website: https://www.bmguk.com
Website: https://www.facebook.com/brummedia

Represents: Artists/Bands

Genres: Alternative Pop; Indie; Rock

Dedicated to nurturing and promoting the vibrant music talent emerging from the West Midlands. Specialize in comprehensive music management services tailored to the unique needs of upcoming artists and bands. Send demos as links only (no physical submissions or MP3s).

Bulldozer Media Ltd
Email: info@bulldozermedia.com
Website: https://www.bulldozermedia.com
Website: https://soundcloud.com/bulldozermedia

Represents: Artists/Bands; DJs

Genres: All types of music

Artist management agency and music publisher.

Catalyst Management
Website: https://www.facebook.com/officalcatalystmanagment/
Website: https://instagram.com/catalyst.management

Represents: Artists/Bands; Producers

Genres: All types of music

Management and marketing for UK artists aiming for mainstream success.

Chaos & Bedlam Management
Email: liza@chaosandbedlam.com
Website: https://www.musicglue.com/chaos-and-bedlam-consultancy/
Website: https://www.facebook.com/chaosandbedlam/

Represents: Artists/Bands

Genres: Rock

Contact: Liza Buddy

Rock management and consultancy company.

Chosen Music
Website: https://www.chosenmusic.com

Represents: Artists/Bands

Genres: All types of music

An independent boutique artist partnerships company encompassing label, publishing and management.

Closer Artists Management & Publishing
Matrix Studios
91 Peterborough Road
London
SW6 3BU
Email: info@closerartists.com
Website: https://www.closerartists.co.uk
Website: https://twitter.com/closerartists

Represents: Artists/Bands

Genres: All types of music

Contact: Paul McDonald; Ryan Lofthouse

Management, record label and publishing company based in London.

CMG Music
Website: https://www.c-m-g.com/music
Website: https://www.instagram.com/music.cmg/

Represents: Artists/Bands; Producers; Songwriters

Genres: All types of music

Manages artists, producers, writers, composers, and mixers.

CMP Entertainment
Liverpool
Email: info@cmplive.com
Email: info@cmpentertainment.com
Website: https://www.cmpentertainment.com
Website: https://www.facebook.com/CMPEntertainment

Represents: Artists/Bands; Tribute Acts

Genres: All types of music

Contact: Chas Cole

A boutique live music entertainment company, promoting and producing over 500 shows per year.

Conchord
London
Email: info@conchordmanagement.com
Website: https://conchordmanagement.com
Website: https://www.facebook.com/conchordmgmt

Represents: Artists/Bands

Genres: All types of music

Management company based in London.

Consolidated Artists
PO Box 87
Tarporley
CW6 9FN
Fax: +44 (0) 1829 730499
Email: alecconsol@aol.com
Email: ross@consolidatedartists.co.uk
Website: http://www.consolidatedartists.co.uk

Represents: Artists/Bands

Genres: Pop; Rock

Contact: Alec Leslie

Management company based in Tarporley.

Covert Talent Management
Email: covertdemos@gmail.com
Email: simon@coverttalent.com
Website: http://www.coverttalent.com
Website: https://www.instagram.com/coverttalent

Represents: Artists/Bands; Producers; Songwriters

Genres: All types of music

Contact: Simon King

A music management and publishing company that focuses on the creative, strategic and brand development of its hand-picked roster of clients.

Craft Management
Email: enquiries@craftmgmt.com
Website: https://craftmgmt.com

Represents: Artists/Bands; Producers

Genres: Alternative

Represents alternative artists and producers.

Creative International Artist Management
Email: info@cruisin.co.uk
Website: http://www.cruisin.co.uk

Represents: Artists/Bands

Genres: Metal; Pop; Rock

Management company set in 250 acres of countryside on the Wiltshire/Somerset border.

Creative Sounds UK
Email: ade2creativesoundsuk@gmail.com
Website: https://www.creativesoundsuk.com
Website: https://www.facebook.com/CSUK1/

Represents: Artists/Bands

Genres: All types of music

Send query by email with links to your music online, a bio / onesheet / press kit, and your full contact information.

Creeme Entertainments
First Floor
293 Darwen Road
Bromley Cross
Bolton
BL7 9BT
Email: anthony@creeme.co.uk
Email: victoria@creeme.co.uk
Website: https://creeme.co.uk
Website: https://www.facebook.com/creemeentertainmentsltd

Represents: Artists/Bands; Comedians; Other Entertainers; Tribute Acts

Genres: All types of music

Contact: Anthony Ivers

Manages acts including music, tribute acts, lookalikes, comedians, after-dinner speakers, etc. for corporate events, and the pub and club circuits.

dandomanagement
Northamptonshire
Website: https://twitter.com/managementdando
Website: https://www.facebook.com/introducing.dandomanagement

Represents: Artists/Bands

Genres: Indie Rock; Singer-Songwriter

Contact: Martin Dando

Management company based in Northamptonshire.

Danny Brittain Band Management (DBBM)
10B Hollington Park Road
St Leonards on Sea
East Sussex
TN38 0SG
Website: http://www.dbbm.co.uk

Represents: Artists/Bands

Genres: All types of music

Contact: Danny Brittain

Management company based in St Leonards on Sea. Describes itself as "The premier live music booking agency for any occasion".

Darkspin Music Management
Email: info@darkspin.co
Website: https://www.darkspinmusic.com
Website: https://linktr.ee/darkspin.co

Represents: Artists/Bands

Genres: All types of music

Contact: Laura Mckay

Independent artist management and unsigned artist development.

Dawson Breed Music
Website: http://www.dawsonbreedmusic.com
Website: https://twitter.com/DawsonBreed

Represents: Artists/Bands

Genres: Americana; Folk; Indie; Pop; Acoustic

Contact: Debra Downes

A live music agency, we work with emerging acts and established acts, but only acts we are passionate about.

Deathless MGMT

Website: https://deathless-mgmt.com
Website: https://www.instagram.com/deathless_mgmt/

Represents: Artists/Bands

Genres: Metal; Rock

A UK based artist management and consultancy service with a focus on rock and metal music. Works with artists through all aspects of their music career including planning appropriate music and show design for live performances, PR, advertising, promotion, use of digital media, image and branding, booking agencies on behalf of the artist, and selection of other key members of the artists' team.

DEF (Deutsch Englische Freundschaft)

Email: info@d-e-f.com
Website: https://d-e-f.com
Website: https://www.facebook.com/DEFallesistgut

Represents: Artists/Bands

Genres: Dance; Electronic

Concentrates on electronic dance, but willing to consider all types of music.

Defenders Ent

Email: music@defendersent.com
Website: https://www.defendersent.com
Website: https://www.facebook.com/DefendersEnt/

Represents: Artists/Bands

Genres: Dance; Reggae; R&B; Rap

Formed in 2001 as an independent record label, has since been involved in managing, releasing and consulting for many acts/brands.

Deluxxe Management

Email: info@deluxxe.co.uk
Website: https://www.deluxxe.co.uk/
Website: http://www.facebook.com/DeluxxeArtistManagement

Represents: Artists/Bands

Genres: All types of music

Happy to receive new artist submissions. Send email with link to four songs, and social media links. Include message about why you think this is the right time to work with a manager. Response not guaranteed.

Deuce Management & Promotion

Email: rob@deucemusic.com
Website: https://www.deucemusic.com
Website: https://www.facebook.com/deucepr/

Represents: Artists/Bands

Genres: All types of music

Contact: Rob Saunders

Has established itself as one of the leading companies to offer services to unsigned/newly signed bands and artists worldwide. With a growing reputation of being at the forefront of the best new music on the scene and with its idyllically placed office in London, they aim to ensure bands and artists are offered ways and means to get their music heard to a wider audience.

For a FREE evaluation on your music please send a link to your material by email.

DFJ Artists

Studio 114
17 Amhurst Terrace
London
E8 2BT
Website: http://www.dfjartists.com

Represents: Artists/Bands; Producers; Songwriters

Genres: Jazz

Music management and consultancy services across jazz and related music genres.

Digimix Music
Website: https://www.digimixmusic.com

Represents: Artists/Bands; DJs; Film / TV
Composers; Producers; Songwriters

Genres: All types of music

A music media entertainment company,
comprising of commercial music publishers,
library production music publishers, record
companies, management and media
distribution facilities. We work
internationally with songwriters, composers,
performing songwriters, bands, musicians,
electronic dance music DJ/producers, who
are songwriting, producing, recording
working and/or performing in all styles of
music. We also work with composers who
write production library music for use in the
radio, TV, film, audio-visual, advertising,
multimedia and games industry worldwide.

DMF Music Ltd
51 Queen Street
Exeter
Devon
EX4 3SR
Email: info@dmfmusic.co.uk
Website: https://dmfmusic.co.uk
Website: https://www.facebook.com/
DMFMusicTeam

Represents: Artists/Bands

Genres: Ska; Folk; Indie; World; Jazz;
Reggae

Contact: David Farrow; Laura Farrow

Undertake a diverse range of services
including album campaign management,
artist management, live agency, festival
organisation and programming. Work with a
range of established and upcoming artists
from the UK, Europe and the US across
genres including ska, folk, indie, world
music, jazz and reggae.

Don't Try
107-111 Fleet St
London
EC4A 2AB
Email: ben@donttrymusic.com
Website: https://www.donttrymusic.com

Website: https://www.facebook.com/
donttryuk

Represents: Artists/Bands; Producers

Genres: Alternative; Indie; Rock

Music company based in London, managing
artists and producers.

Donatello Music
Email: aaron.trowbridge@
donatellomusic.com
Website: https://www.donatellomusic.com

Represents: Artists/Bands; Songwriters

Genres: Alternative Pop; Country; Guitar
based; Pop

Experts in international artist representation,
we offer end to end management of the
careers of musicians and songwriters.

Down For Life
Email: info@downforlifemusic.co.uk
Website: https://www.
downforlifemusic.co.uk
Website: https://www.facebook.com/
downforlifemusic

Represents: Artists/Bands

Genres: Alternative; Hardcore; Metal; Rock

UK based artist and event management
company.

Steve Draper Entertainments
Email: stevedraperents1@gmail.com
Website: http://www.
stevedraperentertainments.co.uk

Represents: Artists/Bands; Comedians;
Other Entertainers; Tribute Acts

Genres: All types of music

Contact: Steve Draper

Management and entertainment agency
established for over 35 years.

Duroc Media
PO Box 6030
Windsor

SL4 9GD
Email: info@durocmedia.com
Website: http://www.durocmedia.com

Represents: Artists/Bands

Genres: All types of music

Management and public relations
consultants.

East City Management
London
Email: demo@eastcitymanagement.com
Email: hello@eastcitymanagement.com
Website: https://eastcitymanagement.com
Website: https://www.facebook.com/
eastcitymanagement

Represents: Artists/Bands

Genres: Alternative; Dance; Indie

Manager based in London. Send query by
email with links to streaming music online.

Empire Artist Management
16 Tileyard Studios
Tileyard Road
London
N7 9AH
Email: info@empire-management.co.uk
Website: http://www.empire-
management.co.uk
Website: https://twitter.com/EmpireMGMT_

Represents: Artists/Bands; Producers;
Songwriters

Genres: All types of music

Management company based in London,
representing well-known artists, as well as
producers and writers.

Equator Music
London
Website: http://www.equatormusic.com

Represents: Artists/Bands

Genres: Indie; Pop; Rock

London-based management company which
has been managing the affairs of major
artists and writers for over 35 years.

Everybody's Management Ltd
31 Corsica Street
Highbury
London
N5 1JT
Email: info@everybody-s.com
Website: https://www.everybody-s.com
Website: https://www.facebook.com/
everybodysmgmt

Represents: Artists/Bands

Genres: All types of music

Management company based in London.

F&G Management
Website: https://www.facebook.com/
fgdjtrade

Represents: Artists/Bands; DJs

Genres: Alternative; Dance; Electronic;
Experimental; House; Techno

Promoter / Management / Booking DJ
Agency.

Feed Your Head
Website: https://www.fyhpresents.com

Represents: Artists/Bands

Genres: Alternative; Electronic; Dance;
Indie

Management company founded in 2008.

Feraltone
Email: rene@feraltone.co.uk
Website: http://www.feraltone.co.uk

Represents: Artists/Bands

Genres: All types of music

Artist management, records, and consulting.

Ferocious Talent
Email: ferocioustalent@gmail.com
Website: https://www.ferocioustalent.com
Website: https://www.facebook.com/
ferocioustalentlondon/

Represents: Artists/Bands

Genres: All types of music

Artist service company offering artist management, music consultancy, music business development, agency and rights management, label services, and in-house production.

Finger Lickin' Management
67-69 Chalton Street
Somers Town
London
NW1 1HY
Email: info@fingerlickin.co.uk
Email: amie@fingerlickin.co.uk
Website: http://www.fingerlickinmanagement.co.uk
Website: https://soundcloud.com/fingerlickinmanagement

Represents: Artists/Bands

Genres: Dance; Electronic; Hip-Hop; Break Beat

World recognised booking and artist management agency, currently managing a number of award winning artists and labels.

Flat Cap Music
Email: mike@flatcapmusic.com
Website: https://uk.linkedin.com/company/flat-cap-music
Website: https://twitter.com/mikeflatcap

Represents: Artists/Bands

Genres: All types of music

Independent manager based in London.

Flat50
Email: info@flat50.co.uk
Website: http://www.flat50.co.uk
Website: https://www.youtube.com/user/pmj83hatl/videos

Represents: Artists/Bands

Genres: Pop; Rock; Rap

Artist representation, promotion, and management company based in London. Send demos or queries by email.

Flow State Music
Edinburgh
Email: kyle@flowstatemusic.co.uk
Website: https://flowstatemusic.co.uk
Website: https://www.facebook.com/flowstateedinburgh/

Represents: Artists/Bands; DJs

Genres: Alternative Dance; Electronic

Music company based in Edinburgh, offering Event Production; Artist & Tour Management; Live Music Promotion; Music Programming; Digital Communications (Social Media / Direct Marketing).

FP / Fantastic Plastic Music
Unit 6 Trident House
London
SE1 8QW
Email: info@fpmusic.org
Website: https://www.fpmusic.org
Website: https://www.facebook.com/fpmusicco

Represents: Artists/Bands

Genres: Alternative

Music company including record label, publishing, and management services.

Freaks R Us
Email: freaks@freaksrus.net
Website: https://www.facebook.com/freakartists
Website: https://twitter.com/freakartists

Represents: Artists/Bands

Genres: Alternative; Electronic; Experimental; Post Punk

Record label and management company.

Friends Vs Music Ltd
London
Email: pip@friendsvsmusic.com
Website: https://www.friendsvsmusic.com
Website: https://www.facebook.com/friendsvsmusic

Represents: Artists/Bands; Producers

Genres: All types of music

Artist and producer management company and music consultancy based in London. Approach via form on website.

From the Whitehouse
Email: bookings@fromthewhitehouse.com
Email: katie@fromthewhitehouse.com
Website: http://www.fromthewhitehouse.com
Website: https://www.facebook.com/fromtheWhiteHouse/

Represents: Artists/Bands

Genres: Electronic; Folk; Indie; Singer-Songwriter; World

An award-winning music management, artist development, booking and promotion agency, covering all aspects of strategic artist development for musicians.

Front Room Songs
Website: https://frontroomsongs.com
Website: https://twitter.com/Frontroomsongs

Represents: Artists/Bands

Genres: Folk; Pop; Roots; World

Provides artist and project management for a growing roster of emerging artists spanning the folk / roots / world and pop genres. Send query through online contact form with links to music online.

Fruition Music
Email: rod@fruitionmusic.co.uk
Website: https://www.fruitionmusic.co.uk
Website: https://www.facebook.com/FruitionArtists/

Represents: Artists/Bands

Genres: Dance; Indie

Offers artist management and music and media PR.

Future Agency
30 Bloomsbury Street
London
WC1B 3QJ
Email: hello@futureagency.com
Website: https://www.futureagency.com

Website: https://www.instagram.com/futureagencymgmt

Represents: Artists/Bands

Genres: Commercial; Mainstream

A forward-thinking talent representation and live events agency based in London.

Future Songs
London
Email: michael@futuresongs.co.uk
Website: https://www.facebook.com/futuresongspublishing
Website: https://soundcloud.com/future-songs

Represents: Artists/Bands; Producers; Songwriters; Sound Engineers

Genres: Pop; R&B; Singer-Songwriter

A music company specializing in management and music publishing. The company was founded in 2015 and represents a talented roster of clients which includes Grammy Nominated songwriters, producers and mix engineers.

Ganbei Records
Email: paul@ganbeirecords.com
Website: https://ganbeirecords.com
Website: https://www.facebook.com/ganbeirecords

Represents: Artists/Bands

Genres: Alternative; Folk; Post Punk; Psychedelic Rock

Record label and artist management company that aims to help musicians release and promote their music. Query through contact form on website.

Glow Artists
Brighton
Email: martha@glow-artists.com
Website: https://www.glow-artists.com
Website: https://twitter.com/glowartists_

Represents: Artists/Bands

Genres: Alternative; Indie; Jazz; Soul

Contact: Martha Cleary

Strives to help artists grow through day-to-day management, campaign planning and press and radio promotions.

Goo Music Management Ltd
Email: contact@goomusic.net
Website: https://www.goomusic.net
Website: https://www.facebook.com/goomusic

Represents: Artists/Bands

Genres: Alternative; Indie; Rock

Contact: Ben Kirby

Built from a background of gig promotion, festival production and artist liaison. Has trusting relationships with many industry contacts including record labels, publishers, booking agents and tour managers.

Graphite Media
5-6 Greenfield Crescent
Edgbaston
Birmingham
B15 3BE
Email: info@graphitemedia.net
Email: ben@graphitemedia.net
Website: https://www.graphitemedia.net
Website: https://twitter.com/Graphite1

Represents: Artists/Bands; DJs; Producers

Genres: Dance; Electronic

Contact: Ben Turner

A music management and brand services company, based between London and Los Angeles.

Guvnor Management
Email: info@guvnormanagement.co.uk
Website: https://www.guvnormanagement.co.uk
Website: https://www.facebook.com/GuvnorManagement/

Represents: Artists/Bands; Comedians; Other Entertainers; Tribute Acts

Genres: Pop; Rock

An Entertainments Agency established in 2006, covering all aspects of the entertainments business from, cabaret artists, tribute shows, function bands, comedians, sporting and after dinner speakers.

Hal Carter Organisation
41 Horsefair Green
Stony Stratford
Milton Keynes
Bucks
MK11 1JP
Email: artistes@halcarterorg.com
Website: https://www.halcarterorg.com
Website: https://www.facebook.com/halcarterorg/

Represents: Artists/Bands; Tribute Acts

Genres: All types of music

Management company based in Milton Keynes.

Hand in Hive Independent Records & Management
London
Email: contact@handinhive.com
Email: tristan@handinhive.com
Website: https://www.handinhive.com
Website: https://soundcloud.com/hand-in-hive

Represents: Artists/Bands

Genres: Indie; Pop; Rock

Independent music company, formed in 2014 by two friends with a shared love of music, specialising in records, management, publishing and sync.

Handshake Ltd.
2 Holly House
Mill Street,
Uppermill
Greater Manchester
OL3 6LZ
Fax: +44 (0) 1457 810052
Email: info@handshakegroup.com
Website: http://www.Handshakegroup.com
Website: https://www.facebook.com/handshakeltd/

Represents: Artists/Bands; Comedians; DJs; Tribute Acts; Variety Artists

Genres: Pop; Rock and Roll; Commercial

Contact: Stuart Littlewood

Artistes Representation, and Concert Promotion Company, touring shows and events in the UK.

Also offering certain productions on a worldwide basis.

Happy House Management & Marketing Services
Email: happyhousemanagement@gmail.com
Email: dannydeathdisco@googlemail.com
Website: http://happyhousemanagement.weebly.com
Website: https://www.facebook.com/happyhousemgmt

Represents: Artists/Bands

Genres: All types of music

Contact: Danny Watson

Management, marketing and product management company.

Harbourside Artist Management
Email: ben@harboursidemgmt.com
Website: https://harboursidemgmt.com
Website: https://www.facebook.com/Harboursidemgmt/

Represents: Artists/Bands

Genres: All types of music

An international management company with a heartbeat in the city of Bristol, UK. Whether you're an artist seeking management support or a partner looking to collaborate, don't hesitate to reach out by email.

Heard and Seen
Greens Court
West Street
Midhurst
West Sussex
GU29 9NQ
Email: enquiries@heardandseen.com
Website: http://www.heardandseen.com

Website: https://www.facebook.com/Heard-and-Seen-Ltd-197097010394361/

Represents: Artists/Bands

Genres: All types of music

Offers a range of services to artists, including management. See website for full details.

Heist or Hit
12 Hilton Street
Manchester
M1 1JF
Email: submissions@heistorhit.com
Email: team@heistorhit.com
Website: https://www.heistorhit.com
Website: https://www.facebook.com/heistorhit

Represents: Artists/Bands

Genres: Acoustic; Alternative; Indie

Management company based in Manchester. Send demos by email.

Holocene Management
Website: https://www.holocenemgmt.com
Website: https://www.instagram.com/holocenemanagement/

Represents: Artists/Bands

Genres: Electronic; Indie; Pop

Management company founded in November 2019. Also offers consultancy services.

Hope Management
Unit 4.16 The Paintworks
Bath Road
Bristol
BS4 3EH
Email: info@hopemanagement.co.uk
Website: http://www.hopemanagement.co.uk

Represents: Artists/Bands

Genres: Alternative; Dance

Management company based in Bristol, with US offices in Los Angeles.

Hot Gem

Glasgow
Email: sync@hotgem.co.uk
Website: http://www.hotgem.co.uk
Website: https://soundcloud.com/
hotgemtunes

Represents: Artists/Bands

Genres: Ambient; Dance; Electronic;
Experimental; Pop

Musician management and label based in
Glasgow. Accepts demos, but must have
difference / unique sound. No indie guitar
bands. Send demos by email as MP3
attachments, or via soundcloud.

On hiatus as at April 2023.

Hot House Music Ltd

33 Duke Street
Marylebone
London
W1U 1JY
Email: info@hot-house-music.com
Website: https://www.hot-house-music.com
Website: https://www.facebook.com/
HotHouseMusicLtd/

Represents: Film / TV Composers;
Supervisors

Genres: All types of music

Management company based in London,
representing film and TV composers / music
supervisors / score co-ordinators.

Hot Vox

London
Email: info@hotvox.co.uk
Website: https://hotvox.co.uk
Website: https://www.facebook.com/hotvox

Represents: Artists/Bands

Genres: All types of music

We work hard to create events that showcase
the talents of our acts across the full range of
genres, creating a great atmosphere for both
musician and fan alike.

We also specialise in management, video

production and work as consultants for
branding, advertising, TV and film.

House of Us

London
Email: us@houseofus.co.uk
Website: https://www.facebook.com/
houseofusmanagement/

Represents: Artists/Bands

Genres: Dance; House; Indie; Pop

London-based music management,
consultancy, and PR company.

HQ Familia

38 Charles Street
Leicester
LE1 1FB
Email: yasin@hqrecording.co.uk
Website: https://www.hqrecording.co.uk/hq-
familia/
Website: http://soundcloud.com/hqrecording

Represents: Artists/Bands

Genres: Electronic; Urban

Contact: Yasin El Ashrafi

Collective of like minded artists with
associated record label and recording studio.

Humans & Other Animals

Website: https://
humansandotheranimals.com
Website: https://instagram.com/
listentohumans

Represents: Artists/Bands

Genres: Indie; Rock; Folk; Electronic

We offer a range of services to help raise the
profile of independent recording artists and
record labels, from one-off consultancy and
advice sessions to strategic campaign and
label management. We work with artists and
labels to raise your profile. We only work
with those we believe can compete at the
highest level of the music industry. In other
words, we become strategic partners in your
musical journey.

Ignition Management
London
Website: https://www.ignition.co.uk
Website: https://twitter.com/
IgnitionMusicUK

Represents: Artists/Bands

Genres: Alternative; Indie; Pop; Rock

Management company with offices in London and LA. Approach via online contact form, including as many links to your social media as possible. Response not guaranteed.

Impact Artist Management
Website: http://impactartist.com/#artist-management-banner
Website: https://www.facebook.com/impactartistmanagement

Represents: Artists/Bands

Genres: All types of music

Our focus is on guiding the long-term career of our artists towards critical and commercial success by linking our clients' unique vision to satisfying and successful projects on a global scale.

Incendia Music
Email: Lulu@incendia-management.co.uk
Website: https://www.incendiamusic.co.uk
Website: https://soundcloud.com/incendia-music-management

Represents: Artists/Bands; Songwriters

Genres: Metal; Rock; Progressive; Experimental; Heavy

Contact: Lulu Davis

Artist Management, Publicity, and Consultancy services for Rock, Prog and Metal bands and artists.

Infinite Future Mgmt
Email: info@infinitefuture.co.uk
Website: https://infinitefuture.co.uk

Represents: Artists/Bands

Genres: Alternative Dance; Alternative Pop; Dance; Electronic; Pop

An artist management company with a clear and unflinching focus: to discover and nurture untapped musical talent, and to lead them to worldwide success.

Innate – Music Ltd
Email: nathan@soundvault.tv
Website: https://www.innate-music.com/

Represents: Artists/Bands

Genres: All types of music

Contact: Nathan Graves

Creative strategy, project management, marketing and media consultancy established in 2003.

Insomnia Music UK
Email: management@insomniamusic.co.uk
Website: http://insomniamusic.co.uk
Website: https://www.facebook.com/InsomniaMusicUK/

Represents: Artists/Bands

Genres: Commercial; Pop

Music management company specialising in pop and commercial.

Intune Addicts
Email: info@intuneaddicts.com
Website: https://www.intuneaddicts.com
Website: https://www.facebook.com/intuneaddicts

Represents: Artists/Bands

Genres: All types of music

Contact: Mark Smutz Smith

A cutting-edge artistic development company. Provides handpicked musicians with holistic and forward-thinking management services.

Involved Management
London
Email: info@involvedmanagement.com
Website: https://involvedmanagement.com

Represents: Artists/Bands

Genres: Chill; Electronic; House; Trance;
Progressive House

Management company with offices in
London and Los Angeles.

IQ Artist Management
1 Northumberland Avenue
Trafalgar Square
London
WC2N 5BW
Email: contact@iqmgmnt.com
Email: info@iqmgmnt.com
Website: https://iqmgmnt.com

Represents: Artists/Bands

Genres: All types of music

Management company based in London.
Send streaming links (soundcloud or similar)
through online form. Strongly advises
against sending physical media.

JBLS Management
Unit 13, The Tay Building
2A Wrentham Avenue
London
NW10 3HA
Email: louise@jblsmanagement.com
Email: jo@jblsmanagement.com
Website: http://www.jblsmanagement.com
Website: https://www.facebook.com/
JBLSManagement/

Represents: Artists/Bands; Producers;
Songwriters

Genres: Electronic; Alternative; Pop; Singer-
Songwriter

Contact: Louise Smith

London management company representing
artists, producers, remixers, mixers, and
writers.

Jelli Records
Email: jellirecords@yahoo.co.uk
Website: https://www.jelli-records.com
Website: https://www.facebook.com/Jelli.
Records/

Represents: Artists/Bands

Genres: Acoustic; Folk; Roots

Record label and entertainment agency
offering stage management, open mic nights
and songwriter evenings, and consultancy
services, as well as hosting two radio shows
every weeks.

Jude Street Management
Email: info@judestreet.com
Email: paul@judest.com
Website: https://judestreet.com
Website: https://twitter.com/judestreetmusic

Represents: Artists/Bands; Film / TV
Composers; Producers

Genres: Alternative; Pop; Indie; Classical

Contact: Paul Devaney

Music services and management company
based in East London and established in
2005. Provides professional representation
for bands, artists, producers and
composers/arrangers in the fields of
Alt/Pop/Indie, Classical, Games, Film and
TV. Send query by email and follow up with
demos upon request.

Kaleidoscope
3-5 Stepney Bank
Newcastle upon Tyne
NE1 2PW
Email: info@kaleidoscope-music.co.uk
Website: https://www.kaleidoscope-
music.co.uk
Website: https://www.facebook.com/
KaleidoscopeUK/

Represents: Artists/Bands

Genres: All types of music

An artist management company and record
label established in 2015 and based in
Newcastle upon Tyne, UK. Established a
sister company in Bangkok, Thailand, in
2021.

Karma Artists Music LLP
Unit 31, Tileyard Studios
Tileyard Road
Kings Cross
London
N7 9AH
Email: info@karmaartists.co.uk

Website: https://www.karmaartists.co.uk
Website: https://www.facebook.com/
karmaartistsuk

Represents: Artists/Bands; Producers;
Songwriters

Genres: All types of music

Contact: Jordan Jay; Ross Gautreau; Jess
Miller

Multi-faceted entertainment company based
in London, representing a roster with
combined sales of over 400 million units.

Key Music Management
Suite 403, Bonded Warehouse
18 Lower Byrom Street
Manchester
M3 4AP
Email: contact@kmmltd.com
Email: contact@keymusicmanagement.com
Website: https://www.
keymusicmanagement.com
Website: https://www.facebook.com/
keymusicmanagement

Represents: Artists/Bands

Genres: Alternative

Contact: Richard Jones; Ryan Terpstra; Will
Hanson; Marcus Jones

Management company based in Manchester.

KMY (Keep Me Young)
Website: https://www.keepmeyoung.uk
Website: https://www.instagram.com/
KeepMeYoungUK/

Represents: Artists/Bands

Genres: Pop

Art first collective.

KRMB Management & Consultancy
Metropolis Studios
70 Chiswick High Road
London
W4 1SY
Email: kreynolds@krmbmanagement.com
Website: https://www.krmbmanagement.com

Website: https://www.facebook.com/
krmbmanagement

Represents: Artists/Bands

Genres: All types of music

Contact: Kevin Reynolds

Management and consultancy company
offering artist development, creative
direction, talent management, corporate
entertainment, and consultancy.

Laissez Faire Club
London
Email: jeremy@laissezfaireclub.com
Website: https://laissezfaireclub.tumblr.com
Website: https://www.facebook.com/jilloyd

Represents: Artists/Bands

Genres: All types of music

Contact: Jeremy Lloyd

Originally a live promotions company, now
focuses solely on artist management.

Lazy Daze
Email: studio@lazydaze.co.uk
Website: http://www.lazydaze.co.uk
Website: https://www.facebook.com/
LazyDazeRecs

Represents: Artists/Bands

Genres: Indie; Rock; Rock and Roll

Provide music management and label
services for up and coming bands.

Legacy Records
Cambridge
Email: jeremy@legacyrecords.uk
Email: info@legacyrecords.uk
Website: https://www.legacyrecords.uk
Website: https://www.facebook.com/
OfficialLegacyRecords

Represents: Artists/Bands

Genres: All types of music

With over 20 years industry experience we
can help you take the next step towards your
goal, with direct contacts to labels,

producers, song writers and more our team can not only help you but we can put you with the right people for you.

Leodis Talent
Website: https://www.leodistalent.com
Website: https://instagram.com/leodistalent/

Represents: Artists/Bands

Genres: All types of music

We are a talent management company that represents an exciting mix of performers and creative clients, who work across all aspects of the entertainment industries. We pride ourselves on always going the extra mile, to work alongside our clients and partners to forge long lasting careers and relationships.

Line-Up pmc
10 Matthew Close
Newcastle upon Tyne
NE6 1XD
Email: chrismurtagh@line-up.co.uk
Website: http://www.line-up.co.uk

Represents: Artists/Bands

Genres: World

Contact: Chris Murtagh

Promotions and marketing consultancy company with over 25 years of experience specialising in live arts performance, ethnic and World Music. May not necessarily offer representation, but may pass your demo on to relevant contacts if potential is seen.

Liquid Management
Email: david@liquidmanagement.net
Email: steve@Liquidmanagement.net
Website: https://www.musicglue.com/liquidmanagement
Website: https://twitter.com/liquidmgmnt

Represents: Artists/Bands; DJs; Producers

Genres: All types of music

Contact: David Manders; Steve Dix

Management company with 20 years of managing artists through all levels of the music industry.

Lonewolf Talent Management
Email: rob@theboywiththelionhead.co.uk
Website: https://www.lonewolftalentmanagement.com
Website: https://www.facebook.com/lonewolftalent

Represents: Artists/Bands

Genres: Alternative; Ambient; Indie; Post Punk; Punk; Punk Rock

An artist management company focused on developing and supporting new and emerging artists to achieve their goals and help them through the various stages of their career in the music industry. Contact through form on website. No reply unless interested.

The Lost Atlantis Records
Email: Thelostatlantisrecords@gmail.com
Website: https://www.thelostatlantisrecords.com
Website: https://twitter.com/crystalchild01

Genres: Hip-Hop; House; Rap; Soul; Techno; Urban

Contact: Charlene Jones

Artist development and management. Send query by email.

Lucky House Management
Bristol
Email: luckyhousemanagement@gmail.com
Website: https://www.luckyhousemanagement.com/
Website: https://www.facebook.com/luckyhousemanagement

Represents: Artists/Bands

Genres: Grime; Hip-Hop; Rap; Soul; Urban

Contact: Jade Fearon

Personalised artist management, booking and casting agency.

Lucky Number Music Limited
Unit 1.6, Islington Studios
Marlborough Rd
London
N19 4NF
Email: contact@luckynumbermusic.com

Website: https://www.
luckynumbermusic.com/
Website: https://www.facebook.com/
luckynumbermusic/

Represents: Artists/Bands

Genres: Indie; Pop; Electronic

Provide management and producer services, and also operate a record label.

Lyricom
Website: https://lyricom.co.uk

Represents: Artists/Bands; Producers; Songwriters

Genres: Indie; Singer-Songwriter; Urban

Managing a roster that spans both independent and major label Recording Artists, Digital Talents, Producers and Writers.

Offering expertise across Production, Distribution, Digital, Promotion, Brand & Franchise Extensions, Live, Merch, Team Architecture and Administration.

MaDa Music Entertainment
Email: press@madamusic.com
Website: https://madamusic.com
Website: https://twitter.com/madamusicent

Represents: Artists/Bands; Producers

Genres: All types of music

Multi divisional entertainment company specialising in Artist and Producer Management, Events, PR and Consultancy. Particularly interested in pop, indie, and rock, but will consider most genres.

Major Labl
Website: https://www.majorlabl.com
Website: https://www.facebook.com/
MajorLabl/

Represents: Artists/Bands

Genres: All types of music

Offers marketing and management services for unsigned and independent artists. Apply through online form.

Manana Music Management
Email: lyle@mananamusicmanagement.com
Email: nathan@
mananamusicmanagement.com
Website: https://www.
mananamusicmanagement.com
Website: https://www.facebook.com/
mananamusicmgmt

Represents: Artists/Bands

Genres: All types of music

Music management service.

Manners McDade Artist Management
3rd floor, 12 Greenhill Rents
London
EC1M 6BN
Email: submissions@mannersmcdade.co.uk
Email: info@mannersmcdade.co.uk
Website: http://mannersmcdade.co.uk
Website: https://www.facebook.com/
mannersmcdademusic/

Represents: Film / TV Composers

Genres: All types of music

Management company based in London, representing composers for film and TV. Send submissions by email. Response only if interested.

MBM (Music Business Management Ltd)
Labrican
Healey Dell Nature Reserve
Rochdale
OL12 6BG
Email: anne@mbmcorporate.co.uk
Email: phil@mbmcorporate.co.uk
Website: https://www.mbmcorporate.co.uk
Website: https://www.facebook.com/
MBMCorporate

Represents: Artists/Bands; DJs; Tribute Acts

Genres: All types of music

Contact: Anne Barrett; Phil Barrett

Entertainment consultancy and artiste management. Specialises in Tributes and Tribite shows.

Memphia Music Management
Bristol
Email: jp@memphia.com
Website: https://www.memphia.com
Website: https://www.facebook.com/
MemphiaMM/

Represents: Artists/Bands

Genres: Indie; Rock

Management company based in Bristol.
Query by email or via contact us page on
website.

Miller Music Management
Fax: +44 (0) 20 8964 4965
Email: info@m-music-m.com
Website: http://www.m-music-m.com

Represents: Artists/Bands

Genres: Indie; Rock; Singer-Songwriter

Contact: Carrie Hustler

Management company with offices in
London and Los Angeles.

MJM Agency
Email: demos@mjmagency.co.uk
Email: info@mjmagency.co.uk
Website: http://www.mjmagency.co.uk

Represents: Artists/Bands; DJs; Other
Entertainers

Genres: All types of music

Contact: Mike Jones

Management agency run on a part-time
basis. Handles musical entertainers and
performing acts. Send demos and/or band
details by email.

Moksha Management
PO Box 102
London
E15 2HH
Email: info@moksha.co.uk
Website: https://www.moksha.co.uk
Website: https://twitter.com/mokshamgt

Represents: Artists/Bands

Genres: Alternative Electronic Fusion;
Contemporary; Dance

Demos preferred as streaming weblinks.

Morningstar
Email: enquiries@morningstarpro.co.uk
Email: artists@morningstarpro.co.uk
Website: https://www.morningstarpro.co.uk
Website: https://www.facebook.com/
Mstarliveevents

Represents: Artists/Bands

Genres: Indie; Rock

Management agency based on the key values
of honesty and a more personal touch with
everyone they choose to represent.

Mother Artist Management
Email: info@motherartists.com
Website: https://www.motherartists.com
Website: https://www.facebook.com/
motherartistsltd/

Represents: Artists/Bands

Genres: All types of music

Artist management and live music agency.

Music by Design
48 Home Hill
Hextable
Kent
BR8 7RR
Email: info@musicbydesign.co.uk
Website: http://www.musicbydesign.co.uk

Represents: Artists/Bands

Genres: All types of music

"Innovative out of the box thinkers required.
Send us your idea, receive a song. Let's
create something good together".

Music Media Events
Website: https://www.
musicmediaevents.com
Website: https://twitter.com/musicmediasean

Represents: Artists/Bands

Genres: Pop; Acoustic; Alternative; Folk

We have booked artists in to arenas, clubs, art centres, theatres, colleges, stadiums, festivals, Christmas switch-ons, store openings, charity, private and corporate events.

N.O.W. Music Management
1st Floor
25 Commercial Street
Brighouse
HD6 1AF
Email: info@now-music.com
Website: https://www.now-music.com

Represents: Artists/Bands; Tribute Acts

Genres: Pop; Rock

A management company based in Brighouse, West Yorkshire, with strong connections in Europe and with a small independent record company.

Nettwerk Management UK
15 Adeline Place, Ground Floor
London
WC1B 3AJ
Fax: +44 (0) 20 7456 9501
Website: https://nettwerk.com
Website: https://www.facebook.com/nettwerkmusicgroup

Represents: Artists/Bands

Genres: All types of music

Management company headquartered in Vancouver, with offices in London, Hamburg, LA, and New York.

New Champion Management
Oh Yeah Centre
Belfast
BT1 2LG
Email: newchampionmanagement@gmail.com
Website: https://www.facebook.com/newchampionmanagement/
Website: https://www.instagram.com/newchampionmanagement/

Represents: Artists/Bands

Genres: Electronic; Folk; Indie; Pop; Punk

Provides artist management, PR and music consultancy services. Based in Northern Ireland.

NewLevel Management
Oxford
Email: newlevelmgmt@gmail.com
Website: https://www.facebook.com/NewLevelMgmt
Website: https://twitter.com/NewLevelMgmt

Represents: Artists/Bands

Genres: All types of music

Music management company based in Oxford. Offers artist management, tour booking, professional guidance, tour management, PR, label mailouts, release campaign co-ordination, and contract negotiation.

Night Owl Music Promotions & Management
Glasgow
Website: https://juvan834.wixsite.com/nightowlmusicpromos
Website: https://linktr.ee/nightowlmusicpromos

Represents: Artists/Bands

Genres: Alternative; Indie; Rock

We manage from the "heart" and with a "music first" attitude! We feel too many managers think about "money first" and forget about the MUSIC because they are too obsessed in making as much money from the band as they possibly can! We manage for the love and joy of music! We always work hard for the bands, with a duty of self care and an absolute determination to see you succeed!

No Half Measures Ltd
1st Floor
5 Eagle Street
Glasgow
G4 9XA
Email: info@nohalfmeasures.com
Website: https://nohalfmeasures.com/
Website: https://www.facebook.com/nohalfmeasures

Represents: Artists/Bands

Genres: All types of music

A company registered in Scotland, U.K. and based in Glasgow. The firm has a general structure based on its artist management, music publishing, record label and photography divisions. Works with a diverse range of artists and operates in huge variety of areas. These include artist management; intellectual property and rights management; music composition and publishing; audio and audio visual recording, mixing, and mastering; design, manufacturing, distribution and sale of audio and audio visual products, merchandise, clothing, apparel, and printed products; photography; marketing, promotion and advertising of these goods; sponsorship and branding; live entertainment performances, presentations and touring; event logistics, consultancy, management and promotion; sale of tickets; training and education.

Northern Music Co. Ltd
Piazza Offices, Salts Mill
Victoria Road
Saltaire, Shipley
West Yorkshire
BD18 3LA
Fax: +44 (0) 1274 593546
Email: demos@northernmusic.co.uk
Email: info@northernmusic.co.uk
Website: https://www.northernmusic.co.uk
Website: https://www.facebook.com/NMCLtd

Represents: Artists/Bands

Genres: Metal; Rock

Contact: Andy Farrow

Send query by email with your band/act's name in the subject line, with details on what you are looking for; links to stream your music; a brief bio of your band/act; links to your website / social media / videos; and any details of existing industry partners / releases / live dates, etc.

Nowhere Talent
Email: andy@nowheretalent.com
Website: https://facebook.com/nowheretalent
Website: https://twitter.com/nowheretalent

Represents: Artists/Bands

Genres: All types of music

Exclusive talent management, offering services in consulting, development, media, and touring.

Off the Chart Promotions
Email: tim@offthechart.co.uk
Website: https://www.offthechart.co.uk
Website: https://www.facebook.com/offthechartmanagement

Represents: Artists/Bands

Genres: Folk; Pop; Rock; Indie; Singer-Songwriter

Management company based in Cambridge. Works with artists from the East of England and London.

One Fifteen
A&R
1 Globe House
Middle Lane Mews
London
N8 8PN
Email: enquiry@onefifteen.com
Website: https://www.onefifteen.com

Represents: Artists/Bands

Genres: All types of music

Prefers links to your SoundCloud, Spotify, or YouTube page. If you insist on sending MP3s, send no more than three. Include short bio and photo. Aims to listen to everything, but response not guaranteed if not interested.

141a Management
Email: admin@art19.co.uk
Website: https://www.141amanagement.co.uk
Website: https://www.facebook.com/141amanagementcompany/?fref=ts

Represents: Artists/Bands

Genres: All types of music

Music management company representing artists from all music genres.

140dB Management Limited
London
Email: ros@140db.co.uk
Website: https://www.biglifemanagement.com/140db
Website: https://www.facebook.com/140dBManagement/

Represents: Artists/Bands; Producers

Genres: All types of music

Contact: Ros Earls

Management company based in London. Represents artists and producers.

Opre Roma
Email: info@opreroma.co.uk
Website: https://opreroma.co.uk
Website: https://www.facebook.com/OpreRomaSounds

Represents: Artists/Bands

Genres: Acoustic; Americana; Folk; Guitar based; Indie

Contact: Nayfe Slusjan

Aims to help artists build long-term stability into their music careers, with 24/7 access to business management services and global representation. Send links to your music through online submission form.

Orean Music Ltd
Email: adrian@oreanmusic.com
Email: ah@oreanmusic.com
Website: https://oreanmusic.com
Website: https://www.facebook.com/oreanmusic/

Represents: Artists/Bands

Genres: Alternative; Dance; Electronic; Indie; Pop

Artist management company dedicated to helping independent artists grow and succeed in the music industry.

Ornadel Management
Email: info@ornadel.com
Email: guy@ornadel.com
Website: https://ornadel.com
Website: https://www.facebook.com/OrnadelMGM/

Represents: Artists/Bands; DJs

Genres: Dance

Contact: Guy Ornadel

Mainly works with DJs.

Parade Music
Email: leonwright@parademusic.co
Website: https://www.parademusic.co/
Website: http://www.instagram.com/parademusic.co

Represents: Artists/Bands

Genres: Electronic; Pop; Soul

Management company based in the UK.

Park Promotions
PO Box 651
Oxford
OX2 9RB
Email: parkoffice@parkrecords.com
Website: https://parkrecords.com
Website: https://www.facebook.com/Park-Promotions-141933172641365/

Represents: Artists/Bands

Genres: Folk; Singer-Songwriter; Roots; Acoustic; Folk Rock

Music company including record label and management and PR services.

Perfect Havoc Ltd
Email: info@perfecthavoc.com
Website: https://perfecthavoc.com
Website: https://www.facebook.com/perfecthavocmusic/

Represents: Artists/Bands

Genres: Dance; Disco; House

London-based music entertainment management, record label, and events.

Submit demos as soundcloud links using online form on website.

Petty Music Management
Email: hello@pettymanagement.com
Website: https://pettymanagement.com

Represents: Artists/Bands

Genres: All types of music

UK management company.

Phono Sounds UK
Email: phonosounds@gmail.com
Website: https://phono.uk/
Website: https://www.facebook.com/phonosounds

Represents: Artists/Bands

Genres: Electronic; Pop; House; Trance; Dance

Independent minded label, also providing publishing, management, and distribution. Send demos by email.

Pierce Entertainment
Pierce House
London Apollo Complex
Queen Caroline Street
London
W6 9QH
Email: info@pierce-entertainment.com
Website: https://www.pierce-entertainment.com
Website: https://www.facebook.com/PierceEnt/

Represents: Producers; Sound Engineers

Genres: Pop; R&B

Management company based in London, home to award winning producers and engineers.

Pillar Artists
Newcastle upon Tyne
Email: pillar.artists@gmail.com
Website: https://www.musicglue.com/pillar-artists
Website: https://facebook.com/PillarArtists

Represents: Artists/Bands

Genres: Acoustic; Alternative; Guitar based; Indie

Management agency based in Newcastle Upon Tyne. Also involved with independent gig promotion, PR, and booking.

PMS Music Management
122 London Road
Rayleigh
Essex
SS6 9BN
Fax: +44 (0) 1268 784807
Email: pmsmusicmgt@yahoo.co.uk
Website: https://pmsmusicmanagement.weebly.com

Represents: Artists/Bands; Tribute Acts

Genres: All types of music

Contact: Peter Scott

Send demo by post or email. MP3 preferred but not essential. Currently managing Indie/pop/rock but open to all genres. 'If I like it, I can represent it!' Welcomes all submissions in the form of CD, MP3 or video on DVD together with a biography and links to your Website, and any other relevant links. Particularly keen to work with unsigned bands.

Program Music, Ltd
197 Queen's Crescent
London
NW5 4DS
Email: info@program-music.co.uk
Website: https://www.program-music.co.uk
Website: https://www.facebook.com/programproducts

Represents: Artists/Bands; DJs

Genres: All types of music

Specialises in the production of immersive video domes and 3D experiences, large-scale audiovisual work and interactive installations, and voice-activated applications.

Prolifica Management
London
Email: info@prolifica.co.uk
Website: http://www.
prolificamanagement.co.uk
Website: https://www.instagram.com/
prolificamanagement/

Represents: Artists/Bands

Genres: All types of music

London-based Music Management and
Production Company.

Psycho Management Company
Email: patrick@psycho.co.uk
Website: https://www.psycho.co.uk/
Website: https://twitter.com/psychomanco

Represents: Artists/Bands; Comedians; DJs;
Other Entertainers; Tribute Acts

Genres: All types of music

Management company representing circus
acts, entertainment acts, lookalikes, music
acts, name acts, and tribute acts.

Push Music Management
London
Email: info@pushmusicmanagement.com
Website: https://pushmusicmanagement.com
Website: https://twitter.com/pushmusicmgmt

Represents: Artists/Bands

Genres: All types of music

Management company based in London.

Quest Management
London
Email: quest@maverick.com
Website: http://www.quest-management.com
Website: https://www.instagram.com/
questartistmgmt/

Represents: Artists/Bands

Genres: All types of music

A collective of experienced management
executives with offices in London, Los
Angeles, and Milan, renowned for

innovations in creating lasting revenue
strategies for artists.

Radius Music Ltd
Email: info@radiusmusic.co.uk
Website: https://www.radiusmusic.co.uk
Website: https://www.facebook.com/
radiusmusic

Represents: Artists/Bands; Producers;
Songwriters

Genres: All types of music

UK based music industry management
representing Songwriters and Producers.
Send SoundCloud / DISCO / Spotify links.
No response unless interested.

Raw Power Management
London
Website: https://rawpowermanagement.com/
Website: https://www.facebook.com/
rawpowermanagement

Represents: Artists/Bands

Genres: Punk Rock; Alternative; Metal;
Rock

Punk rock management company with
offices in London and Los Angeles.

Reaction Management
Email: jay.burnett@reaction-
management.com
Email: jedd.lefthander@reaction-
management.com
Website: https://www.reaction-
management.com
Website: https://www.facebook.com/
ReactionManagement

Genres: Alternative; Guitar based; Indie;
Metal; Pop Punk; Rock; Singer-Songwriter

Joining the roster isn't a fast track to success
but what we will do will set you up for a
professional career in music. There are no
contracts and you can stay with us for as
long or short a period of time as you feel
necessary. We have great contacts across the
industry and have built up solid relationships
with bookers, promoters, venues, PR and

media not only in the UK, but across the globe.

Real Media Music
Email: info@realmediamusic.co.uk
Website: https://www.realmediamusic.co.uk
Website: https://www.facebook.com/RealMediaMusic

Represents: Artists/Bands

Genres: All types of music

International artist booking and management.

Reckless Yes
Email: pete@recklessyes.com
Email: sarah@recklessyes.com
Website: https://recklessyes.com/artist-management/
Website: https://www.facebook.com/RecklessYes/

Represents: Artists/Bands

Genres: Acoustic; Alternative; Guitar based; Indie

Contact: Pete; Sarah

Independent record label, management and live music agency. Closed to submissions as at July 2022.

Red Afternoon Music
Email: info@redafternoonmusic.co.uk
Email: lewis@redafternoonmusic.co.uk
Website: https://www.redafternoonmusic.co.uk
Website: https://www.facebook.com/RedAfternoonMusic/

Represents: Artists/Bands

Genres: All types of music

Contact: Lewis Forrest

An Independent Record Company based in Central Scotland and London, UK. Provides label services, distribution, music publishing, specialist consultancy, artist development, artist management and live/ touring services. All genres accepted, but with a particular background in indie/ alternative, pop,

EDM/house, Americana, country, jazz and R&B.

Revolt Artist Management
Email: demos@revoltartists.com
Website: https://www.revoltartists.com

Represents: Artists/Bands; Film / TV Composers; Lyricists; Producers; Songwriters; Studio Musicians; Studio Vocalists

Genres: Emo; Garage; Guitar based; Hardcore; Indie; Metal; Nostalgia; Pop; Punk; Rock; Rock and Roll; Singer-Songwriter; Surf

Contact: Lisa Mckeown

Artist Management and Development company based in the UK, providing exclusive worldwide representation to musicians. We offer services in artist management, social media management and artist development.

We've worked with 80's legend 'Tiffany', known for the 1987 Billboard #1 'I Think We're Alone Now', as well as 'Cellar Door Moon Crow', 'The Last Internationale', 'GUN', 'The Graveltones' and 'Silverkord' (just to name a few!)

Our artists have played Download Festival, Lollapalooza, Hellfest, Nova Rock, BST Hyde Park, Venoge Festival, Rock Werchter, Pinkpop Festival, Let's Rock 80's Festival, Forever Young Festival, Impact Festival.

Our artists have supported KISS, Rage Against The Machine, Deep Purple, The Picturebooks, Skindred.

Our artists have had their music featured in Umbrella Academy, TED, The Tonight Show Featuring Jimmy Fallon, The Masked Singer, McDonald's adverts.

Our artists have made TV appearances across the world including I'm a Celebrity Get Me Out of Here!, Strictly Come Dancing: It Takes Two, Lorraine, Loose Women, Good Morning Britain, This Morning, The Morning Show, Celebrity Boot Camp, Wogan.

Please send your music and social links by email.

Rhythmic Records Management and Production

Email: info@rhythmic-records.co.uk
Website: https://www.rhythmic-records.co.uk
Website: https://www.facebook.com/rhythmicrecordsuk

Represents: Artists/Bands

Genres: Dance; Hip-Hop; House; Pop

Contact: Zac Bikhazi

Independent record label and management company based in London. Submit query with links to music online through form on website or by email.

Rock Artist Management (RAM)

Email: colinrockartistmgmt@aol.com
Email: bandmgmt@aol.com
Website: http://www.rockartistmanagement.com
Website: https://www.facebook.com/RAMRockArtistManagement/

Represents: Artists/Bands

Genres: Classic Rock; Blues; Pop; Rock

Contact: Peter Barton; Colin Black; Peter Hughes

Management company formed in the late eighties, specialising in retro rock, blues, and pop.

Rock People Management (RPM)

Email: terri@rockpeoplemanagement.com
Email: heidi@rockpeoplemanagement.com
Website: https://www.rockpeoplemanagement.com
Website: https://www.facebook.com/rockpeoplemanagement/

Represents: Artists/Bands

Genres: Blues; Rock

Contact: Terri Chapman; Heidi Kerr

With almost 14 years of experience in the music industry and a hands on approach, we can offer a wealth of knowledge, skills and opportunities to todays artists and bands.

Over those 14 years we have amassed a wealth of invaluable industry contacts from Radio to Press, Festivals to Merch Design and everything in between. We take immense pride and care in what we do, and always put your needs and requirements first.

Get in touch today to see how we can help you.

Rockstar Management

Email: hello@rockstar.management
Website: http://www.rockstar.management
Website: https://twitter.com/RockstarMGMT

Represents: Artists/Bands

Genres: All types of music

As an artist-centric, full-service management firm, we offer always-on support to new talent and established stars alike. We build careers from the ground up, engaging with the best in the business to empower the full scope of our clients' creative vision, amplifying their art to a global audience.

Rosier Artist Management (RAM)

Hillgrove House Winbrook
Bewdley
DY12 2BA
Website: https://twitter.com/steverosier
Website: https://suite.endole.co.uk/insight/company/13784719-rosier-artist-management-ltd

Represents: Artists/Bands

Genres: Americana; Rock

Contact: Steve Rosier

UK manager focusing on Rock and Americana.

Roundface Music Management
Scotland
Email: george@roundfacemusic.com
Website: https://www.roundfacemusic.com
Website: https://www.facebook.com/
RFmusicmanagement/

Represents: Artists/Bands

Genres: All types of music

Contact: George Murray

Music management company based in Scotland.

Royal Artists Management
Email: info@royalartists.co
Website: https://www.facebook.com/
royalartistsco
Website: https://twitter.com/royalartistsco

Represents: Artists/Bands

Genres: Alternative; Indie; Punk

Artist management and consultancy established in 2022.

Run the Sound
Manchester
Website: https://www.runthesound.com/
Website: https://www.instagram.com/
runthesoundmgmt/

Represents: Artists/Bands

Genres: Commercial; Hip-Hop; Pop; Rap

Contact: Zak Akram

A full-service entertainment company, based in the heart of Manchester inclusive of artist and management, label, publishing, touring, film / TV and new ventures. Provides aspiring stars with the opportunities and support they need to bring their talents directly into the spotlight. Also offers consultancy services.

Saga Entertainment
35 Berkeley Square
Mayfair
London
W1J 5BF

Email: info@sagaentertainment.tv
Website: https://www.sagaentertainment.tv
Website: http://www.facebook.com/
SagaMusicUK

Represents: Artists/Bands

Genres: Electronic; Pop; Rock

Operates a production company, publishing house and record label with offices in London, England. Specialising in music management, artist development and label services.

Sarah Lipman Management Ltd
Website: https://sarahlipmanmgmt.com
Website: https://www.facebook.com/
sarahlipmanmgmt

Represents: Artists/Bands

Genres: Electronic; Hip-Hop; Pop; Alternative Pop; Singer-Songwriter

Management company based in London. Contact via online form on website.

SAS Entertainment
Email: serena@sas-ents.com
Email: steve@sas-ents.com
Website: https://www.sas-ents.com
Website: https://www.facebook.com/
SASbackstage

Represents: Artists/Bands

Genres: Americana; Dance; Indie; Pop; Rock

Contact: Steve Hughes; Serena Catapano

Offers Artist Management, Tour Management, Music Consultancy, and Event / Festival Booking.

Saviour Management
London
Email: james@svrmgmt.com
Email: designs@svrmgmt.com
Website: https://www.svrmgmt.com
Website: https://www.facebook.com/
saviourmanagement

Represents: Artists/Bands

Genres: Alternative; Metal; Pop Punk

Contact: James Illsley; Jay Harris

Management company based in London.
Send query via form on website.

SB Management
Email: info@sb-management.com
Website: https://www.sb-management.com/
Website: https://twitter.com/sbmanagement

Represents: Artists/Bands; Producers;
Songwriters

Genres: All types of music

Artist, writer, and producer management.

Second Sun Management
Bristol
Email: enquiries@
secondsunmanagement.co.uk
Website: https://www.instagram.com/
secondsunmgmt/
Website: https://linktr.ee/secondsunmgmt

Represents: Artists/Bands

Genres: All types of music

Management company based in Bristol.

September Management (UK)
London
Email: info@sept.com
Website: https://sept.com

Represents: Artists/Bands; Producers; Sound
Engineers

Genres: All types of music

Represents a roster of internationally
renowned recording artists, producers and
mix engineers who have collectively
amassed 44 Grammys, 12 Brit Awards, 2
Oscars, 2 Golden Globes and sold over 100
million albums worldwide. The company has
offices in London, New York and Los
Angeles.

Serious
Pill Box
Unit 503

115 Coventry Road
London
E2 6GG
Website: https://serious.org.uk
Website: https://www.facebook.com/
seriouslivemusic

Represents: Artists/Bands

Genres: Jazz; World; Contemporary

Management company based in London
producing jazz, international, and
contemporary music, and offering
management, music publishing and the
production of concerts, tours and special
events.

74 Promotions
Brighton
Email: andy@74promotions.com
Website: http://www.74promotions.com
Website: https://www.facebook.com/74-
Promotions-181204548583646/

Represents: Artists/Bands

Genres: All types of music

Contact: Andy Hollis

Management company based in Brighton.

SGM Music Group Ltd
Unit 4, Forest Industrial Park,
Crosbie Grove
Kidderminster
Worcestershire
DY11 7FX
Email: info@sgmmusicgroup.com
Website: https://www.sgmmusicgroup.com
Website: https://www.facebook.com/
sgmmusicgroup/

Represents: Artists/Bands

Genres: Pop; Rock

Contact: Scott Garrett

Over 20 years experience working in the
music industry, primarily in the areas of live
event production, management, record label
services, and education.

SGO Ltd
Website: https://www.sgomusic.com
Website: https://www.facebook.com/
SGOMusic

Represents: Artists/Bands

Genres: All types of music

Offers music publishing, rights management, and label services.

Shaw Thing Management
20 Coverdale Road
London
N11 3FG
Email: info@shawthingmanagement.com
Website: https://www.
shawthingmanagement.com
Website: https://www.facebook.com/profile.
php?id=100067377485649

Represents: Artists/Bands

Genres: Pop

Management company based in London.
Send submissions and enquiries by email.

Sidewinder Management Ltd
Email: sdw@sidewindermgmt.com
Website: http://www.sidewindermgmt.com

Represents: Artists/Bands

Genres: All types of music

Contact: Simon Watson

An Artist management company with over thirty years experience managing a broad range of bands and solo artists.

Silverword Music Group
Website: https://www.silverword.co.uk

Represents: Artists/Bands

Genres: Urban; Dance; Pop; Rock; Jazz; Soul; Classical; Country; Gospel; R&B

Part of music group incorporating record label, promotion, publishing, distribution, etc.

Siren Artist Management (UK)
Email: ace@sirenmanagement.com
Email: adam@sirenmanagement.com
Website: https://www.sirenmanagement.com
Website: https://www.facebook.com/profile.
php?id=100063474578473

Represents: Artists/Bands

Genres: Alternative; Rock

UK office of US management company based in California.

sm-mgmt
Liverpool
Website: https://twitter.com/smmmgmt
Website: https://www.instagram.com/
smmmgmt

Represents: Artists/Bands

Genres: All types of music

Management company based in Liverpool.

Smashing Buttons
Belfast
Northern Ireland
Email: hadouken@smashingbuttons.com
Email: onboard@smashingbuttons.com
Website: https://smashingbuttons.com
Website: https://www.facebook.com/
SmashingButtonsLtd

Represents: Artists/Bands

Genres: Dance; Hip-Hop; Jazz; Pop; Rock

Music production, management, and events company based in Belfast.

Solar Management
Unit 10 Union Wharf
23 Wenlock Road
London
N1 7SB
Email: info@solarmanagement.co.uk
Website: https://www.
solarmanagement.co.uk
Website: https://www.facebook.com/
solarmanagement/

Represents: Artists/Bands; Producers

Genres: All types of music

Eexperience in producer and artist development, recording, touring, budgeting and all producer and artist contracts.

Sounds Like A Hit Ltd
Email: info@soundslikeahit.com
Website: http://www.slahit.com

Represents: Artists/Bands

Genres: Pop; Dance; Country

Contact: Steve Crosby

Has previously worked with artists such as Steps, Dixie Chicks, and Shania Twain.

Steady Management
London
Website: https://www.instagram.com/steadymgmt
Website: https://www.linkedin.com/company/steady-management/

Represents: Artists/Bands

Genres: Hip-Hop; Indie; Pop; Post Punk; Rock

Artist management company based in London, founded in 2021.

Steve Allen Entertainments
The Coach House
163 Broadway
Peterborough
PE1 4DH
Email: sales@sallenent.co.uk
Website: https://steveallenentertainments.co.uk
Website: https://www.facebook.com/steveallenentertainments/

Represents: Artists/Bands; Comedians; Other Entertainers; Tribute Acts

Genres: All types of music

Contact: Steve Allen

Based in Peterborough, in Cambridgeshire. Supplies entertainers and entertainments for private events and corporate occasions. Client base includes many National companies as well as most of the major Hotel Chains.

Stormcraft Music
Email: info@stormcraftmusic.com
Website: https://www.stormcraftmusic.com
Website: https://www.facebook.com/stormcraftmusic

Represents: Artists/Bands

Genres: Alternative Pop; Singer-Songwriter; Guitar based

We specialise in the management and development of up and coming talented artists.

Covering a wide range of the musical spectrum we strive to develop the careers of the next generation of original musicians.

With over 10 years worth of industry experience we are able to closely work with each artist to help shape their career and be their gateway into both the music industry and into the public eye.

Talent Everywhere
Bentinck House
3-8 Bolsover Street
London
W1W 6AB
Email: info@talenteverywhere.com
Website: https://www.talenteverywhere.com
Website: https://twitter.com/TalentEvrywhere

Represents: Artists/Bands

Genres: Commercial; Indie; Pop

We are a passionate team of managers and agents dedicated to proudly showcasing the very best of our clients' talents.

Tap Music
Email: info@tapmgmt.com
Website: https://tap-music.com
Website: https://www.facebook.com/tapmusicofficial/

Represents: Artists/Bands; Producers; Songwriters

Genres: All types of music

Music management company with offices in London, Berlin, LA and Sydney.

This Is Music Ltd
408 Brickfields
37 Cremer Street
London
E2 8HD
Email: simon@thisismusicltd.com
Website: http://thisismusicltd.com
Website: https://www.soundcloud.com/this-is-music

Represents: Artists/Bands; Producers

Genres: Electronic; Underground; Indie; Pop

Contact: Simon Gold

Music company based in London and Los Angeles. Provides management and label services for artists and producers.

Toonteen Industries: Management & Promotions
Bury St Edmunds
Suffolk
Email: demos@toonteen.co.uk
Email: joe@toonteen.co.uk
Website: https://www.toonteen.co.uk
Website: https://www.facebook.com/toonteenAM

Represents: Artists/Bands

Genres: Acoustic Alternative Heavy Progressive Ambient Emo Hardcore Indie Metal Pop Punk Rock

Contact: Joe Weaver

Management company based in Bury St Edmunds. Promotes shows with various bands in venues all over East Anglia, but mainly focused within Bury St Edmunds. Also manages bands and solo artists. Send query by email with links to music online. No attachments. Response not guaranteed.

Top Draw Music Management
Email: james@tdmm.co.uk
Website: https://www.facebook.com/TopDrawMusicManagement

Represents: DJs; Producers

Genres: Dance; Electronic

Contact: James Hamilton

A creative, connected and multi-faceted agency. Works with artists in electronic music, along with brands, where music, fashion and technology intersect, providing consultancy and direction.

Touchdown Management
London
Website: https://www.touchdownmanagement.com
Website: https://twitter.com/TouchdownMGMT

Represents: Artists/Bands

Genres: All types of music

Management company based in London. Open to all genres but particularly pop and rock. Send submissions by email. Prefers links to attachments.

Trak Image Music Ltd
12 Hilton Street
Manchester
M1 1JF
Email: submissions@heistorhit.com
Email: team@heistorhit.com
Website: https://www.heistorhit.com
Website: https://www.facebook.com/heistorhit

Represents: Artists/Bands

Genres: Shoegaze; Chill; Indie; Acoustic; Alternative

Music company based in Manchester. Send demos by email.

Transgressive
Email: general@transgressiverecords.com
Website: https://transgressiverecords.com
Website: https://www.facebook.com/transgressiverecords

Represents: Artists/Bands

Genres: All types of music

An independent music group comprising a record label, publisher and management company.

Travelled Music
Email: alan@travelledmusic.co.uk
Email: ian@travelledmusic.co.uk
Website: https://www.travelledmusic.co.uk
Website: https://twitter.com/travelledmusic

Represents: Artists/Bands

Genres: Alternative; Rock; Electronic; Indie

Contact: Alan Thompson; Ian Thompson

Music company offering artist and tour management, websites and social media, direct-to-fan marketing, bookings and promotions, event management.

Trinifold Management
12 Oval Road
London
NW1 7DH
Website: https://www.trinifold.co.uk

Represents: Artists/Bands

Genres: All types of music

Submit demo via form on website.

Triple Threat Management
Email: neil@triplethreatmgmt.com
Website: https://www.triplethreatmgmt.com
Website: https://www.facebook.com/triplethreatmgmt/

Represents: Artists/Bands

Genres: All types of music

Offers management, label services, A&R, touring, production, events, brand building, legal, marketing, press and strategic partnerships expertise all in-house.

Twenty Music Roots
Email: info@twentymusicroots.com
Website: https://www.twentymusicroots.com
Website: https://www.facebook.com/twentymusicroots

Represents: Artists/Bands

Genres: Americana; Country; Roots

Providers of booking agent, promotion, and management services, focussing on the Roots genre.

Underplay
Email: chrisbellam@underplay.co.uk
Website: https://www.underplay.co.uk
Website: https://www.instagram.com/u_n_d_e_r_p_l_a_y/

Represents: Artists/Bands

Genres: All types of music

Contact: Chris Bellam

Artist management and promotion.

Up On Mars
Brighton
Email: hello@uponmars.com
Website: https://uponmars.com
Website: https://www.linkedin.com/company/up-on-mars/

Represents: Artists/Bands

Genres: Electronic; Pop

Artist management company based in Brighton. Send demos via form on website.

Upside Management Ltd
18 Cherrington Gardens
Stourbridge
West Midlands
DY9 0QB
Email: denise@upsideuk.com
Email: simon@upsideuk.com
Website: https://www.upsideuk.com
Website: https://www.facebook.com/upsideuk

Represents: Artists/Bands

Genres: Dance; Pop

Contact: Denise Beighton; Simon Jones

Management company based in Stourbridge, West Midlands.

Various Artists Management
37 Lonsdale Road
London
NW6 6RA
Email: info@variousartistsmanagement.com
Website: https://variousartistsmanagement.com

Website: https://www.facebook.com/
variousartistsmanagement

Represents: Artists/Bands; Producers

Genres: All types of music

Management company with offices in
London, Los Angeles, and Hong Kong.

Viral Music
Brunswick Mill
Manchester
M40 7EZ
Email: info@viralmusicuk.com
Website: https://www.viralmusicuk.com
Website: https://www.facebook.com/
ViralMusicUK/

Represents: Artists/Bands; DJs

Genres: Dance; House; Commercial

Management company providing
conservatoire-trained, professionally-
accomplished musicians to the nightlife
entertainment industry, as well as for a wide
range of other events, including weddings
and private/corporate functions.

Virtually Pop
VO2, 22 Jordan Street
Baltic Creative Quarter
Liverpool
Merseyside
L1 0BP
Email: info@virtuallypop.com
Website: https://www.virtuallypop.com
Website: https://www.facebook.com/
virtuallypopmusicgroup

Represents: Artists/Bands

Genres: Acoustic; Folk; Jazz; Pop; Rock

Music company based in Liverpool, offering
Artist Management, Tour Promotion and
Publishing.

We Like Oliver
London
Email: olly@welikeoliver.com
Website: https://welikeoliver.com
Website: https://www.facebook.com/
welikeoliver

Represents: Artists/Bands

Genres: All types of music

Contact: Olly Andrews

Offers "Complete digital Marketing & IT
Solutions for your creative business".

The Weird and the Wonderful
London
Email: info@theweirdandthewonderful.com
Website: https://www.andthewonderful.com
Website: https://www.facebook.com/
theweirdandthewonderfulofficial

Represents: Artists/Bands

Genres: Electronic; Folk; House; Techno;
Urban

An international, multi-faceted talent
consultancy, record label, events curation
and management collective, dealing with all
things weird and wonderful.

West Midlands Media Group
Grosvenor House
11 St Pauls Square
Birmingham
B3 1RB
Email: press@wmmg.uk
Email: info@wmmg.uk
Website: https://www.wmmg.uk
Website: https://www.facebook.com/
ukwmmg

Represents: Artists/Bands

Genres: All types of music

We are the local experts in managing music
careers for local, new and upcoming artists
and bands all over the west midlands. Our
experienced artist management team deal
with everything from organising rehearsal
studios, booking gigs and building on our
existing portfolio and social media profiles.

Wildlife Entertainment Ltd
Email: info@wildlife-entertainment.com
Website: https://www.wildlife-
entertainment.com

Represents: Artists/Bands

Genres: Indie; Rock; R&B

Management company based in South West London.

XVII Music Group
Email: info@xviimusic.com
Website: https://xviimusic.com
Website: https://soundcloud.com/xviimusicgroup

Represents: Artists/Bands

Genres: All types of music

Artists development and record label.

Yellowbrick Music
Email: info@yellowbrickmusic.com
Email: meredith@yellowbrickmusic.com
Website: https://yellowbrickmusic.com
Website: https://twitter.com/YellBrickMusic

Represents: Artists/Bands

Genres: All types of music

Label service company based in London, offering artists a creative range of support and tools. Send query by email or via online contact form.

YMU Group
Clifton Works
23 Grove Park Terrace
Chiswick
London
W4 3QE

180 Great Portland Street
London
W1W 5QZ

3rd Floor Colwyn Chambers
19 York Street
Manchester
M2 3BA
Email: enquiries@ymugroup.com
Website: https://www.ymugroup.com

Represents: Artists/Bands; DJs; Producers; Songwriters

Genres: Alternative Rock; Dance; Electronic; Pop

Management company with offices in London, Manchester, Washington DC, California, and New York.

Young Guns
2 Princes Street
Mayfair
London
W1B 2LB
Email: hello@younggunsgroup.com
Website: https://www.younggunsgroup.com
Website: https://www.facebook.com/YoungGunsLtd

Represents: Artists/Bands; Producers; Studio Musicians

Genres: Classical; Jazz; Pop; Fusion

A music agency that creates acts and sources musicians from all genres for the events, record and TV industries.

Youthquake
Email: contact@youthquake.london
Website: https://youthquake.london/
Website: https://www.instagram.com/youthquakemgmt/

Represents: Artists/Bands

Genres: Alternative; Guitar based

Artist management company based in Isleworth.

Z Management
Email: alex@zman.co.uk
Email: daniela@zman.co.uk
Website: http://www.zman.co.uk
Website: https://www.facebook.com/zmanagementuk

Represents: Artists/Bands; DJs; Producers; Songwriters

Genres: All types of music

Management company based in London, handling song writers, producers, mixers, remixers, and artists. Send demo by email.

Zero Myth
Website: https://www.zeromyth.co.uk
Website: https://twitter.com/ZeroMythUK

Represents: Artists/Bands

Genres: Alternative; Pop; Rock

A creative music management company, specialising in artist development and project management. Aims to create sustainable artist led campaigns by managing strategic development, distribution and partnerships. Offers fixed-fee consultation sessions.

Zulu Music
Email: thando@zulumusic.uk
Website: https://zulumusic.uk
Website: https://www.instagram.com/zulumusicuk

Genres: Mainstream; Pop

Contact: Thando Zulu

As a company we exist to help our clients reach their full holistic potential.

We follow a relationship-first approach to working with current and prospective clients, remebering before we are artists, clients or creators...first we are humans.

I believe that trust is the foundation of good leadership and that we can build trust by consistently exemplifying competence, connection and character.

My Vision is to build a company that is excellent in it's execution (competence), integral in its dealings (character) and is built on authentic relationships (connection).

In this way, the aim is not only commercial success but the holistic flourishing of all involved.

Canadian Managers

For the most up-to-date listings of these and hundreds of other managers, visit https://www.musicsocket.com/managers

*To claim your **free** access to the site, please see the back of this book.*

Bedlam Music Management
864 Eastern Ave
Toronto, ON M4L 1A3
Email: info@bedlammusicmgt.com
Website: https://www.bedlammusicmgt.com

Represents: Artists/Bands

Genres: All types of music

A full service artist management company based in Toronto, Canada.

Bruce Allen Talent
#500-425 Carrall Street
Vancouver, BC
V6B 6E3
Fax: +1 (604) 688-7118
Email: info@bruceallen.com
Website: https://www.bruceallen.com

Represents: Artists/Bands; Producers

Genres: All types of music

Contact: Bruce Allen

Talent agency based in Vancouver, British Columbia. Not accepting unsolicited material as of December 2024.

Coalition Music
200-310 Spadina Ave
Toronto ON, M5T 2E8
Email: info@coalitionmusic.com
Website: https://www.coalitionmusic.com

Website: https://www.facebook.com/CoalitionMUS

Represents: Artists/Bands

Genres: Contemporary; Indie; Pop; Rock; Singer-Songwriter; Alternative; Jazz; Punk; R&B; Rap; Hip-Hop

Artists are always welcome to submit demos for consideration. Please use the online form on the website to provide your full contact information. No MP3s via email or CD press kits via mail / courier. Unfortunately, because of the volume of submissions we receive, we aren't able to give status updates. You will be contacted if we have anything to request from you, please do not contact us.

Macklam Feldman Management
#200 – 1505 West 2nd Avenue
Vancouver, BC
V6H 3Y4
Email: info@mfmgt.com
Website: https://www.mfmgt.com
Website: https://www.facebook.com/macklamfeldmanmgmt

Represents: Artists/Bands; Producers

Genres: Pop; Rock; Jazz; World; Alternative; Indie

Contact: Sam Feldman; Steve Macklam

Management company based in Vancouver, Canada. Send demos by email with links to music online (soundcloud, spotify, etc.).

Nettwerk Management
1675 West 2nd Ave, 2nd Floor
Vancouver, BC. V6J 1H3
Website: https://nettwerk.com
Website: https://www.facebook.com/
nettwerkmusicgroup

Represents: Artists/Bands; Film / TV Composers; Producers; Songwriters; Sound Engineers; Studio Technicians

Genres: Contemporary; Christian; Electronic; Folk; Indie; Latin; Pop; Punk; Rap; Rock; Hip-Hop; Dance; Singer-Songwriter

Music company based in Vancouver, Canada (head office), with other offices in the US and Europe. Includes label, management, and publishing arms.

Talk's Cheap Management
Website: https://talks-cheap.com/contact
Website: https://www.facebook.com/Voivod

Represents: Artists/Bands

Genres: Metal; Punk; Hardcore; Rock; Roots

Management company based in Canada.

Australian Managers

For the most up-to-date listings of these and hundreds of other managers, visit https://www.musicsocket.com/managers

*To claim your **free** access to the site, please see the back of this book.*

Open Door Management

Email: chris.obrien@destroyalllines.com
Email: joshua@opendoormgmt.com.au
Website: https://opendoormgmt.com.au/
Website: https://www.facebook.com/
OpenDoorMgt/

Represents: Artists/Bands

Genres: All types of music

Contact: Chris O'Brien; Joshua Smith

Management company established by an industry veteran and a self-managed musician.

Wanted Management

Email: wantedgregg@gmail.com
Website: https://www.facebook.com/
WantedMgmt
Website: https://soundcloud.com/
wantedmgmt

Represents: Artists/Bands

Genres: Pop; Punk; Rock; Soul; Roots; Rock and Roll

Contact: Gregg Bell

Management company formed originally in the US in 2001, now based in Perth, Australia.

Managers Index

This section lists managers by their genres, with directions to the section of the book where the full listing can be found.

You can create your own customised lists of managers using different combinations of these subject areas, plus over a dozen other criteria, instantly online at https://www.musicsocket.com.

*To claim your **free** access to the site, please see the back of this book.*

All types of music
!K7 (*UK*)
2k Management (*UK*)
360 Artist Development (*UK*)
4 Tunes Ltd (*UK*)
7pm Management (*UK*)
A&R Factory (*UK*)
ACA Music & Entertainment (*US*)
Aesthetic V (*US*)
Amber Artists (*UK*)
American Artiste (UK) (*UK*)
Amour:Music (*UK*)
AMW Group Inc. (*US*)
Anger Management (*UK*)
The Animal Farm (*UK*)
APA (Agency for the Performing Arts) (*US*)
Artistes International Representation (AIR) Ltd (*UK*)
ASM Talent (*UK*)
ATC Management (*UK*)
Autonomy Music Group (*UK*)
Avenoir Records (*UK*)
Backer Entertainment (*US*)
Backstage Entertainment (*US*)
Bedlam Music Management (*Can*)
Big Hug Management (*UK*)
Big Life Management (*UK*)
Big Noise (*US*)
BiGiAM Promotions & Management (*UK*)

Bill Silva Management (*US*)
Blinding Talent (*UK*)
BLOCS (*UK*)
Blue Raincoat Music (*UK*)
Brian Yeates Associates Ltd (*UK*)
BrightonsFinest (*UK*)
Bruce Allen Talent (*Can*)
Bsquared MGMT (*US*)
Bulldozer Media Ltd (*UK*)
C Management (*US*)
Catalyst Management (*UK*)
Celebrity Enterprises (CE) Inc. (*US*)
Century Artists Management Agency, LLC (*US*)
Chosen Music (*UK*)
Closer Artists Management & Publishing (*UK*)
CMG Music (*UK*)
CMP Entertainment (*UK*)
Conchord (*UK*)
Covert Talent Management (*UK*)
Creative Artists Agency (CAA) (*US*)
Creative Sounds UK (*UK*)
Creeme Entertainments (*UK*)
Crush Music Media Management (*US*)
Culler Talent Management (*US*)
Danny Brittain Band Management (DBBM) (*UK*)
Darkspin Music Management (*UK*)
Deluxxe Management (*UK*)

Deuce Management & Promotion (*UK*)
Digimix Music (*UK*)
Dog & Pony Industries (*US*)
Steve Draper Entertainments (*UK*)
Duroc Media (*UK*)
East Coast Entertainment (ECE) (*US*)
Elevation Group Inc. (*US*)
Empire Artist Management (*UK*)
Everybody's Management Ltd (*UK*)
Feraltone (*UK*)
Ferocious Talent (*UK*)
Flat Cap Music (*UK*)
Friends Vs Music Ltd (*UK*)
Funzalo Music / Mike's Artist
Management (*US*)
Gary Stamler Management (*US*)
Gayle Enterprises, Inc. (*US*)
The Gorfaine/Schwartz Agency, Inc. (*US*)
Hal Carter Organisation (*UK*)
Happy House Management & Marketing
Services (*UK*)
Harbourside Artist Management (*UK*)
Headline Talent Agency (*US*)
Heard and Seen (*UK*)
Hoffman Entertainment (*US*)
Hot House Music Ltd (*UK*)
Hot Vox (*UK*)
Howard Rosen Promotion, Inc. (*US*)
Impact Artist Management (*UK*)
In Touch Entertainment (*US*)
Innate – Music Ltd (*UK*)
Intune Addicts (*UK*)
Invasion Group, Ltd (*US*)
IQ Artist Management (*UK*)
James Joseph Music Management LA
(*US*)
Jampol Artist Management (*US*)
Jay Anthony's Next Level Booking and
Entertainment Agency, LLC (*US*)
Kaleidoscope (*UK*)
Karma Artists Music LLP (*UK*)
KBH Entertainment (*US*)
KRMB Management & Consultancy (*UK*)
LA Personal Development (*US*)
Laissez Faire Club (*UK*)
Lake Transfer Artist & Tour Management
(*US*)
Larro Media (*US*)
Legacy Records (*UK*)
Leodis Talent (*UK*)
Leonard Business Management (*US*)
Liquid Management (*UK*)
MaDa Music Entertainment (*UK*)
Madison House Inc. (*US*)
Major Labl (*UK*)

Manana Music Management (*UK*)
Manners McDade Artist Management
(*UK*)
MBM (Music Business Management Ltd)
(*UK*)
MJM Agency (*UK*)
Mother Artist Management (*UK*)
Murphy to Manteo (MTM) Music
Management (*US*)
Music by Design (*UK*)
Music City Artists (*US*)
Music Group Entertainment Worldwide,
LLC (*US*)
MusicBizMentors (*US*)
Nettwerk Management UK (*UK*)
New Heights Entertainment (*US*)
NewLevel Management (*UK*)
Nightside Entertainment, Inc. (*US*)
No Half Measures Ltd (*UK*)
Nowhere Talent (*UK*)
One Fifteen (*UK*)
141a Management (*UK*)
140dB Management Limited (*UK*)
Open All Nite Entertainment (*US*)
Open Door Management (*Aus*)
Pacific Talent (*US*)
Paradigm Talent Agency (*US*)
Persistent Management (*US*)
Petty Music Management (*UK*)
Platinum Star Management (*US*)
PMS Music Management (*UK*)
Primary Wave (*US*)
Program Music, Ltd (*UK*)
Prolifica Management (*UK*)
Psycho Management Company (*UK*)
Push Music Management (*UK*)
Quest Management (*UK*)
Radius Music Ltd (*UK*)
Real Media Music (*UK*)
Red Afternoon Music (*UK*)
Regime Seventy-Two (*UK*)
Rockstar Management (*UK*)
Roundface Music Management (*UK*)
SB Management (*UK*)
Second Sun Management (*UK*)
Selak Entertainment, Inc. (*US*)
Self Group (*US*)
September Management (UK) (*UK*)
September Management (US) (*US*)
74 Promotions (*UK*)
SGO Ltd (*UK*)
Sherrod Artist Management (*US*)
Sidewinder Management Ltd (*UK*)
SKH Music (*US*)
sm-mgmt (*UK*)

SMC Artists (*US*)
Solar Management (*UK*)
Solid Music Company (*US*)
Sparks Entertainment Management Co.
(*US*)
Steve Allen Entertainments (*UK*)
Stiletto Entertainment (*US*)
Take Out Management (*US*)
Talent Source (*US*)
Tap Music (*UK*)
Tenth Street Entertainment (*US*)
That's Entertainment International Inc.
(TEI Entertainment) (*US*)
Threee (*US*)
Tom Callahan & Associates (TCA) (*US*)
Touchdown Management (*UK*)
A Train Entertainment (*US*)
Transgressive (*UK*)
Trinifold Management (*UK*)
Triple Threat Management (*UK*)
Tsunami Entertainment (*US*)
Uncle Booking (*US*)
Underplay (*UK*)
United Talent Agency (*US*)
Universal Attractions Agency (*US*)
Various Artists Management (*UK*)
Velvet Hammer Music & Management
Group (*US*)
Walker Entertainment Group (*US*)
We Like Oliver (*UK*)
West Midlands Media Group (*UK*)
Whiplash PR and Management (*US*)
William Morris Endeavor (WME) (*US*)
Wolfson Entertainment, Inc. (*US*)
XVII Music Group (*UK*)
Yellow Couch Management (*US*)
Yellowbrick Music (*UK*)
Z Management (*UK*)
Acoustic
A2E – Artists 2 Events (*UK*)
Aspire Music Management (*UK*)
Dawson Breed Music (*UK*)
Fat City Artists (*US*)
HardKnockLife Entertainment (*US*)
Heist or Hit (*UK*)
Hello! Booking, Inc. (*US*)
Jelli Records (*UK*)
Kari Estrin Management & Consulting
(*US*)
Music Media Events (*UK*)
Nashville Records, LLC (*US*)
Opre Roma (*UK*)
Outrider Music, LLC (*US*)
Park Promotions (*UK*)
Pillar Artists (*UK*)

Reckless Yes (*UK*)
TAC Music Management (*US*)
Toonteen Industries: Management &
Promotions (*UK*)
Trak Image Music Ltd (*UK*)
Virtually Pop (*UK*)
Alternative
Advanced Alternative Media (AAM) (*US*)
Allure Media Entertainment Group (*US*)
Associated London Management (*UK*)
Bad Apple Music Group (*UK*)
Big Hassle Management (*US*)
Bitchin' Entertainment (*US*)
Brum Media Group (*UK*)
Burgess World Co. (*US*)
Coalition Music (*Can*)
Craft Management (*UK*)
DDB Productions (*US*)
Deep South Artist Management (*US*)
Don't Try (*UK*)
Donatello Music (*UK*)
Down For Life (*UK*)
East City Management (*UK*)
F&G Management (*UK*)
Feed Your Head (*UK*)
5B Artist Management (*US*)
Flow State Music (*UK*)
FP / Fantastic Plastic Music (*UK*)
Freaks R Us (*UK*)
Ganbei Records (*UK*)
Glow Artists (*UK*)
Goo Music Management Ltd (*UK*)
Hardin Entertainment (*US*)
Heist or Hit (*UK*)
Hope Management (*UK*)
Hornblow Group USA, Inc. (*US*)
Ignition Management (*UK*)
Impact Artist Management (*US*)
Infinite Future Mgmt (*UK*)
JBLS Management (*UK*)
Jude Street Management (*UK*)
Key Music Management (*UK*)
Kuper Personal Management (*US*)
Lonewolf Talent Management (*UK*)
Macklam Feldman Management (*Can*)
MOB Agency (*US*)
Moksha Management (*UK*)
Monqui Presents (*US*)
Music Gallery International (*US*)
Music Media Events (*UK*)
Night Owl Music Promotions &
Management (*UK*)
Orean Music Ltd (*UK*)
Outrider Music, LLC (*US*)
Pillar Artists (*UK*)

Position Music (*US*)
Prodigal Son Entertainment (*US*)
Q Prime Management, Inc. (*US*)
Raw Power Management (*UK*)
Reaction Management (*UK*)
Reckless Yes (*UK*)
Royal Artists Management (*UK*)
Russell Carter Artist Management (*US*)
Sarah Lipman Management Ltd (*UK*)
Saviour Management (*UK*)
Semaphore Mgmt & Consulting (*US*)
Silva Artist Management (SAM) (*US*)
Siren Artist Management (UK) (*UK*)
Steven Scharf Entertainment (SSE) (*US*)
Stormcraft Music (*UK*)
Sweet! Music Management (*US*)
TAC Music Management (*US*)
Toonteen Industries: Management &
Promotions (*UK*)
Trak Image Music Ltd (*UK*)
Travelled Music (*UK*)
Trunk Bass Entertainment (*US*)
Union Entertainment Group (*US*)
Vector Management (*US*)
YMU Group (*UK*)
Youthquake (*UK*)
Zero Myth (*UK*)
Ambient
Bitchin' Entertainment (*US*)
Hot Gem (*UK*)
Lonewolf Talent Management (*UK*)
Outrider Music, LLC (*US*)
Toonteen Industries: Management &
Promotions (*UK*)
Tuscan Sun Music (*US*)
Americana
Aguia Music (*UK*)
Bitchin' Entertainment (*US*)
Brighthelmstone Promotions (*UK*)
Brilliant Productions (*US*)
Dawson Breed Music (*UK*)
Deep South Artist Management (*US*)
Grassy Hill Entertainment (*US*)
Hard Head Management (*US*)
Hardin Entertainment (*US*)
Kari Estrin Management & Consulting
(*US*)
Kuper Personal Management (*US*)
Mike's Artist Management (*US*)
Music Gallery International (*US*)
Myriad Artists (*US*)
Nashville Records, LLC (*US*)
Opre Roma (*UK*)
Rosier Artist Management (RAM) (*UK*)
Russell Carter Artist Management (*US*)

SAS Entertainment (*UK*)
Steven Scharf Entertainment (SSE) (*US*)
Sweet! Music Management (*US*)
TAC Music Management (*US*)
Twenty Music Roots (*UK*)
Vector Management (*US*)
Atmospheric
Outrider Music, LLC (*US*)
Semaphore Mgmt & Consulting (*US*)
Avant-Garde
Semaphore Mgmt & Consulting (*US*)
Blues
A2E – Artists 2 Events (*UK*)
Act 1 Entertainment (*US*)
Artist Representation and Management
(ARM) Entertainment (*US*)
Big Bear Music (*UK*)
Bitchin' Entertainment (*US*)
Blind Ambition Management, Ltd (*US*)
Brilliant Productions (*US*)
Burgess World Co. (*US*)
Cantaloupe Music Productions, Inc. (*US*)
Collin Artists (*US*)
Concerted Efforts (*US*)
Emcee Artist Management (*US*)
Fat City Artists (*US*)
Fleming Artists (*US*)
Gold Mountain Entertainment (*US*)
Hardin Entertainment (*US*)
Harmony Artists (*US*)
Impact Artist Management (*US*)
The Kurland Agency (*US*)
Max Bernard Management (*US*)
Myriad Artists (*US*)
Q Prime Management, Inc. (*US*)
Red Light Management (RLM) (*US*)
Rock Artist Management (RAM) (*UK*)
Rock People Management (RPM) (*UK*)
Ron Rainey Management Inc. (*US*)
Russell Carter Artist Management (*US*)
Sterling Artist Management (*US*)
Steven Scharf Entertainment (SSE) (*US*)
Sweet! Music Management (*US*)
TAC Music Management (*US*)
Union Entertainment Group (*US*)
Universal Tone Management (*US*)
Val's Artist Management (VAM) (*US*)
Westwood Music Group (*US*)
Break Beat
Finger Lickin' Management (*UK*)
Nexus Artist Management (*US*)
Celtic
A2E – Artists 2 Events (*UK*)
Fat City Artists (*US*)
Worldsound, LLC (*US*)

Chill
Involved Management (*UK*)
Trak Image Music Ltd (*UK*)
Christian
25 Artist Agency (*US*)
Deep South Artist Management (*US*)
Hardin Entertainment (*US*)
Jeff Roberts & Associates (*US*)
MTS Management (*US*)
Nashville Records, LLC (*US*)
Nettwerk Management (*US*)
Nettwerk Management (*Can*)
Prodigal Son Entertainment (*US*)
Proper Management (*US*)
Red Light Management (RLM) (*US*)
Classic
Act 1 Entertainment (*US*)
Arslanian & Associates, Inc. (*US*)
Artist Representation and Management
(ARM) Entertainment (*US*)
Big Beat Productions, Inc. (*US*)
Entertainment Services International (*US*)
IMG Artists (*US*)
Michael Anthony's Electric Events (*US*)
Rock Artist Management (RAM) (*UK*)
Suncoast Music Management (*US*)
TAC Music Management (*US*)
Classical
American International Artists, Inc. (*US*)
Askonas Holt Ltd (*UK*)
BBA Management & Booking (*US*)
Bitchin' Entertainment (*US*)
Columbia Artists Music LLC (CAMI
Music) (*US*)
Dawn Elder Management (*US*)
Domo Music Group Management (*US*)
Jude Street Management (*UK*)
Opus 3 Artists (*US*)
Pinnacle Arts Management, Inc. (*US*)
Silverword Music Group (*UK*)
Val's Artist Management (VAM) (*US*)
Young Guns (*UK*)
Commercial
Future Agency (*UK*)
Handshake Ltd. (*UK*)
Insomnia Music UK (*UK*)
MTS Management (*US*)
Run the Sound (*UK*)
TAC Music Management (*US*)
Talent Everywhere (*UK*)
Viral Music (*UK*)
Contemporary
Amour:Music (*UK*)
Big Beat Productions, Inc. (*US*)
Booking Entertainment (*US*)

Chapman & Co. Management (*US*)
Coalition Music (*Can*)
Collin Artists (*US*)
David Belenzon Management, Inc. (*US*)
Domo Music Group Management (*US*)
Fleming Artists (*US*)
Gold Mountain Entertainment (*US*)
Hardin Entertainment (*US*)
Impact Artist Management (*US*)
Magus Entertainment Inc. (*US*)
MBK Entertainment (*US*)
Michael Hausman Artist Management Inc.
(*US*)
MM Music Agency (*US*)
Moksha Management (*UK*)
Nettwerk Management (*US*)
Nettwerk Management (*Can*)
Riot Artists (*US*)
Ron Rainey Management Inc. (*US*)
Russell Carter Artist Management (*US*)
Serious (*UK*)
Stiefel Entertainment (*US*)
Val's Artist Management (VAM) (*US*)
Vector Management (*US*)
Country
Act 1 Entertainment (*US*)
Aguia Music (*UK*)
American Artists Entertainment Group
(*US*)
Artist Representation and Management
(ARM) Entertainment (*US*)
Big Beat Productions, Inc. (*US*)
Bitchin' Entertainment (*US*)
Brick Wall Management (*US*)
Bulletproof Artist Management (*US*)
Deep South Artist Management (*US*)
Donatello Music (*UK*)
Fat City Artists (*US*)
Hardin Entertainment (*US*)
Hello! Booking, Inc. (*US*)
Impact Artist Management (*US*)
Maine Road Management (*US*)
Major Bob Music, Inc. (*US*)
Mascioli Entertainment (*US*)
McGhee Entertainment (*US*)
Michael Anthony's Electric Events (*US*)
Modern Management (*US*)
Monqui Presents (*US*)
Morris Higham Management (*US*)
MTS Management (*US*)
Nashville Records, LLC (*US*)
Prodigal Son Entertainment (*US*)
Red Light Management (RLM) (*US*)
Ron Rainey Management Inc. (*US*)
Silverword Music Group (*UK*)

Sounds Like A Hit Ltd (*UK*)
Spinning Plates (*US*)
Sweet! Music Management (*US*)
TAC Music Management (*US*)
Third Coast Talent (*US*)
TKO Artist Management (*US*)
Twenty Music Roots (*UK*)
Union Entertainment Group (*US*)
Val's Artist Management (VAM) (*US*)
Vector Management (*US*)
Westwood Music Group (*US*)
Dance
1 2 One Entertainment (*UK*)
2-Tone Entertainment (2TE) (*UK*)
AuthorityMGMT (*UK*)
Celebrity Talent Agency Inc. (*US*)
DEF (Deutsch Englische Freundschaft)
(*UK*)
Defenders Ent (*UK*)
East City Management (*UK*)
F&G Management (*UK*)
Feed Your Head (*UK*)
Finger Lickin' Management (*UK*)
Flow State Music (*UK*)
Fruition Music (*UK*)
Graphite Media (*UK*)
Hardin Entertainment (*US*)
Hope Management (*UK*)
Hot Gem (*UK*)
House of Us (*UK*)
Infinite Future Mgmt (*UK*)
Michael Anthony's Electric Events (*US*)
Moksha Management (*UK*)
Nettwerk Management (*US*)
Nettwerk Management (*Can*)
Orean Music Ltd (*UK*)
Ornadel Management (*UK*)
Perfect Havoc Ltd (*UK*)
Phono Sounds UK (*UK*)
Position Music (*US*)
Red Light Management (RLM) (*US*)
Rhythmic Records Management and
Production (*UK*)
SAS Entertainment (*UK*)
Silverword Music Group (*UK*)
Smashing Buttons (*UK*)
Sounds Like A Hit Ltd (*UK*)
Spectrum Talent Agency (*US*)
Stiefel Entertainment (*US*)
Top Draw Music Management (*UK*)
Upside Management Ltd (*UK*)
Val's Artist Management (VAM) (*US*)
Viral Music (*UK*)
YMU Group (*UK*)

Deep Funk
Sweet! Music Management (*US*)
Disco
Big Beat Productions, Inc. (*US*)
Perfect Havoc Ltd (*UK*)
Suncoast Music Management (*US*)
Dubstep
Nexus Artist Management (*US*)
Electronic
AJM (*UK*)
AprilSeven Music (*UK*)
Bitchin' Entertainment (*US*)
DEF (Deutsch Englische Freundschaft)
(*UK*)
F&G Management (*UK*)
Feed Your Head (*UK*)
Finger Lickin' Management (*UK*)
Flow State Music (*UK*)
Freaks R Us (*UK*)
From the Whitehouse (*UK*)
Graphite Media (*UK*)
Hard Head Management (*US*)
Hardin Entertainment (*US*)
Holocene Management (*UK*)
Hot Gem (*UK*)
HQ Familia (*UK*)
Humans & Other Animals (*UK*)
Infinite Future Mgmt (*UK*)
Involved Management (*UK*)
JBLS Management (*UK*)
Lucky Number Music Limited (*UK*)
Magus Entertainment Inc. (*US*)
Moksha Management (*UK*)
Music + Art Management (*US*)
Nettwerk Management (*US*)
Nettwerk Management (*Can*)
New Champion Management (*UK*)
Nexus Artist Management (*US*)
Orean Music Ltd (*UK*)
Outrider Music, LLC (*US*)
Parade Music (*UK*)
Phono Sounds UK (*UK*)
Position Music (*US*)
Red Light Management (RLM) (*US*)
Saga Entertainment (*UK*)
Sarah Lipman Management Ltd (*UK*)
Semaphore Mgmt & Consulting (*US*)
This Is Music Ltd (*UK*)
Top Draw Music Management (*UK*)
Travelled Music (*UK*)
Up On Mars (*UK*)
Waxploitation (*US*)
The Weird and the Wonderful (*UK*)
YMU Group (*UK*)

Emo
Music Gallery International (*US*)
Outrider Music, LLC (*US*)
Revolt Artist Management (*UK*)
Toonteen Industries: Management &
Promotions (*UK*)
Ethnic
Domo Music Group Management (*US*)
Experimental
Bitchin' Entertainment (*US*)
F&G Management (*UK*)
Freaks R Us (*UK*)
Hot Gem (*UK*)
Incendia Music (*UK*)
Music + Art Management (*US*)
Semaphore Mgmt & Consulting (*US*)
Folk
21st Century Artists, Inc. (*US*)
Aguia Music (*UK*)
Bitchin' Entertainment (*US*)
Blind Ambition Management, Ltd (*US*)
Brighthelmstone Promotions (*UK*)
Bulletproof Artist Management (*US*)
Concerted Efforts (*US*)
Dawson Breed Music (*UK*)
DCA Productions (*US*)
DMF Music Ltd (*UK*)
Domo Music Group Management (*US*)
Fat City Artists (*US*)
Fleming Artists (*US*)
From the Whitehouse (*UK*)
Front Room Songs (*UK*)
Ganbei Records (*UK*)
Gold Mountain Entertainment (*US*)
Grassy Hill Entertainment (*US*)
Hardin Entertainment (*US*)
Hello! Booking, Inc. (*US*)
Humans & Other Animals (*UK*)
IMG Artists (*US*)
Impact Artist Management (*US*)
Jelli Records (*UK*)
Kari Estrin Management & Consulting
(*US*)
Kuper Personal Management (*US*)
Maine Road Management (*US*)
Mike's Artist Management (*US*)
Music Media Events (*UK*)
Myriad Artists (*US*)
Nettwerk Management (*US*)
Nettwerk Management (*Can*)
New Champion Management (*UK*)
NSI Management (*US*)
Off the Chart Promotions (*UK*)
Opre Roma (*UK*)
Park Promotions (*UK*)

Q Prime Management, Inc. (*US*)
Russell Carter Artist Management (*US*)
Steven Scharf Entertainment (SSE) (*US*)
Sweet! Music Management (*US*)
TAC Music Management (*US*)
Val's Artist Management (VAM) (*US*)
Variety Artists International (*US*)
Vector Management (*US*)
Virtually Pop (*UK*)
The Weird and the Wonderful (*UK*)
Worldsound, LLC (*US*)
Funk
Bitchin' Entertainment (*US*)
Fat City Artists (*US*)
Nexus Artist Management (*US*)
Pyramid Entertainment Group (*US*)
Sweet! Music Management (*US*)
TAC Music Management (*US*)
Funky
Sweet! Music Management (*US*)
TAC Music Management (*US*)
Fusion
Moksha Management (*UK*)
Sweet! Music Management (*US*)
TAC Music Management (*US*)
Young Guns (*UK*)
Garage
Music Gallery International (*US*)
Revolt Artist Management (*UK*)
Glam
MTS Management (*US*)
Semaphore Mgmt & Consulting (*US*)
Gospel
Blind Ambition Management, Ltd (*US*)
Celebrity Talent Agency Inc. (*US*)
Concerted Efforts (*US*)
Enlight Entertainment, Inc. (*US*)
Fat City Artists (*US*)
Fresh Flava Entertainment (*US*)
IMG Artists (*US*)
Len Weisman Personal Management (*US*)
MBK Entertainment (*US*)
Nashville Records, LLC (*US*)
Pyramid Entertainment Group (*US*)
RAM Talent Group (*US*)
Silverword Music Group (*UK*)
Vector Management (*US*)
Westwood Music Group (*US*)
Gothic
Bitchin' Entertainment (*US*)
Music Gallery International (*US*)
Grime
Lucky House Management (*UK*)
Guitar based
Donatello Music (*UK*)

MTS Management (*US*)
Opre Roma (*UK*)
Pillar Artists (*UK*)
Reaction Management (*UK*)
Reckless Yes (*UK*)
Revolt Artist Management (*UK*)
Stormcraft Music (*UK*)
TAC Music Management (*US*)
Youthquake (*UK*)
Hard
MTS Management (*US*)
Music Gallery International (*US*)
Outrider Music, LLC (*US*)
Prodigal Son Entertainment (*US*)
Semaphore Mgmt & Consulting (*US*)
Sweet! Music Management (*US*)
TAC Music Management (*US*)
Hardcore
Down For Life (*UK*)
Hardin Entertainment (*US*)
Music Gallery International (*US*)
Outrider Music, LLC (*US*)
Position Music (*US*)
Red Light Management (RLM) (*US*)
Revolt Artist Management (*UK*)
Singerman Entertainment (*US*)
Talk's Cheap Management (*Can*)
Toonteen Industries: Management &
Promotions (*UK*)
Heavy
Incendia Music (*UK*)
Music Gallery International (*US*)
Outrider Music, LLC (*US*)
Semaphore Mgmt & Consulting (*US*)
Singerman Entertainment (*US*)
TAC Music Management (*US*)
Toonteen Industries: Management &
Promotions (*UK*)
Hip-Hop
Aguia Music (*UK*)
Allure Media Entertainment Group (*US*)
Bitchin' Entertainment (*US*)
Celebrity Talent Agency Inc. (*US*)
Coalition Music (*Can*)
DAS Communications Ltd (*US*)
Def Ro Inc. (*US*)
Finger Lickin' Management (*UK*)
First Access Entertainment (*US*)
Fresh Flava Entertainment (*US*)
HardKnockLife Entertainment (*US*)
Hello! Booking, Inc. (*US*)
Len Weisman Personal Management (*US*)
Lippman Entertainment (*US*)
The Lost Atlantis Records (*UK*)
Lucky House Management (*UK*)

Magus Entertainment Inc. (*US*)
Mauldin Brand Agency (*US*)
MBK Entertainment (*US*)
Nettwerk Management (*US*)
Nettwerk Management (*Can*)
Nexus Artist Management (*US*)
Position Music (*US*)
Pyramid Entertainment Group (*US*)
Red Light Management (RLM) (*US*)
Rhythmic Records Management and
Production (*UK*)
Run the Sound (*UK*)
Sarah Lipman Management Ltd (*UK*)
Smashing Buttons (*UK*)
Spectrum Talent Agency (*US*)
Steady Management (*UK*)
Steven Scharf Entertainment (SSE) (*US*)
Trunk Bass Entertainment (*US*)
Union Entertainment Group (*US*)
Val's Artist Management (VAM) (*US*)
Waxploitation (*US*)
Wright Entertainment Group (WEG) (*US*)
House
Bitchin' Entertainment (*US*)
F&G Management (*UK*)
House of Us (*UK*)
Involved Management (*UK*)
The Lost Atlantis Records (*UK*)
Nexus Artist Management (*US*)
Perfect Havoc Ltd (*UK*)
Phono Sounds UK (*UK*)
Rhythmic Records Management and
Production (*UK*)
Spectrum Talent Agency (*US*)
Viral Music (*UK*)
The Weird and the Wonderful (*UK*)
House
Bitchin' Entertainment (*US*)
F&G Management (*UK*)
House of Us (*UK*)
Involved Management (*UK*)
The Lost Atlantis Records (*UK*)
Nexus Artist Management (*US*)
Perfect Havoc Ltd (*UK*)
Phono Sounds UK (*UK*)
Rhythmic Records Management and
Production (*UK*)
Spectrum Talent Agency (*US*)
Viral Music (*UK*)
The Weird and the Wonderful (*UK*)
Indie
Advanced Alternative Media (AAM) (*US*)
Bad Apple Music Group (*UK*)
Big Hassle Management (*US*)
Bold Management (*UK*)

Brighthelmstone Promotions (*UK*)
Brilliant Corners Artist Management (*US*)
Brum Media Group (*UK*)
Coalition Music (*Can*)
dandomanagement (*UK*)
Dawson Breed Music (*UK*)
DMF Music Ltd (*UK*)
Domo Music Group Management (*US*)
Don't Try (*UK*)
East City Management (*UK*)
Equator Music (*UK*)
Feed Your Head (*UK*)
Fire Tower Entertainment (*US*)
From the Whitehouse (*UK*)
Fruition Music (*UK*)
Glow Artists (*UK*)
Gold Mountain Entertainment (*US*)
Goo Music Management Ltd (*UK*)
Hand in Hive Independent Records &
Management (*UK*)
Hardin Entertainment (*US*)
Heist or Hit (*UK*)
Hello! Booking, Inc. (*US*)
Holocene Management (*UK*)
Hornblow Group USA, Inc. (*US*)
House of Us (*UK*)
Humans & Other Animals (*UK*)
Ignition Management (*UK*)
Impact Artist Management (*US*)
In De Goot Entertainment (*US*)
Jude Street Management (*UK*)
Lazy Daze (*UK*)
Lonewolf Talent Management (*UK*)
Lucky Number Music Limited (*UK*)
Lyricom (*UK*)
Macklam Feldman Management (*Can*)
Magus Entertainment Inc. (*US*)
Maine Road Management (*US*)
Max Bernard Management (*US*)
Media Five Entertainment (*US*)
Memphia Music Management (*UK*)
Mike's Artist Management (*US*)
Miller Music Management (*UK*)
Monqui Presents (*US*)
Morningstar (*UK*)
Nettwerk Management (*US*)
Nettwerk Management (*Can*)
New Champion Management (*UK*)
Night Owl Music Promotions &
Management (*UK*)
NSI Management (*US*)
Off the Chart Promotions (*UK*)
Opre Roma (*UK*)
Orean Music Ltd (*UK*)
Outrider Music, LLC (*US*)

Pillar Artists (*UK*)
Reaction Management (*UK*)
Reckless Yes (*UK*)
Red Light Management (RLM) (*US*)
Revolt Artist Management (*UK*)
Royal Artists Management (*UK*)
Russell Carter Artist Management (*US*)
SAS Entertainment (*UK*)
Silva Artist Management (SAM) (*US*)
Steady Management (*UK*)
Steven Scharf Entertainment (SSE) (*US*)
Stiefel Entertainment (*US*)
Street Smart Management (*US*)
Sweet! Music Management (*US*)
TAC Music Management (*US*)
Talent Everywhere (*UK*)
Thirty Tigers (*US*)
This Is Music Ltd (*UK*)
Toonteen Industries: Management &
Promotions (*UK*)
Trak Image Music Ltd (*UK*)
Travelled Music (*UK*)
Val's Artist Management (VAM) (*US*)
Waxploitation (*US*)
Wildlife Entertainment Ltd (*UK*)
Industrial
Music Gallery International (*US*)
Semaphore Mgmt & Consulting (*US*)
Instrumental
Bitchin' Entertainment (*US*)
Collin Artists (*US*)
Columbia Artists Music LLC (CAMI
Music) (*US*)
Outrider Music, LLC (*US*)
Prodigal Son Entertainment (*US*)
Westwood Music Group (*US*)
Jazz
Act 1 Entertainment (*US*)
American International Artists, Inc. (*US*)
AprilSeven Music (*UK*)
B.H. Hopper Management Ltd. (*UK*)
BBA Management & Booking (*US*)
Big Bear Music (*UK*)
Big Beat Productions, Inc. (*US*)
Bitchin' Entertainment (*US*)
Booking Entertainment (*US*)
Burgess World Co. (*US*)
Cantaloupe Music Productions, Inc. (*US*)
Celebrity Talent Agency Inc. (*US*)
Chaney Gig Affairs (CGA) (*US*)
Chapman & Co. Management (*US*)
Coalition Music (*Can*)
Collin Artists (*US*)
Columbia Artists Music LLC (CAMI
Music) (*US*)

Concerted Efforts (*US*)
Dawn Elder Management (*US*)
DDB Productions (*US*)
DFJ Artists (*UK*)
DMF Music Ltd (*UK*)
Emcee Artist Management (*US*)
Entourage Talent Associates, Ltd (*US*)
Fat City Artists (*US*)
Fresh Flava Entertainment (*US*)
Glow Artists (*UK*)
Harmony Artists (*US*)
Hello! Booking, Inc. (*US*)
IMG Artists (*US*)
Impact Artist Management (*US*)
Ina Dittke & Associates (*US*)
The Kurland Agency (*US*)
Macklam Feldman Management (*Can*)
Maine Road Management (*US*)
The Major Group (*US*)
The Management Ark, Inc. (*US*)
Mars Jazz Booking (*US*)
Mascioli Entertainment (*US*)
Max Bernard Management (*US*)
MM Music Agency (*US*)
Music + Art Management (*US*)
Myriad Artists (*US*)
Opus 3 Artists (*US*)
PRA [Patrick Rains & Associates] (*US*)
Pyramid Entertainment Group (*US*)
RPM Music Productions (*US*)
Russell Carter Artist Management (*US*)
Serious (*UK*)
Silverword Music Group (*UK*)
Smashing Buttons (*UK*)
Sterling Artist Management (*US*)
Steven Scharf Entertainment (SSE) (*US*)
TAC Music Management (*US*)
Val's Artist Management (VAM) (*US*)
Variety Artists International (*US*)
Virtually Pop (*UK*)
Westwood Music Group (*US*)
Young Guns (*UK*)
Kraut
Semaphore Mgmt & Consulting (*US*)
Latin
BBA Management & Booking (*US*)
Cantaloupe Music Productions, Inc. (*US*)
Celebrity Talent Agency Inc. (*US*)
Collin Artists (*US*)
Hardin Entertainment (*US*)
Harmony Artists (*US*)
IMG Artists (*US*)
Impact Artist Management (*US*)
Ina Dittke & Associates (*US*)
Magus Entertainment Inc. (*US*)

Nettwerk Management (*US*)
Nettwerk Management (*Can*)
Once 11 Entertainment (*US*)
RAM Talent Group (*US*)
Red Light Management (RLM) (*US*)
Universal Tone Management (*US*)
Val's Artist Management (VAM) (*US*)
Westwood Music Group (*US*)
Leftfield
Semaphore Mgmt & Consulting (*US*)
Mainstream
Future Agency (*UK*)
Max Bernard Management (*US*)
Music Gallery International (*US*)
Sweet! Music Management (*US*)
Zulu Music (*UK*)
Melodic
Aspire Music Management (*UK*)
MTS Management (*US*)
Outrider Music, LLC (*US*)
Metal
Artist Representation and Management
(ARM) Entertainment (*US*)
Bitchin' Entertainment (*US*)
Ciulla Management, Inc. (*US*)
Creative International Artist Management
(*UK*)
Deathless MGMT (*UK*)
Down For Life (*UK*)
5B Artist Management (*US*)
In De Goot Entertainment (*US*)
Incendia Music (*UK*)
McGhee Entertainment (*US*)
MTS Management (*US*)
Music Gallery International (*US*)
Northern Music Co. Ltd (*UK*)
Outrider Music, LLC (*US*)
Position Music (*US*)
Q Prime Management, Inc. (*US*)
Raw Power Management (*UK*)
Reaction Management (*UK*)
Red Light Management (RLM) (*US*)
Revolt Artist Management (*UK*)
Saviour Management (*UK*)
Silva Artist Management (SAM) (*US*)
Singerman Entertainment (*US*)
Steven Scharf Entertainment (SSE) (*US*)
Street Smart Management (*US*)
TAC Music Management (*US*)
Talk's Cheap Management (*Can*)
Toonteen Industries: Management &
Promotions (*UK*)
Vector Management (*US*)
Modern
Sweet! Music Management (*US*)

New Age
Domo Music Group Management (*US*)
Tuscan Sun Music (*US*)
New Wave
Semaphore Mgmt & Consulting (*US*)
Non-Commercial
Semaphore Mgmt & Consulting (*US*)
Nostalgia
Revolt Artist Management (*UK*)
Pop
1 2 One Entertainment (*UK*)
2-Tone Entertainment (2TE) (*UK*)
Advanced Alternative Media (AAM) (*US*)
AJM (*UK*)
Allure Media Entertainment Group (*US*)
American Artists Entertainment Group (*US*)
Aspire Music Management (*UK*)
AuthorityMGMT (*UK*)
Big Hassle Management (*US*)
Bitchin' Entertainment (*US*)
Bold Management (*UK*)
Booking Entertainment (*US*)
Brick Wall Management (*US*)
Brum Media Group (*UK*)
Bulletproof Artist Management (*US*)
Coalition Music (*Can*)
Consolidated Artists (*UK*)
Creative International Artist Management (*UK*)
D. Bailey Management, Inc. (*US*)
DAS Communications Ltd (*US*)
David Belenzon Management, Inc. (*US*)
Dawn Elder Management (*US*)
Dawson Breed Music (*UK*)
DCA Productions (*US*)
Deep South Artist Management (*US*)
Def Ro Inc. (*US*)
Direct Management Group (DMG) (*US*)
Domo Music Group Management (*US*)
Donatello Music (*UK*)
Entourage Talent Associates, Ltd (*US*)
Equator Music (*UK*)
Fat City Artists (*US*)
Fire Tower Entertainment (*US*)
First Access Entertainment (*US*)
Flat50 (*UK*)
Fleming Artists (*US*)
Front Room Songs (*UK*)
Future Songs (*UK*)
Gold Mountain Entertainment (*US*)
Good Guy Entertainment (*US*)
Guvnor Management (*UK*)
Hand in Hive Independent Records & Management (*UK*)

Handshake Ltd. (*UK*)
Hardin Entertainment (*US*)
HardKnockLife Entertainment (*US*)
Hello! Booking, Inc. (*US*)
Holocene Management (*UK*)
Hornblow Group USA, Inc. (*US*)
Hot Gem (*UK*)
House of Us (*UK*)
Ignition Management (*UK*)
IMC Entertainment Group (*US*)
In De Goot Entertainment (*US*)
Infinite Future Mgmt (*UK*)
Insomnia Music UK (*UK*)
JBLS Management (*UK*)
Jude Street Management (*UK*)
KMY (Keep Me Young) (*UK*)
Laffitte Management Group (*US*)
Lippman Entertainment (*US*)
Lucky Number Music Limited (*UK*)
Macklam Feldman Management (*Can*)
Magus Entertainment Inc. (*US*)
Major Bob Music, Inc. (*US*)
The Major Group (*US*)
Mauldin Brand Agency (*US*)
MBK Entertainment (*US*)
Michael Anthony's Electric Events (*US*)
Michael Hausman Artist Management Inc. (*US*)
Mike's Artist Management (*US*)
Moksha Entertainment and Music Management (US) (*US*)
Monqui Presents (*US*)
MTS Management (*US*)
Music Media Events (*UK*)
N.O.W. Music Management (*UK*)
Nashville Records, LLC (*US*)
Nettwerk Management (*US*)
Nettwerk Management (*Can*)
New Champion Management (*UK*)
Off the Chart Promotions (*UK*)
Orean Music Ltd (*UK*)
Outrider Music, LLC (*US*)
Parade Music (*UK*)
Paradise Artists (*US*)
Phono Sounds UK (*UK*)
Pierce Entertainment (*UK*)
Position Music (*US*)
PRA [Patrick Rains & Associates] (*US*)
Progressive Global Agency (PGA) (*US*)
Q Prime Management, Inc. (*US*)
Rainmaker Artists (*US*)
Reaction Management (*UK*)
Red Light Management (RLM) (*US*)
Revolt Artist Management (*UK*)

Rhythmic Records Management and
Production (*UK*)
Rock Artist Management (RAM) (*UK*)
Ron Rainey Management Inc. (*US*)
RPM Music Productions (*US*)
Run the Sound (*UK*)
Russell Carter Artist Management (*US*)
Saga Entertainment (*UK*)
Sarah Lipman Management Ltd (*UK*)
SAS Entertainment (*UK*)
Saviour Management (*UK*)
SGM Music Group Ltd (*UK*)
Shaw Thing Management (*UK*)
Silva Artist Management (SAM) (*US*)
Silverword Music Group (*UK*)
Smashing Buttons (*UK*)
Sound Management, Inc. (*US*)
Sounds Like A Hit Ltd (*UK*)
Spectrum Talent Agency (*US*)
Starkravin' Management (*US*)
Steady Management (*UK*)
Steven Scharf Entertainment (SSE) (*US*)
Stiefel Entertainment (*US*)
Stormcraft Music (*UK*)
Street Smart Management (*US*)
Sweet! Music Management (*US*)
Talent Everywhere (*UK*)
This Day And Age Management (*US*)
This Is Music Ltd (*UK*)
Toonteen Industries: Management &
Promotions (*UK*)
Trunk Bass Entertainment (*US*)
Tuscan Sun Music (*US*)
Union Entertainment Group (*US*)
Universal Tone Management (*US*)
Up On Mars (*UK*)
Upside Management Ltd (*UK*)
Val's Artist Management (VAM) (*US*)
Variety Artists International (*US*)
Vector Management (*US*)
Virtually Pop (*UK*)
Wanted Management (*Aus*)
Westwood Music Group (*US*)
Worldsound, LLC (*US*)
Wright Entertainment Group (WEG) (*US*)
YMU Group (*UK*)
Young Guns (*UK*)
Zero Myth (*UK*)
Zulu Music (*UK*)
Post
Freaks R Us (*UK*)
Ganbei Records (*UK*)
Lonewolf Talent Management (*UK*)
Outrider Music, LLC (*US*)
Semaphore Mgmt & Consulting (*US*)

Steady Management (*UK*)
Power
MTS Management (*US*)
Music Gallery International (*US*)
Progressive
Incendia Music (*UK*)
Involved Management (*UK*)
MTS Management (*US*)
Nexus Artist Management (*US*)
Outrider Music, LLC (*US*)
Toonteen Industries: Management &
Promotions (*UK*)
Psychedelic
Ganbei Records (*UK*)
Moksha Entertainment and Music
Management (US) (*US*)
Semaphore Mgmt & Consulting (*US*)
Punk
Bitchin' Entertainment (*US*)
Coalition Music (*Can*)
Freaks R Us (*UK*)
Ganbei Records (*UK*)
Gold Mountain Entertainment (*US*)
Lonewolf Talent Management (*UK*)
Magus Entertainment Inc. (*US*)
Media Five Entertainment (*US*)
Moksha Entertainment and Music
Management (US) (*US*)
Music Gallery International (*US*)
Nettwerk Management (*US*)
Nettwerk Management (*Can*)
New Champion Management (*UK*)
Outrider Music, LLC (*US*)
Raw Power Management (*UK*)
Reaction Management (*UK*)
Revolt Artist Management (*UK*)
Royal Artists Management (*UK*)
Saviour Management (*UK*)
Silva Artist Management (SAM) (*US*)
Steady Management (*UK*)
Sweet! Music Management (*US*)
Talk's Cheap Management (*Can*)
Toonteen Industries: Management &
Promotions (*UK*)
Val's Artist Management (VAM) (*US*)
Wanted Management (*Aus*)
R&B
Act 1 Entertainment (*US*)
Aguia Music (*UK*)
Allure Media Entertainment Group (*US*)
American Artists Entertainment Group
(*US*)
Big Beat Productions, Inc. (*US*)
Bitchin' Entertainment (*US*)
Booking Entertainment (*US*)

Celebrity Talent Agency Inc. (*US*)
Chaney Gig Affairs (CGA) (*US*)
Coalition Music (*Can*)
Collin Artists (*US*)
D. Bailey Management, Inc. (*US*)
David Belenzon Management, Inc. (*US*)
Def Ro Inc. (*US*)
Defenders Ent (*UK*)
Enlight Entertainment, Inc. (*US*)
Fat City Artists (*US*)
First Access Entertainment (*US*)
Fresh Flava Entertainment (*US*)
Future Songs (*UK*)
HardKnockLife Entertainment (*US*)
IMC Entertainment Group (*US*)
Impact Artist Management (*US*)
Laffitte Management Group (*US*)
Len Weisman Personal Management (*US*)
Lippman Entertainment (*US*)
Magus Entertainment Inc. (*US*)
Major Bob Music, Inc. (*US*)
The Major Group (*US*)
Mascioli Entertainment (*US*)
Mauldin Brand Agency (*US*)
Max Bernard Management (*US*)
MBK Entertainment (*US*)
Pierce Entertainment (*UK*)
Position Music (*US*)
Pyramid Entertainment Group (*US*)
Silverword Music Group (*UK*)
Spectrum Talent Agency (*US*)
Starkravin' Management (*US*)
TAC Music Management (*US*)
This Day And Age Management (*US*)
True Talent Entertainment (*US*)
Trunk Bass Entertainment (*US*)
Val's Artist Management (VAM) (*US*)
Westwood Music Group (*US*)
Wildlife Entertainment Ltd (*UK*)
Wright Entertainment Group (WEG) (*US*)

Rap
Aguia Music (*UK*)
Bitchin' Entertainment (*US*)
Coalition Music (*Can*)
Defenders Ent (*UK*)
Enlight Entertainment, Inc. (*US*)
First Access Entertainment (*US*)
Flat50 (*UK*)
HardKnockLife Entertainment (*US*)
Lippman Entertainment (*US*)
The Lost Atlantis Records (*UK*)
Lucky House Management (*UK*)
Magus Entertainment Inc. (*US*)
The Major Group (*US*)
Mauldin Brand Agency (*US*)

MBK Entertainment (*US*)
Nettwerk Management (*US*)
Nettwerk Management (*Can*)
Position Music (*US*)
Red Light Management (RLM) (*US*)
Run the Sound (*UK*)
Steven Scharf Entertainment (SSE) (*US*)
This Day And Age Management (*US*)
Union Entertainment Group (*US*)
Val's Artist Management (VAM) (*US*)
Variety Artists International (*US*)
Waxploitation (*US*)
Wright Entertainment Group (WEG) (*US*)

Reggae
Act 1 Entertainment (*US*)
Celebrity Talent Agency Inc. (*US*)
Defenders Ent (*UK*)
DMF Music Ltd (*UK*)
Fat City Artists (*US*)
Gold Mountain Entertainment (*US*)
MBK Entertainment (*US*)
Nexus Artist Management (*US*)
Waxploitation (*US*)

Regional
Big Beat Productions, Inc. (*US*)
Brilliant Productions (*US*)
Cantaloupe Music Productions, Inc. (*US*)
MM Music Agency (*US*)
TAC Music Management (*US*)

Rhythm and Blues
TAC Music Management (*US*)

Rock and Roll
Fat City Artists (*US*)
Handshake Ltd. (*UK*)
Lazy Daze (*UK*)
Paradise Artists (*US*)
Revolt Artist Management (*UK*)
Singerman Entertainment (*US*)
Sweet! Music Management (*US*)
TAC Music Management (*US*)
Wanted Management (*Aus*)
Worldsound, LLC (*US*)

Rock
21st Century Artists, Inc. (*US*)
Act 1 Entertainment (*US*)
Advanced Alternative Media (AAM) (*US*)
Allure Media Entertainment Group (*US*)
American Artists Entertainment Group
(*US*)
Arslanian & Associates, Inc. (*US*)
Artist Representation and Management
(ARM) Entertainment (*US*)
Aspire Music Management (*UK*)
Bad Apple Music Group (*UK*)
BBA Management & Booking (*US*)

Big Beat Productions, Inc. (*US*)
Big Hassle Management (*US*)
Bitchin' Entertainment (*US*)
Bold Management (*UK*)
Booking Entertainment (*US*)
Brick Wall Management (*US*)
Brilliant Corners Artist Management (*US*)
Brum Media Group (*UK*)
Bulletproof Artist Management (*US*)
Burgess World Co. (*US*)
Chaos & Bedlam Management (*UK*)
Ciulla Management, Inc. (*US*)
Coalition Music (*Can*)
Concerted Efforts (*US*)
Consolidated Artists (*UK*)
Creative International Artist Management (*UK*)
D. Bailey Management, Inc. (*US*)
dandomanagement (*UK*)
DAS Communications Ltd (*US*)
Dave Kaplan Management (*US*)
David Belenzon Management, Inc. (*US*)
Dawn Elder Management (*US*)
DCA Productions (*US*)
Deathless MGMT (*UK*)
Deep South Artist Management (*US*)
Domo Music Group Management (*US*)
Don't Try (*UK*)
Down For Life (*UK*)
Emcee Artist Management (*US*)
Entertainment Services International (*US*)
Entourage Talent Associates, Ltd (*US*)
Equator Music (*UK*)
5B Artist Management (*US*)
Flat50 (*UK*)
Fleming Artists (*US*)
Fresh Flava Entertainment (*US*)
Ganbei Records (*UK*)
Gold Mountain Entertainment (*US*)
Goo Music Management Ltd (*UK*)
Guvnor Management (*UK*)
Hand in Hive Independent Records & Management (*UK*)
Hard Head Management (*US*)
Hardin Entertainment (*US*)
Hello! Booking, Inc. (*US*)
Hornblow Group USA, Inc. (*US*)
Humans & Other Animals (*UK*)
Ignition Management (*UK*)
Impact Artist Management (*US*)
In De Goot Entertainment (*US*)
Incendia Music (*UK*)
Kuper Personal Management (*US*)
Laffitte Management Group (*US*)
Lazy Daze (*UK*)

Lippman Entertainment (*US*)
Lonewolf Talent Management (*UK*)
Macklam Feldman Management (*Can*)
Magus Entertainment Inc. (*US*)
Maine Road Management (*US*)
The Major Group (*US*)
Mascioli Entertainment (*US*)
McDonough Management LLC (*US*)
McGhee Entertainment (*US*)
Media Five Entertainment (*US*)
Memphia Music Management (*UK*)
Michael Anthony's Electric Events (*US*)
Michael Hausman Artist Management Inc. (*US*)
Mike's Artist Management (*US*)
Miller Music Management (*UK*)
MOB Agency (*US*)
Moksha Entertainment and Music Management (US) (*US*)
Monqui Presents (*US*)
Morningstar (*UK*)
MTS Management (*US*)
Music + Art Management (*US*)
Music Gallery International (*US*)
N.O.W. Music Management (*UK*)
Nettwerk Management (*US*)
Nettwerk Management (*Can*)
Nice Management (*US*)
Night Owl Music Promotions & Management (*UK*)
Northern Music Co. Ltd (*UK*)
NSI Management (*US*)
Off the Chart Promotions (*UK*)
Outrider Music, LLC (*US*)
Paradise Artists (*US*)
Park Promotions (*UK*)
Position Music (*US*)
PRA [Patrick Rains & Associates] (*US*)
Prodigal Son Entertainment (*US*)
Progressive Global Agency (PGA) (*US*)
Q Management (*US*)
Q Prime Management, Inc. (*US*)
Rainmaker Artists (*US*)
Raw Power Management (*UK*)
Reaction Management (*UK*)
Red Light Management (RLM) (*US*)
Revolt Artist Management (*UK*)
Rock Artist Management (RAM) (*UK*)
Rock People Management (RPM) (*UK*)
Ron Rainey Management Inc. (*US*)
Rosier Artist Management (RAM) (*UK*)
Russell Carter Artist Management (*US*)
Saga Entertainment (*UK*)
SAS Entertainment (*UK*)
SGM Music Group Ltd (*UK*)

Silva Artist Management (SAM) (*US*)
Silverword Music Group (*UK*)
Singerman Entertainment (*US*)
Siren Artist Management (UK) (*UK*)
Smashing Buttons (*UK*)
Sound Management, Inc. (*US*)
Spinning Plates (*US*)
Starkravin' Management (*US*)
Steady Management (*UK*)
Steven Scharf Entertainment (SSE) (*US*)
Stiefel Entertainment (*US*)
Street Smart Management (*US*)
Suncoast Music Management (*US*)
Sweet! Music Management (*US*)
TAC Music Management (*US*)
Talk's Cheap Management (*Can*)
Thirty Tigers (*US*)
Toonteen Industries: Management &
Promotions (*UK*)
Travelled Music (*UK*)
Union Entertainment Group (*US*)
Universal Tone Management (*US*)
Val's Artist Management (VAM) (*US*)
Variety Artists International (*US*)
Vector Management (*US*)
Virtually Pop (*UK*)
Wanted Management (*Aus*)
Waxploitation (*US*)
Westwood Music Group (*US*)
Wildlife Entertainment Ltd (*UK*)
Worldsound, LLC (*US*)
Wright Entertainment Group (WEG) (*US*)
YMU Group (*UK*)
Zero Myth (*UK*)
Rockabilly
Act 1 Entertainment (*US*)
Fat City Artists (*US*)
Hello! Booking, Inc. (*US*)
TAC Music Management (*US*)
Roots
21st Century Artists, Inc. (*US*)
Act 1 Entertainment (*US*)
Blind Ambition Management, Ltd (*US*)
Brilliant Productions (*US*)
Dawn Elder Management (*US*)
Fleming Artists (*US*)
Front Room Songs (*UK*)
Grassy Hill Entertainment (*US*)
Hardin Entertainment (*US*)
Impact Artist Management (*US*)
Jelli Records (*UK*)
Kari Estrin Management & Consulting
(*US*)
Kuper Personal Management (*US*)
Park Promotions (*UK*)

Steven Scharf Entertainment (SSE) (*US*)
TAC Music Management (*US*)
Talk's Cheap Management (*Can*)
Twenty Music Roots (*UK*)
Val's Artist Management (VAM) (*US*)
Wanted Management (*Aus*)
Shoegaze
Trak Image Music Ltd (*UK*)
Singer-Songwriter
Amour:Music (*UK*)
AuthorityMGMT (*UK*)
Bitchin' Entertainment (*US*)
Blind Ambition Management, Ltd (*US*)
Brick Wall Management (*US*)
Brilliant Corners Artist Management (*US*)
Burgess World Co. (*US*)
Coalition Music (*Can*)
Concerted Efforts (*US*)
dandomanagement (*UK*)
Domo Music Group Management (*US*)
Entourage Talent Associates, Ltd (*US*)
Fire Tower Entertainment (*US*)
From the Whitehouse (*UK*)
Future Songs (*UK*)
Gold Mountain Entertainment (*US*)
Grassy Hill Entertainment (*US*)
Hardin Entertainment (*US*)
Hornblow Group USA, Inc. (*US*)
IMG Artists (*US*)
Impact Artist Management (*US*)
JBLS Management (*UK*)
Lippman Entertainment (*US*)
Lyricom (*UK*)
Magus Entertainment Inc. (*US*)
Max Bernard Management (*US*)
McGhee Entertainment (*US*)
Michael Hausman Artist Management Inc.
(*US*)
Miller Music Management (*UK*)
Nettwerk Management (*US*)
Nettwerk Management (*Can*)
NSI Management (*US*)
Off the Chart Promotions (*UK*)
Park Promotions (*UK*)
Position Music (*US*)
Q Prime Management, Inc. (*US*)
Reaction Management (*UK*)
Red Light Management (RLM) (*US*)
Revolt Artist Management (*UK*)
Russell Carter Artist Management (*US*)
Sarah Lipman Management Ltd (*UK*)
Sterling Artist Management (*US*)
Steven Scharf Entertainment (SSE) (*US*)
Stiefel Entertainment (*US*)
Stormcraft Music (*UK*)

Sweet! Music Management (*US*)
TAC Music Management (*US*)
Vector Management (*US*)
Wright Entertainment Group (WEG) (*US*)
Ska
DMF Music Ltd (*UK*)
Fat City Artists (*US*)
Soul
Act 1 Entertainment (*US*)
AprilSeven Music (*UK*)
Chaney Gig Affairs (CGA) (*US*)
Concerted Efforts (*US*)
Glow Artists (*UK*)
The Lost Atlantis Records (*UK*)
Lucky House Management (*UK*)
Major Bob Music, Inc. (*US*)
Max Bernard Management (*US*)
Parade Music (*UK*)
Silverword Music Group (*UK*)
Sweet! Music Management (*US*)
Wanted Management (*Aus*)
Soulful
Max Bernard Management (*US*)
TAC Music Management (*US*)
Soundtracks
First Artists Management (*US*)
Kraft-Engel Management (*US*)
Max Bernard Management (*US*)
Soundtrack Music Associates (SMA) (*US*)
Steven Scharf Entertainment (SSE) (*US*)
Spoken Word
Bitchin' Entertainment (*US*)
Surf
Revolt Artist Management (*UK*)
Swing
Act 1 Entertainment (*US*)
Big Bear Music (*UK*)
Cantaloupe Music Productions, Inc. (*US*)
Collin Artists (*US*)
Fat City Artists (*US*)
Harmony Artists (*US*)
Mascioli Entertainment (*US*)
Techno
Bitchin' Entertainment (*US*)
F&G Management (*UK*)
The Lost Atlantis Records (*UK*)
The Major Group (*US*)
Nexus Artist Management (*US*)
The Weird and the Wonderful (*UK*)
Thrash
Semaphore Mgmt & Consulting (*US*)
Singerman Entertainment (*US*)
Traditional
Dawn Elder Management (*US*)
Riot Artists (*US*)

TAC Music Management (*US*)
Trance
Bitchin' Entertainment (*US*)
Involved Management (*UK*)
Phono Sounds UK (*UK*)
Underground
In De Goot Entertainment (*US*)
Semaphore Mgmt & Consulting (*US*)
This Is Music Ltd (*UK*)
Urban
1 2 One Entertainment (*UK*)
2-Tone Entertainment (2TE) (*UK*)
Bitchin' Entertainment (*US*)
Good Guy Entertainment (*US*)
HQ Familia (*UK*)
Lippman Entertainment (*US*)
The Lost Atlantis Records (*UK*)
Lucky House Management (*UK*)
Lyricom (*UK*)
Magus Entertainment Inc. (*US*)
Max Bernard Management (*US*)
MBK Entertainment (*US*)
Position Music (*US*)
Pyramid Entertainment Group (*US*)
RAM Talent Group (*US*)
Silverword Music Group (*UK*)
Thirty Tigers (*US*)
Val's Artist Management (VAM) (*US*)
The Weird and the Wonderful (*UK*)
World
Bitchin' Entertainment (*US*)
Cantaloupe Music Productions, Inc. (*US*)
Collin Artists (*US*)
Columbia Artists Music LLC (CAMI Music) (*US*)
Concerted Efforts (*US*)
Dawn Elder Management (*US*)
DDB Productions (*US*)
DMF Music Ltd (*UK*)
Domo Music Group Management (*US*)
Fat City Artists (*US*)
From the Whitehouse (*UK*)
Front Room Songs (*UK*)
Gold Mountain Entertainment (*US*)
Hardin Entertainment (*US*)
IMG Artists (*US*)
Impact Artist Management (*US*)
Ina Dittke & Associates (*US*)
Line-Up pmc (*UK*)
Macklam Feldman Management (*Can*)
McGhee Entertainment (*US*)
Music + Art Management (*US*)
Nettwerk Management (*US*)
Once 11 Entertainment (*US*)
Position Music (*US*)

Progressive Global Agency (PGA) (*US*)
Red Light Management (RLM) (*US*)
Riot Artists (*US*)
Serious (*UK*)

Steven Scharf Entertainment (SSE) (*US*)
Val's Artist Management (VAM) (*US*)
Worldsound, LLC (*US*)

Get Free Access to the MusicSocket Website

To claim your free access to the **MusicSocket** website simply go to https://www. musicsocket.com/subscribe and begin the subscription process as normal. When you are given the opportunity to enter a voucher / coupon enter the following code:

- MSC-CJG-552

You should then be able to take out a subscription for free, or a longer term subscription at a reduced price.

Please note that this code will only remain valid until the release of the next edition, and is only permitted for use in the creation of one account for the owner of this book.

If you need any assistance please email support@musicsocket.com.

If you have found this book useful, please consider leaving a review on the website where you bought it!

What you get

Once you have set up access to the site you will be able to benefit from all the following features:

Databases

All our databases are updated almost every day and include powerful search facilities to help you find exactly what you need. Searches that used to take you hours or even days in print books or on search engines can now be done in seconds and produce more accurate and up-to-date information. You can try out any of our databases before you subscribe:

- Search **over 1,200 record labels**
- Search **over 500 managers**

PLUS advanced features to help you with your search:

- Save searches and save time – set up to 15 search parameters specific to your work, save them, and then access the search results with a single click whenever you log in. You can even save multiple different searches if you have different types of work you are looking to place.
- Add personal notes to listings, visible only to you and fully searchable – helping you to organise your actions.

- Set reminders on listings to notify you when to submit your work, when to follow up, when to expect a reply, or any other custom action.
- Track which listings you've viewed and when, to help you organise your search – any listings which have changed since you last viewed them will be highlighted for your attention!

Daily email updates

As a subscriber you will be able to take advantage of our email alert service, meaning you can specify your particular interests and we'll send you automatic email updates when we change or add a listing that matches them. So if you're interested in labels dealing in hard rock in the United States you can have us send you emails with the latest updates about them – keeping you up to date without even having to log in.

User feedback

Our databases all include a user feedback feature that allows our subscribers to leave feedback on each listing – giving you not only the chance to have your say about the markets you contact but giving a unique artist's perspective on the listings.

Save on copyright protection fees

If you're sending your work away to record labels or managers, you should consider first protecting your copyright. As a subscriber to **MusicSocket** you can do this through our site and save 10% on the copyright registration fees normally payable for protecting your work internationally through the Intellectual Property Rights Office.

Terms and conditions

The promotional code contained in this publication may be used by the owner of the book only to create one subscription to MusicSocket at a reduced cost, or for free. It may not be used by or disseminated to third parties. Should the code be misused then the owner of the book will be liable for any costs incurred, including but not limited to payment in full at the standard rate for the subscription in question. The code may be used at any time until the end of the calendar year named in the title of the publication, after which time it will become invalid. The code may be redeemed against the creation of a new account only – it cannot be redeemed against the ongoing costs of keeping a subscription open. In order to create a subscription a method of payment must be provided, but there is no obligation to make any payment. Subscriptions may be cancelled at any time, and if an account is cancelled before any payment becomes due then no payment will be made. Once a subscription has been created, the normal schedule of payments will begin on a monthly, quarterly, or annual basis, unless a life Subscription is selected, or the subscription is cancelled prior to the first payment becoming due. Subscriptions may be cancelled at any time, but if they are left open beyond the date at which the first payment becomes due and is processed then payments will not be refundable.